The Ancient Chinese Super State of Primary Societies

Taoist Philosophy for the 21st Century

The Second Edition

YOU-SHENG LI

The Ancient Chinese Super State of Primary Societies:
Taoist Philosophy for the 21st Century
Copyright © 2024 by You-Sheng Li

ISBN: 978-1962497633(hc)
ISBN: 978-1962497503(sc)
ISBN: 978-1962497473(e)

The Reading Glass Books
1-888-420-3050
www.readingglassbooks.com
fulfillment@readingglassbooks.com

Contents

Preface and Key Terms Including a List of Chinese Dynasties

Unlike any other major civilizations, Chinese civilization started with a super state in their isolated world, and this super state functioned as police to keep peace among tribes and vassal states just as the United Nations does in today's world. If all human societies are divided into genetically coded primary society and man-made secondary society, this relatively peaceful environment allowed the Chinese people to still live in primary society until the Warring States Period (476-221 BC). Chinese Taoist philosophy or Taoism summarizes the lifestyle of those who lived in the ancient primary society. Taoism sees the world and interprets human experience from the basis of human nature and self enjoyment while modern secondary society is goal-oriented.

The twelve essays (or chapters) in this book provide a further reading along the same line of thought of my previous book *A New Interpretation of Chinese Taoist philosophy*, which explains this ancient Taoist wisdom in modern terms. Although the two books can each be read alone, it is recommended that the reader read *A New Interpretation of Chinese Taoist philosophy* first, since it is an introduction to this newly interpreted theory.

Again those essays pursue high originality and academic value, but the author has made every effort to accommodate general readers and their reading interest. In line with the lifestyle of primary society, the author tries to convey information, insights along with emotional experience and images. The author drew the illustrations himself, and he also talks about his own life experience. The four long academic essays, Nos. 3, 5, 7, and 10, all start with a summary, and present detailed data to outline the different pathway Chinese civilization took in comparison with the West while the other essays serve as a much lighter reading to bridge the gap between the Taoist ideology and modern daily life of ordinary people. The first essay gives a more general view to serve as an introduction. The Appendix includes the

i

revised versions of three previous essays of the same titles that are included in the previous book but they are now almost twice as long.

Key Terms:

Ancient Super State: An ancient state that became by far the largest state of the known world to its people. It usually became the major politically stabilizing force and functioned as police to keep peace among local powers. In ancient China, such a super state had no vision of secondary society and had no need to construct one. This super state of primary societies hatched the first Chinese philosophy, Taoism, and deeply influenced Confucianism.

Primary Society and Secondary Society*:** Primary society is genetically coded society, and secondary society is any society that is created by man or human culture. Although there is no real primary society for us to examine, it is not difficult to outline the features of a primary society through its definition and by the study of animal societies and human society before civilization.

In primary society, human nature and instinct are enough to keep the society harmonious and functional. Primary society is the basic social organization of men immediately above families, and the ideal number of people in a primary society is believed to be around 150. Members are linked together emotionally and psychologically, and thus they are a whole at the subconscious level, since they interacted with each other face-to-face. Bands and tribes are regarded as primary societies, which were headed by headmen. Those headmen had no power to force their will on others, and their leadership was based on persuasion and consensus. The culture of primary society has no power to modify human nature. Secondary society is created by man, and so it has an ideology and a corresponding social structure to support the ideology. As a creation by man, it has limitless possible types while primary society, dictated by genetics, has only one type. Social stratification and institutionalized violence such as police and army are often necessary to keep a secondary society stable in its present type and restrain its members from seeking other types of society.

Spare Time: Here we define spare time as time left after one's basic biological needs such as food and water are fulfilled. Spare time is essential for the development and advancement of human culture and civilization. If culture is defined as how to spend spare time, and it is found that there is no law to guide humans on how to spend their spare time. As a result, culture plus social power can organize a society to do the most absurd thing for ages even though it goes against the basic human nature. Human nature is essentially peaceful and self-contained but has a wide range of peripheral potentials. A goal-oriented secondary society tends to force its members to explore their peripheral potentials.

Taoism: Taoism is a philosophy, a religion, and a way of life. As a philosophy, it was first founded by Lao Tzu (?604-484 BC) and Chuang Tzu (?369-286 BC). It emphasizes the natural way and advocates pristine simplicity. It developed into an organized religion during the Eastern Han dynasty (25-220 AD). Confucianism, Buddhism, and Taoism were the three major religions or ideologies in Chinese history.

Chinese Dynasties: The first three dynasties, Hsia, Shang, Chou, were confederations of independent states with a super state functioning as police. The subsequent dynasties were empires with a centralized government supervising provinces and counties. The economic basis of both types of dynasties was the same: small-scale peasant economy of self-sufficiency. The government was run on the tax collected from the peasants. Dating of Chinese history was considered to be approximate before 841 BC.

Yangshao (Revere-Beauty) Culture	5000-2400 BC
Longshan (Dragon-Hills) Culture	2600-1900 BC
Yellow Emperor (legendary)	
Yao	
Shun	
Yu	
Hsia	2200-1766 BC

Shang	1766-1122 BC
Chou	1122-256 BC
Spring and Autumn Period	770-476 BC
Warring States Period	476-221 BC
Qin	221-207 BC
Han	206 BC-220 AD
Jin	265-420
North/South	420-589
Sui	581-618
Tang	618-907
Song	960-1279
Yuan	1271-1368
Ming	1368-1644
Qing	1644-1911

1

Taoist Philosophy for the 21ˢᵗ Century

During the Warring States Periods (476-221 BC), the vast area along the Yangtze River valley was the territory of State Chu, which was lagging behind other states in social reform. It was the ideal environment to cultivate Taoist ideology, since the favorable climate allowed an idle lifE there.

Once a man lost his bow but was reluctant to find it back, saying, "A man of State Chu lost his bow but another man of State Chu got it. Why do I have to bother myself looking for it?"

Confucius heard this and said, "It is okay if the words 'State Chu' are omitted." Confucianism embraces all humanity. Lao Tzu heard this and said, "It is okay if the word 'man' is omitted too." Taoism embraces both man and nature. (Adapted from Lu's Spring and Autumn Annals: The Public is Highly Valued) [1]

When people meet unexpectedly far from their hometown, they say, "It is a small world." People also say, our world has shrunk to a village, a global village. Modern communication technology has brought people closer than ever before, especially since the end of the Cold War. Airway services allow us to reach any corner of the earth within the same day, and modern communication enables us to talk to our friends face-to-face in spite of the fact that they are on the other side of the planet. We are facing a new world that humans have never faced before. Do you think we need a new way of life? Many scholars say YES, and they predict that different cultures will replace nations to compete with each other on the upcoming stage of this new world.

Yes, we have entered a new era, and we need a new way of life. What is this new lifestyle we are going to adapt to? Although there is no simple answer, I believe that the ancient wisdom of Chinese Taoist philosophy provides a good choice. At least, it is worthwhile to learn a little bit more about this ancient way of life. Taoist philosophy emphasizes the value of naturalness and simplicity, which are well complementary to the Western philosophy of materialism. Some emerging trends indicate that the world is coming closer to Taoist ideology. I will, however, tell you the lobefin fish story first to show our position in the bio-evolutionary world.

(1)   Lobefin Fish and Human Self-Transcendence

When I was in school, we were taught that what distinguished humans from animals was, humans had consciousness and animals did not. Animals were unable to think and unaware of what they were doing. Now, we all know that animals can think too, and they know well what they are doing. They make c hoices in their lives just as we do in our lives. They also have creative thinking. The captive gorilla Koko mastered over a thousand words of American Sign Language and was able to link them up in statements of up to eight words in a creative way. It happened in a laboratory setting. In the wild, animals show creative thinking too.

In the African jungle, Jane Goodall first observed that chimpanzees carefully stripped leaves off a tree twig to make a stick and then used it to fish out termites from their holes. A similar type of tool making was observed in other apes too, even in some birds. A particular type of tool making is usually limited to certain groups and is not observed in other groups of the same species of animals. It was apparently invented and learned.

Scientists have been able to observe the actual process by which behavioral innovations spread from individual to individual and became part of a troop's culture independently of genetic transmission. This happened at the Primate Research Institute of Kyoto University in Japan in the 1960s. They dropped sweet potatoes on a beach to attract monkeys for observation. One day, a young female began to wash sand off the potato by plunging it into a small brook that ran through the beach. This washing technique spread throughout the group and gradually replaced the former habit of rubbing the sand off by hand. Nine years later, 80 to 90 percent of those monkeys were washing their potatoes, ether in the brook or in the sea.

A few animals such as apes and dolphins are even self-conscious, and they can recognize their own images in a mirror. Then the question is why humans are able to build secondary society while animals are not. The answer is humans have the ability of self-transcendence: They are continuously looking for something higher than themselves and their real life. This eventually lets them create new worlds for themselves. Under certain circumstances, animals may be able to use language in a creative way like Gorilla Koko did. However, they use language just as other tools to enrich their lives. Humans use language to create totally new worlds such as in many novels, especially science fictions. Each novel literally represents a new world created by humans. Our secondary society is also one of those worlds created by humans. But this one is a real one, created not by one person but by numerous people over thousands of years.

Here I will show you that animals have the ability of self-transcendence too: the lobefin fish story. The long bio-evolutionary course was stagnant for most time but punctuated by short phases of rapid changes, which were triggered either by environmental change or by major favorable mutations including recombination and expressive alteration of genes. The transition from aquatic animals or water animals to land animals (terrestrial animals) combines the two triggering factors: Mutation led animals to a new environment, which triggered more mutations.

From water to land, there were several critical changes animals had to acquire such as limbs to support body weight, lungs to breathe, a neck to turn the head. Those changes could not take place overnight but could not last forever ether, as it was an extra burden to those animals that carried those preliminary changes. Lobefin fish carry those changes and serve as a living fossil to illustrate how animals moved from sea to land in ancient time.

Lobefin fish (coelancath, Figure 1) first appeared some 400 million years ago and once flourished in shallow seas all over the world but vanished about 70 million years ago. On 23 December 1938, a fisherman caught an unusual fish along the east coast of South Africa. The local museum was informed, and a scientist came to examine the specimen. Without any doubt, this was a lobefin fish, which was thought to be extinct at that time. When I studied zoology in university in the 1960s, a total of three or five lobefins had been caught, and there was only a sentence trailing at the end to mention it in the textbook. Divers have now observed them in massive numbers in the deep sea, and a new species was found in Indonesian seas in 1997. Those living fossil fish live in sea caves and only come out to feed themselves at night but still avoid moonlight

Some lobefin fish, such as the Australian lungfish, have primitive lungs in addition to gills. Their fins have a muscular root base with bones and are able to turn in different directions. In comparison with other fish, lobefin fish have little advantage, since they have to nourish and support those extra parts that are only useful under special circumstances. On land, they may survive a little longer than other fish but will eventually die as well. Apparently, they are still aquatic animals. There is a long evolutionary way to go before they become a real land animal.

In history, lobefin fish did not climb onto land themselves but were trapped in enclosed water, which dried out later. They were forced to land by environmental changes. Under such circumstances, most lobefin fish died off except for few with further mutations. The chance for those few may be in the range of one in a million.

How was the life when lobefin fish first moved onto land? The following shall apply:

1. *They are forced unto land by circumstances.*
2. *They have a hard time, since they are not fully land animals yet.*
3. *Their future is uncertain, and they are in a phase of rapid change.*
4. *Their evolutionary pathways leading to mammals, reptiles, birds, or amphibians are determined by nature and chance, not by themselves.*
5. *Once lobefin fish become fully land animals, their lives are as comfortable as those of any fish in the sea.*

All of the above except 5) also apply to humans when they moved from primary society to secondary society, which is exactly like lobefin fish moving from water onto land. Humans first formed secondary society because of population expansion, either the general density exceeded the limit or too many people crowded in one place. Secondary society is apparently not the suitable social environment for humans, so that scientists have recently found that civilization triggered rapid genetic changes in human, and judged from the variation of the size of our brain, our brains are still in the rapid phase of genetic evolution.

Both moves, man's from primary society to secondary society and fish's move from sea onto land, are major steps in their evolutionary process, leading to new directions and opening to new dimensions. Dr. Shubin and his colleagues discovered a fossil fish on the Ellesmere Island in northern Canada after six years of searching. They persisted for so long because the rocks they were looking at in these areas were deposited some 375 million years ago when lobefin fish lived and were in the process of moving onto land. The fossil fish they found had gills and lungs, the neck to turn, and strong lobefins. Dr. Shubin and his colleague studied a living but ancient fish known as the paddlefish. They found that those thoroughly fishy fish were turning on control genes known as hox genes, in a manner characteristic of the four-limbed land animals. They believe major steps in evolution like the transition from water to land are not necessarily set off by genetic mutations inside the genes but by the right ecological situation or habitat, since the appearance of four limbs are critical if animals move from water onto land. Nevertheless, such transition needs numerous generations to accomplish, and meanwhile those half-fish and half-land animals had to struggle in their unfamiliar environment to survive.

We can easily list out numerous evidences indicating that we are having a hard time, which forces us to adapt to rapid change, genetically and culturally. One of the obvious is that we are doing a lot against human nature. We are born resistant to killing other human beings, but such killing is not only institutionalized in our society but also often accelerates into massive scales such as in the two world wars. Nearly a hundred millions died in the Second World War alone. It makes us happy and healthy if we live in a friendly atmosphere, but our society encourages the opposite, competition.

Humans have been on earth for two or three million years, and our species, the Homo Sapiens, appeared some two hundred thousand years ago while our secondary society has a history of only five or six thousand years. During such a short period, the genetic change, though took place, was very limited. We adapt to our secondary society largely by cultural modification and by switching on the survival kit, running on our peripheral potentials. It is no wonder why suicide rates doubled in the twenty century in North America in spite of dramatic improvement in living conditions.

We face nature in primary society, while we face ourselves, competitors and enemies, in secondary society. Unlike the lobefin fish that first move onto land faced environmental challenges from nature, we face challenges from ourselves. As modern technology has brought us so close that we literally live in one village, why cannot we live for a peaceful and meaningful life as villagers did five thousand years ago in primary society? We do not need to go through all the painful genetic changes to become a fully secondary society animal before we can allow us to be as comfortable as those living in primary society.

(2)　The Civilization of War and its Ending

The phrase "tragedy of the commons" originally describes medieval villagers sharing the same pasture ground. Suppose the size of their pasture allowed some fifty villagers each to raise 10 sheep. If one villager raised 11 sheep to increase his income, everyone would soon find out and follow suit, and the pasture would eventually be ruined by over exploitation.

Wars, violent conflicts among different states, start and spread pretty much in the same way, but much faster along an upward spiral.

Only when survival was at risk in prehistoric times, might humans wage a battle on their neighbors, so-called small scale raids, which were driven mostly by hunger. When a conflict could not be solved by other means in primitive society, they performed ritual fighting to settle the dispute. A ritual battle permits the display of courage and the expression of emotion while resulting in relatively few wounds and rarely deaths. Since violence is not part of our nature but one of our peripheral potentials, hunger and unsolvable conflicts were only triggering factors which might and might not end in violence. In ancient primary society, such fighting or battles happened as isolated cases with self-limiting power residing in human nature. They might have been going on for millions of years but their scale remained the same.

However, such violence is not the war we are talking about here. War is a way to access social advantage, get the upper-hand in the conflict-solving process. Such war is in a situation similar to the tragedy of the commons. When a state comes into an advantageous position after waging wars on its neighbors, all the remaining states, whether their original culture is peace-loving or warrior-like, are getting ready for war to protect themselves. War soon breaks out everywhere. Those peace-loving states are the first ones to be engulfed by others, since they are lagging behind in a world of warring culture. When all the states are balanced to the same military level, another state benefits itself by waging a war on its neighbors by militarizing to a new level. Other states soon raise their military level too. The scale of war becomes larger and larger. Meanwhile, other factors such as

7

state size, new technology and so forth come into play as well. In the tragedy of the commons, what is ruined is the pasture ground. It is the peace of life that is ruined in a world of war culture. Our life is enjoyable only when there is peace. Everyone has to fight for his survival during a war.

Like the tragedy of the commons, such wars that happen in secondary society are only limited by the exhaustion of resources. Human nature is no longer a limiting factor.

Anthropologists define civilizations as those cultural traditions that have state structure, monumental buildings, and written records. Those are all hallmarks of secondary society. People who live in primary society have no need to build large monumental constructions though they may have the ability. Equally, nothing prevents primitive people from inventing the writing system, but it is not a useful tool in a primary society.

Human civilizations first appeared five or six thousand years ago in the Middle East, and later in India, China, Europe, and in Americas. There are numerous evidences indicating that more peaceful cultures existed before or in the early years of human civilizations in many places in Asia, Europe, and northern Africa. Here I quote from two authors to support this view, since controversy still exists regarding this issue:

...for millennia – a span of time many times longer than 5,000 years conventionally counted as history – prehistoric societies worshipped the Goddess of nature and spirituality, our great Mother, the giver of life and creator of all. But even more fascinating is that these ancient societies were structured very much like the more peaceful and just society we are now trying to construct.... Contrary to what we have been taught of the Neolithic or first agrarian civilizations as male dominated and highly violent, these were generally peaceful societies in which both women and men lived in harmony with one another and nature. [2]

What was the force which transformed such peaceful cultures into our civilization of war? According to James DeMeo, the second author I quote here, there was a dramatic climate change around

4,000 -3,000 BC which led to desertification in vast areas along central Asia, Arabia, and northern Africa, or so-called Saharasia.

...it can be seen how prolonged drought with its accompanying malnutrition, famine and starvation, provides an important triggering influence whereby massive cultural changes can be initiated, particularly when drought is widespread and incessant, lasting from one generation into the next....And it was precisely during this period of climatic transition that the first widespread evidences of similar social trauma, armoring and patrism appeared within human culture. [3]

It must be pointed out that the isolated aboriginal people who live nowadays in left-over jungles surrounded by the bustling modern world are pretty much in a similar dread situation, shrinking territory and hostile cultural environment. It is not surprising to observe an increased violence among them.

British historian Arnold Joseph Toynbee (1889-1975) raised the so-called challenge and response theory. According to him, civilizations arose in response to some set of challenges of extreme difficulty when "creative minorities" devised solutions that reoriented their entire society. When the Sumerians exploited the intractable swamps of southern Iraq by organizing the Neolithic inhabitants into a society capable of carrying out large-scale irrigation projects, their challenges and responses were physical. When the Catholic Church resolved the chaos of post-Roman Europe by enrolling the new Germanic kingdoms in a single religious community, their challenges and responses were cultural or social. When a civilization responds to challenges, it grows. When it fails to respond to a challenge, it enters its period of decline.

When the Saharasia was drying out, it was a physical challenge, but once the hungry people formed the first raiding army to exploit their neighbours and then seek to maintain their advantageous position over others, the challenge was not physical or social but an ever-growing and rapidly-upgrading hostile mankind itself that humans had never faced before. It is a much tougher challenge as Arnold Joseph Toynbee pointed out: "The human race's prospects of survival were considerably better when we were defenseless against tigers than they are today when we have become defenseless against ourselves."

When humans knew how to wage war to their advantage, it set off the arms' race in the human world with the most militarized and best equipped state as the winner. William Eckhardt (1995) has recently raised the so-called dialectical evolutionary theory to interpret the process of human civilization. He so defines his theory:

A dialectical evolutionary theory tries to relate the concepts of civilization, empire, and war to one another in such a way that their interaction results in positive feedback loops leading them ever upward and onward in a spiraling motion, unless and until it leads them in the opposite direction by way of negative feedback loops which reverse the direction of the spiral.[4]

William Eckhardt found a close correlation between war measured in the frequency of battles, empire measured in the total area of empires, and civilization measured in numbers of geniuses whose superiority was established by the consensus of encyclopedia and textbook authors. While the whole world tended to spiral upward, as a general rule during the last 5,000 years of human civilization, regional areas had their ups and downs, rises and falls. When expenditures exceeded incomes in the evolutionary process, then came the falls, which were characterized by decentralization, feudalization, or foreign conquest. In all cases, the way up not only increased the quantity of civilization, empire, and war, but also changed the social structure to one of greater inequality, indicated by slavery, caste, class, social stratification, and so forth. It is justified to call our civilization the civilization of war. Table 1.1 shows the correlative data on the three parameters along the five thousand years of human civilization:

Table 1.1 Civilizations, Empires, and Wars Between 3000 BC and 2000 with Other Critical Data*

Century	No. of battles	Imperial size (square megameters)	No. of geniuses	population (millions)	Deaths of wars (millions)	Energy consumption (billion kilocalories per day)	Deforested area
-30		0.15	4	50		0.6	
-29		0.20	0				
-28		0.26	3				
-27		0.32	4				
-26		0.37	2				
-25		0.43	4				
-24		0.50	0				
-23		0.90	0				
-22		0.40	0				
-21		0.28	0				
-20		0.50	9				
-19		0.80	6				
-18		1.25	6				
-17		1.10	3				
-16		1.35	3				
-15	0	2.05	3				
-14	0	2.25	3				
-13	1	2.70	9				
-12	0	2.65	1				
-11	0	1.60	0				
-10	0	1.00	2	120			
-9	0	1.15	5				
-8	0	1.15	9				
-7	3	3.10	21				
-6	2	7.85	50				
-5	19	6.25	120			0.16	
-4	29	5.70	114	153		0.35	
-3	43	11.85	49	187		0.13	
-2	22	15.15	65	225		0.56	
-1	34	16.40	61	250		0.31	

1	5	18.40	70	252	0.12		
2	8	13.80	83	257	0.14		
3	25	14.70	38	222	0.24		
4	17	13.70	51	206	0.04		
5	21	17.90	46	207	0.23		
6	17	21.00	49	208	0.01		
7	67	18.00	76	206	0.36		
8	38	24.70	88	224			
9	50	18.50	99	222	0.07		
10	41	17.00	117	253	0.07	6.5	
11	54	17.00	138	299			
12	69	10.10	153	400	2.5		
13	80	32.70	187	431			
14	53	31.80	109	375	0.11		
15	85	17.10	125	461	0.12		
16	148	22.20	424	578	1.0		
17	290	43.80	412	680	6.0		
18	338	61.00	434	954	7.0		25%(1700)
19	449	102.00	795	1,934	19	123	50%(1850)
20		120.35		6,057	118	1380	75%(1915)
Sum	4,511	725.41	4,150				

Data on the world population, deforested area, and energy consumption are from David Christian (2004). The deforested area was 100% in 1985, and the exact year when the data were collected is given in parentheses. The numbers of death in wars are from http://en.wikipedia.org/wiki/. [4, 5, 6]

William Eckhardt did not predict the scale of the next round of world wars according to his upward spiral. Some people say, we have some six billion people now, and it will grow up to 7.5 billions soon but the earth is only able to support 1.5 billion. Therefore, 6 billion human beings have to go, and the next round of world wars will be 60 times of the scale of the last two world wars measured by the number of deaths.

Fortunately, there is evidence that such an upward spiral evolutionary process of warring culture is coming to its end.

Humans were waging wars all along the history of civilization, and their wars were upgraded continually in terms of numbers of people involved as more nations joined in. The maximum size of war humans could have entered was when all humans on earth joined in and when all nations on earth were divided into two huge campuses. This was the two world wars and the Cold War era, which can be regarded as the peak of this upward spiral evolutionary process on war scale.

Similarly, the maximum size of empires also peaked in human history, which was the Mongolian Empire in the 13th century and the British Empire in modern Europe. The history of the British Empire clearly shows that the time of imperialism is over.

The British Empire was the largest empire in history and for a time was the foremost global power. The European age of maritime explorations of the 15th century sparked the era of the European colonial empires with the British as the most successful. By 1921, the British Empire held a population of about 458 million people, approximately one-quarter of the world's population. It covered about 36.6 million km², about a quarter of earth's total land area. It was often said that "the sun never sets on the British Empire" because its span across the globe ensured that the sun was always shining on at least part of its territory. During the five decades following the Second World War, most of the territories of this Empire became independent states, but many of them joined the Commonwealth of Nations, a free association of independent states. If the most powerful empire is no longer able to keep its vast territory, it is impossible to set up new empires. The upward spiral of empire has come to its end.

When moving further away in time from the two world wars, people will become closer to human nature. War makes people work hard for survival, and it makes people feel a sense of urgency. People forget themselves when they have an urgent feeling. They also tend to be more rational and less emotional. I think the relatively peaceful environment, especially after the Cold War was over in 1989, will embrace human nature as a whole not only the parts that fit in the high competitive society. Humans may be lazier than before, but that is in human nature. From the baby boomers to generation X, and to generation Y, people are becoming more relaxed, more distant from materialism but closer to self-happiness or spirituality.

According to the Canadian author, Douglas Coupland and others, generation X who were born in the 1970s are quite different in comparison with the baby boomer generation whose births followed the Second World War. Generation X are less materialistic, less money-oriented, more leisure-seeking, and put more value on individual freedom. In other words, generation X people are closer to human nature while the boomer generation closer to the Western culture.

The wealth-building culture was also part of this upward spiral evolutionary process of war/ empire/civilization, as those three, war, empire, and civilization, needed wealth to support. Since the time when the capitalist system was well established, wealth building has been separated from empires. Thus, it is widely accepted that capitalist expansion led to the two world wars, and it is not the other way around. I think the wealth-building culture was detached from warring culture only after the Renaissance, because such a culture needs a large number of independent and highly educated individuals. The Renaissance created such individuals in massive numbers. The wealth building culture is no longer motivated by the needs of war. The end of the Cold War era did not dampen the wealth building enthusiasm but fueled it.

This wealth building culture will be hindered by resource limitation and environmental problems, and especially by the final realization by humans that wealth provides us convenience and comfort but not happiness. Wealth does not spell happiness at all as the suicide rate doubled during the last century in Canada and the USA while the total wealth of the world doubled several times. The worst part of this wealth-building culture is its consumption of resources and the production of waste. According to the recently released WWF (World Wildlife Fund for Nature) report, we are already moving forward at a speed the earth cannot cope with. It will need two earths to support us by 2050, and it will need five earths if everyone in the world lives their lives as North Americans do today. It is urgent to consider alternative ways to live our life. Taoist philosophy provides a good choice as it stresses the value of naturalness and simplicity, a simple but joyful lifestyle.

(3) The Political Situation of the Modern World is Similar to That of Early Chinese Dynasties When Taoist Philosophy was Popular

Unlike any other major ancient civilizations, Chinese civilization began with a super state in an isolated world. This super state was first started by the Yellow Emperor around 2600 BC and well established by Yu the Great in 2200 BC. The modern world with the powerless United Nations as a platform for countries to work out their differences at various levels is pretty much like the political situation of China from 2600 to 476 BC when a relatively powerless king and his court were trying to keep peace among numerous tribes and vassal states and when human nature was highly respected in politics and in life. If we consider Taoist philosophy as a way of life, Taoist lifestyle was popular from 2600 BC to 476 BC. A sub-school of Taoist philosophy, Huang Lao, is named after the Yellow Emperor and Lao Tzu (?604-484 BC).

William Eckhardt's upward spiral evolutionary process of war/empire/civilization does not apply to the early phase of Chinese civilization from 2600 to 476 BC. Peace and morality were apparently the main voices during this period. The first authoritative volume of Chinese history, *Historical Records*, starts with such words:

>...*When Godly Farmer's (Shen Nong) rule was weakened, states (tribes or federations of tribes) were fighting and conquering each other, and people were devastated, but Godly Farmer was unable to punish them with military actions.*

Now the academic circle considers "Godly Farmer" as a period of history and not a particular ruler. During this time, agriculture was developed and people lived together in peace except for its late years when violent conflicts developed. For a long time, nobody could stop it. In support of this, more than 50 walled towns have been excavated dating from 3000 to 2000 BC. Those town sites were scattered all over China including the Yangtze River valley. Some scholars regarded those towns along with the villages surrounding them as newly emerged states. [7, 8]

In response to this challenge of chaotic situation, the Yellow Emperor appeared and he cracked down two major federations of tribes, who were apparently the peace- violators. Thus the Yellow Emperor restored peace and harmony among ten thousand states, and all respected the Yellow Emperor's leadership afterwards. As the above quotation from *Historical Records* implies, this superpower or super state set up by the Yellow Emperor was to function as police to keep peace among tribes.

More than a thousand archaeological sites have been found all over China from the New Stone Age. Chinese scholars interpret those findings as multiple origins of Chinese civilization. In other words, many different cultures converged to form Chinese civilization rather than a dominant culture conquered and replaced other cultures. It was consistent with the above quoted records. The Yellow Emperor defeated two peace-violators to restore previous peace and he did not conquer all the other states.

According to *Historical Records,* Yu the Great was the seventh national ruler of this super state after the Yellow Emperor. Yu the Great established the first dynasty, Hsia (2200-1766 BC), through cooperation against floods.

The reliability of the Chinese history before the Shang dynasty(1766-1122 BC) is not a concern here. What ancient Chinese people believed to be their history is much more important than what modern scientists can prove to be Chinese history, since the former influenced the thinking of Chinese people and shaped the Chinese society while the latter did not. All Chinese people consider the Yellow Emperor as their ancestor and Yu the Great as a model for the subsequent rulers. The Yellow Emperor, the Hsia people, and the people who established the Chou dynasty (1122-256 BC) are believed to have originated from the same tribal people in western China. The Chou dynasty was critical, since it covered the Axial Age during which the philosophical foundation was laid down for the next two thousand years. Confucius and all other scholars during Confucius's time regarded the three early Chinese dynasties, Hsia, Shang, and Chou, as a period of continuous culture, though the Shang dynasty (1766-1122 BC) seemed to be different.

Such a super state may cover a vast area, since many tribes and independent states wanted to join in for protection. The social structure of this super state was loose, and they lacked the modern concept of territory. They allowed people to move freely, and they required the rulers of states along the bordering areas to report to the central government only once in their life time. Contrary to William Eckhardt's upward spiral evolutionary process of war/empire/civilization, this super state system, like the United Nations in the modern world, allowed the quantity of civilization, empire (the size of this super state) to increase without the increase in battles and conflicts. In Chinese ancient literature, this super state was often referred to as the world (tian xia). They knew nothing beyond this super state. With this loosely constructed super state, human nature was respected and primary society remained intact or near intact.

Consistent with this conclusion, Claudio Cioffi-Revilla and David Lai found in their study, titled *War and Politics in Ancient China, 2700 BC to 722 BC*, "that the Chinese protobellic region experienced an era of stability and change that was unusual when compared to the prevailing instability found in many other regions of time-space... Early China during the period...showed stability similar to that of the cold war era". [9]

Primary society is a genetically coded society, and therefore, humans have a strong tendency to form a primary society unless they are forced to do otherwise. The following is an important assumption:

Primary society or quasi-primary society will form automatically if:
1. The population is less than a few hundreds, and the population is free to divide when it is much larger than the size of a primary society;
2. The population is engaged in face-to-face interaction;
3. No contact with and no ideological influence from secondary society;
4. No outside force threatening their survival.

Based on the above assumption, we have reached an important conclusion that the society was mainly primary or quasi-primary society during the period of the three dynasties Hsia, Shang, and Chou, from 2200 to 476 BC. A quasi-primary society was essentially a primary society based on human nature but has just started its transformation toward secondary society. There was no typical secondary society emerged during this period though this super state functioned as a secondary society. A typical secondary society consists of only independent individuals, and the society is stabilized by a well- defined ideology and corresponding social structure. Primary society is stabilized by human nature such as instincts and subconscious.

The social structure of the period of early Chinese civilization from 2200 to 476 BC was idiographically modeled as follows:

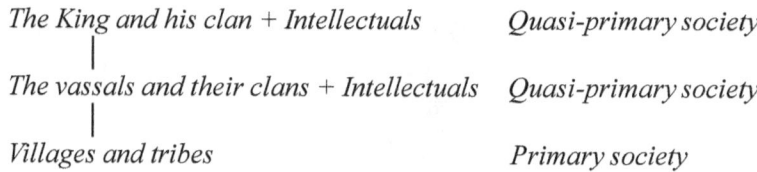

The King and his clan + Intellectuals   *Quasi-primary society*

The vassals and their clans + Intellectuals   *Quasi-primary society*

Villages and tribes   *Primary society*

Although the kings and vassals were in secondary society according to the definition in the section *Preface and Key Terms Including a List of Chinese Dynasties*, they were able to live in quasi-primary society, since all the four "if"s in the above important assumption were met. It is further explained as follows:

1. The king, vassals, villages/tribes, and their clans all lived in primary or quasi- primary society;

2. The king, vassals and their clans lived a better material life than the village/tribal people, but a ten percent tax was well tolerated and was not enough to change their idle lifestyle;

3. The king and vassals did not live together, though they engaged in face-to- face interaction. Their numbers were within a few hundreds, and they formed a quasi- primary society;

4. Similarly, the vassal and his subordinate headmen formed another quasi- primary society; The king ruled his vassals and the vassals ruled their headmen in the same way as a headman ruled his subjects in a primary society, mainly by persuasion and consensus.

5. The relations between the above primary and quasi-primary societies followed the principle of reciprocity and mutual respect;

6. Ideally, the administration and military conflict were optmised to nearly zero according to the Taoist principle: govern by doing nothing.

Under such a social structure, human nature was the main force to stabilize the society. This lifestyle was close to Taoist ideology. Although various philosophies of life were established much later, rudimentary ideology and philosophy were surely present. I tend to think that the major ideology during this period was Taoism with rudimentary Confucianism as the complementary non-official ideology. *Classic of Poetry* and *Book of Mountains and Seas* show clearly that there was not any forceful unified ideology, which is consistant with a primitive lifestyle and Taoist philosophy. Taoism regards neither the authority of heavenly gods nor that of any secular power.

Interestingly, the political situation of the period of early Chinese civilization is similar to the political situation of the modern world. Both the king of ancient China and the United Nations (UN) are relatively powerless, but they play a critical role to keep peace among the local powers. The UN was set up with the same purpose as the first super state in ancient China, and it is to keep peace, and break tension among local powers.

The UN was founded in 1945 to replace the ineffective League of Nations, which was blamed because it failed to prevent the Second World War. Considering that the third world war was widely expected in the 1950s and 1960s, and many countries were struggling to prepare for it, it is remarkable that this third world war eventually did not happen. Without the UN, it would have been most likely a reality.

The Human Security Report 2005, produced by the Human Security Centre at the University of British Columbia with support from several governments and foundations, documented a dramatic, but largely unrecognized, decline in the number of wars, genocides and human rights abuses since the end of the Cold War. Statistics include: a 40% drop in violent conflict; an 80% drop in the most deadly conflicts; and an 80% drop in genocide and politicide.

As mentioned above, a more peaceful international environment cultivates the spirit of freedom and liberty in the new generations. They may appear lazier, less disciplined, but it is in our nature. Humans would be unable to wage war on the same scale of the last two world wars even if they encounter a similar situation in the future. Soldiers will desert on the eve of a battle.on both sides. At least, we hope so.

(4)   The Uniqueness of Chinese Civilization

During the Axial Age around 800-200 BC, different philosophical foundations were laid down in Greece, Israel, Iran, India, and in China that set up the framework of human thinking for the next two thousand years for each of those five cultural traditions. The first four, namely Greece, Israel, Iran, and India, were closely linked together by sea trade, and China was the only one that was isolated from the others.

It is even more commendable that Chinese civilization went through an evolutionary pathway that was fundamentally different from those of all other civilizations. The appearance of the ancient super state of primary societies in China was itself no accident.

There were six primary civilizations in the world, namely Mesopotamia, Egypt, India, China, Mexico, and Peru. There was no higher civilization among the neighbours of a primary civilization. Greek and Hebrew civilizations were secondary but became the philosophical foundation for Western civilization that dominates the world today. Of those eight ancient civilizations, Chinese civilization showed the following characteristics that were lacking in the other seven [10]:

1. The only inland civilization (see Essay 2).
2. Only Chinese history clearly recorded a transformation from a matrilineal to a patriarchal society (see Essay 4).
3. In the six primary civilizations, large-scale irrigation systems were all constructed except in China, where occasional flood control was

often said to have similar effects on the emergence of state structure but in fact, it did not.

4. According to DeMeo [3], the desertification around 4000-3000 BC also occurred in Americas. The patriarchal warriors, who emerged from the affected areas, migrated to the unaffected areas and conquered the original peaceful people and then formed the primary civilizations around the world. China was apparently an exception. According to DeMeo, the Hsia people were the original peaceful people. DeMeo did not know that the Chou people were from the same tribal people as the Hsia. The Axial Age was during the Chou dynasty (1122-256 BC). Ancient Chinese people were not conquered by patriarchal warriors but they transformed from matrilineal to patriarchal society themselves.

5. In the above eight ancient civilizations, China was the only one lacking the geographic/economic barriers to block discontented people from moving out.

6. As a result from the absence of geographic/economic barriers, Chinese people kept their migrating habits of hunters/gathers until the late Axial Age. Confucius once said, "If you were to govern in this way (according to Confucian principles), peasants will come flocking to you from all directions with their babies on their backs." It shows that peasants were migrating freely during Confucius' time.

7. Chinese religious faith remained primitive through Chinese history (see Essay 2).

8. China went through a different pathway leading to the emergence of subjective consciousness (see Essay5).

(5) The Universal Evolutionary Pathways

Our world is a multiple-dimension and multiple-level operation. From the evolutionary view, those levels and dimensions reflect the numerous phases our world has gone through. As shown in Table 1.2, the universe has developed from the physical world, life, culture, and to consciousness, and from non-being, being, atoms and molecules, up to stars, galaxies, and the universe. The non-being and being are concepts from the Chinese Taoist philosophy, and it also agrees with the theory of modern physics. According to the recent superstring theory, all elementary particles are really mini strings that have no area and no thickness but only a length. There are many dimensions in the universe, but those dimensions can fold up. In quantum theory, the elementary particles are only points without any dimension. Nuclear physics sees being and non-being as the two exchangeable states of vacuum, and the cyclotron experiments have confirmed that matter and energy can be created from nothing. Therefore space-taking particles or solid things, in the conventional notion, cease to exist. If the universe can shrink to nothing, it is logical to suppose there was nothing before the Big Bang.

Primary society has culture and its people may also have consciousness but the main force that keeps a primary society harmonious and functional is from unconsciousness, the psychological and emotional social bond everyone feels at the subconscious level. People from a secondary society have both consciousness and unconsciousness but the force that keeps secondary society functional is from consciousness. A secondary society is built on rational thinking systems.

Table 1.2. The Universal Evolutionary Pathways

Content	1. **Physical World**	2. **Life**	2. **Culture**	4. **Consciousness**
Level 1	Non-being			
Level 2	Being			
Level 3	Elementary particles			
Level 4	Atoms and electrons			
Level 5	Molecules	DNA		
Level 6	Matters and objects	Cells		
Level 7	Stars and planets	Tissues		
Level 8	Galaxies	Organs and limbs		
Level 9	Universe	Individuals		
Level 10		Primary society	Culture	Unconscious
Level 11		Secondary society	Civilization	Conscious
Level 12			Transcendence culture	Rational thinking systems
Level 13				Spirituality

(6) The Taoist Ideal Life and Society

Here I would like to say a few words about the different states of the human mind and their influence on our world view and behaviour. As shown in Figure 2, those dogs have three different mental states, namely, resting, goal oriented, and fighting with each other. If you ask those dogs what they see in their world, and what they want in their life, the dogs in rest would say they see the whole world that includes themselves, and they want to enjoy life. If you put their answer in philosophical terms, it will be Taoist philosophy.

The goal oriented dogs only see their target that they run after, and they want to reach their goal. Such goals create conflicts among dogs. When dogs are fighting with each other, they see only each other and want to conquer each other. Since it is impossible to conquer each other at the same time, the only outcome will be that one is conquered by the other except for a tie. Fortunately dogs are still guided by their nature, and they will stop when they are too tired to continue. Civilized humans are beyond human nature, and thus subjected to the upward spiral course described by William Eckhardt.

Thus, the people who lived in the ancient primary society saw the world and interpreted their experience from the basis of human nature and self-enjoyment, or the aesthetic view. When they had an idle mind, they interpreted the world by their memories, their inner experience and their observation. Since such interpretations were also expressions to other members, they stimulated aesthetic feeling or joy in both speakers and the listeners.

The secondary society has an ideology which suits its goals. Since we have all been brought up by the ideology or value system thad has well been established and supported by the social structure, our subjective consciousness, the agent to think and understand the world, is no longer the natural being dictated by our nature but largely a cultural construct by our traditions as Julian Jayness pointed out decades ago. [11] So social scientists claim: "We are, in short, what we make ourselves." [12] Which part we make ourselves, the body or the soul? We make our soul. Unfortunately, the agent that makes our souls is not ourselves but our culture. It is well established that

23

both the appearance of agriculture and the emergence of states in the Middle East were associated with shortened human life spans. According to William Eckhardt, our history of civilization was history of continuously upgrading war with massive numbers of people being killed periodically by wars and disasters. [4] If morden people persue happiness, the doubled suicide rates of the last century in North America indicates clearly that we acted differently, since we were not ourselves anymore but were billions of cultural constructs.

It is most striking if we compared the historical paintings from China and the West. The Chinese paintings were mainly landscapes, flowers and birds with occasional images of people while the Western paintings were exclusively human figures. Therefore, their painters were exactly acted like the resting and fighting dogs respectively. Paintings of landscape appeared first in Holland in the sixteenth century and then after in Britain. Those two coast countries developed sophisticated navigational technology, which led to their contact with more traditional cultures and also enabled them to run away from the threadening millitary forces of the continental Europe. As the result, both Dutch and British people became more relaxed like our ancestors were. A relaxing mind seems to be much broader. The dramatic difference between primary and secondary societies indicates that they are at different levels with an inbridgeable gap between. The people of a secondary society have entered an uncharted territory like lobefin fish moving onto land.

Humans and dogs are, however, the same. They enjoy themselves when there is nothing to worry about; they switch on their survival kit to run on their peripheral potentials when their life is at risk; they switch on death programs when they are in a hopeless situation: The man commits suicide while dogs stop eating when they are terminally ill and stop fighting when they are in front of a hungry tiger. Science and technology have made life much easier. Therefore, we have every reason to enjoy our life, unless we are determined to fight against ourselves as humans did during the past five thousand years of civilization.

Here I only try to interpret the Taoist ideal life and society in modern terms. Lao Tzu, Chuang Tzu and other Taoist classic authors all praised the ancient egalitarian society in which there were no forceful authorities. They even named those who lived in such a society as the real people. It is clear that we cannot accept any "will" forced upon us, whether the "will" is from people in authority, gods, or from faith of any principles. Accordingly, we do not have to work either, since our remote ancestors did not.

In real life, it is often difficult to determine whether an activity is work or pure enjoyment, and whether we are motivated by ourselves or by others' "will". The motto to remember at all times is: enjoy the process and do not care about the result. As long as you enjoy your work and the company of your colleagues at the working place, you may work as long as you like. Do not force yourselves to work hard for the payment.

Therefore, it is up to the secondary society to assemble and integrate all the end products we produce during the activities of our self-enjoyment into something useful and meaningful to us who live in the primary society. As to who have to live in secondary society, and how they achieve this goal, it is beyond my speculation. Ideally, they live their lives exactly the same way as those who live in the primary society. An analogy of the two level societies is that our body tissues are the primary society of cells while the organs such as lungs and livers are the secondary society. Cells live their life in the tissue and it is up to the organs to maintain the macro environment for the cells inside the body.

You may say this is an unrealistic dream. But if you read thoroughly the works by Lao Tzu, Chuang Tzu, and other classic authors, and if you are able to shut off all the ideas that your culture has crammed into your mind and judge it objectively and precisely, you will certainly agree with me that my interpretation is exactly what Lao Tzu, Chuang Tzu, and other classic authors meant in their writings. You will also agree that to keep this ideal life and society in our mind is useful to prevent us from enduring meaningless endeavours. We do not have to labour ourselves like ants before enjoy our lives. We do not have to drive each other into madness.

If our remote ancestors never worked, we need not work either, unless the work itself is a joy. With modern science and technology, such a goal, no work except for enjoyment, is not beyond our reach.

*   *   *

Afterword: My Own Taoist Cultivation and Experience

For a few years, I tried and found some places where I could not see any man- made things such as buildings and electrical wire posts but also had a relatively browd view. I was sitting there meditating Taoist teachings and ideologies. So I was able to live in a pure natural world, and watching how animals and plants to live their lives.

Like water is flowing down the river which is part of the water circulation on earth: Under the sun, sea water evaporates into the air and becomes clouds, from which rain and snow fall on the land and become rivers. Similarly, all plants and animals live their lives in the Taoist natural way like the river flowing to the sea: Plants take **carbon dioxide** from the air to grow and animals eat plants to breathe out **carbon dioxide** into the air.

During my Taoist cultivation, I was watching deers, wild rabits(hares), and squirrels surrounding me. Their lives are idling and do not work except enjoying their lives as part of the natural circulation like water flowing along the river. Whenever the enjoyment is not enough, they will die peacefully since they follow the Taoist teaching: life and death are the same.

At my home yard, there was a cherry tree and there was full of red cherry in the autumn. From time to time, squirrels and crews come to enjoy eating the cherry. I only saw a few of them on this cherry tree while other squirrels and crows were flying nearby and on the nearby pine trees. They apparently do not come to snatch the cherry. For years I never saw a single half-eaten cherry on the ground. So each year, I still have most the cherry on the tree when I picked them up myself.

If Modern humans are in such situation, they will all come together to swallow the tasty cherry though our born naure is not like this. Panda is the most-liked animal by people because their appearance looks like our children and the most popular pests are dogs because their behavior is like our children. Husband and wife have sex thousands of times in their life but only give birth to a few children. It is beyond any doubt that we are born to enjoy ourselves but only the civilization makes us to fight against each other and then exhausting the environment on earth.

References

[1] All quotations from ancient Chinese classics in this book were translated into English by the author. The author consulted the following sources before the translation:

    1) http://chinese.dsturgeon.net.

    2) http://www.toyogakuen_u.ac.jp/~acmuller/contao/analects.htm.

    3) http://chinapage.com/gnl.html.

    4) http://www.his.com/~merkin/DaoGloss.html.

[2] Riane Eisler(2002): Ecofeminism gives life purpose. In: Constructing a life philosophy: opposing view points, ed by M. R. Schmidt. San Diego: Greenhaven Press Inc.

[3] J. DeMeo(2004): Saharasia. Orgone: Orgone Biophysical Research Lab.

[4] William Eckhardt(1995): A dialectical evolutionary theory of civilizations, empires, and wars. In: Civilizations world systems studying world-historical change, ed by S. K. Sanderson. Walnut Creek, USA: AltaMira Press. p75-108.

[5] David Christian(2004): Maps of time: a introduction to big history. Berkeley & Los Angeles: University of California Press.

[6] 1). List of wars; 2). List of battles and other violent events by death toll; 3). List of battles by death toll. (http://en.wikipedia.org/wiki/)[

[7] Zhao Hui, Wei Jun (2002): The Excavation and Study of the Chinese Walled Cities During the New Stone Age. In: Ancient Civilizations, edited by the Archaeology and the Ancient Civilization Centre. Beijing: Cultural Relic Publishing House. (In Chinese)

[8] Zhang Xuehai (2002): On the Emergence and Development of Dongyi Civilization. In: Ancient Civilizations, edited by the Archaeology and the Ancient Civilization Centre.
Beijing: Cultural Relic Publishing House. (In Chinese)

[9] Claudio Cioffi-Revilla and David Lai (1995): War and Politics in Ancient China, 2700 BC to 722 BC: Measurement and Comparative Analysis. Journal of Conflict Resolution, 39:467-494.

[10] You-Sheng Li (2009): The Uniqueness of Chinese Civilization. Xuedeng (Study Lamp), Issue No. 10. (In Chinese)

[11] Julian Jayness (1976): The Origin of Consciousness in the Breakdown of the Bicameral Mind. Boston: Houghton Mifflin.
[12] A. Wolfe (2001) : "Human Nature" in Encyclopedia of Sociology: Human Nature. Oxford: Oxford University Press.

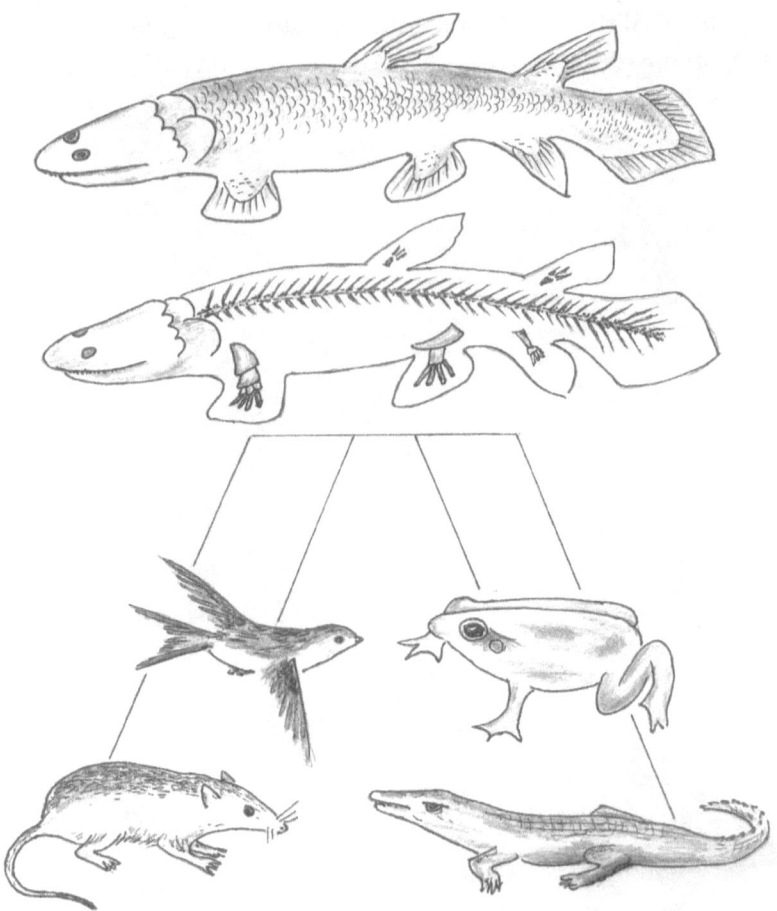

Figure 1. Lobefin fish and their evolutionary prospects.

Figure 2. Dogs and their three states of minds.

2

Life, Culture, and Religion

In her book *A History of God*, the English author and former nun Karen Armstrong says, "When people began to devise their myths and worship their gods, they were not seeking a literal explanation for natural phenomena. The symbolic stories, cave paintings and carvings were an attempt to express their wonder and to link this pervasive mystery with their own lives; indeed, poets, artists and musicians are often impelled by a similar desire today….God was a product of the creative imagination, like the poetry and music that I found so inspiring." [1]

Today a low but substantial percentage of our population indicates that they have no religious faith, and it is certainly conceivable that a culture or a society can easily survive without God or religion. Nevertheless, almost all early recorded cultural traditions have a religious faith in some form or other. In all my extensive reading on ancient human civilizations, I have never come across any non-religious cultural traditions.

Religions, however, are not the only avenue for experiencing awe and wonder. It can also be experienced through arts and through the appreciation of nature. Nobody condemns arts or nature, but today there are those who are condemning religions. One of these is the English man, Richard Dawkins. According to him, "Good people do good things and bad people do bad things, but it takes religion for good people to do bad things". Both Karen Armstrong and Richard Dawkins live in a secondary society, where arts and religions tend to be separated. This was not the case in a primary society. The following is from Chuang Tzu:

In the ancient time, yin and yang were in harmony. 1) Gods and spirits were quiet and did not interfere with people. 2) The four seasons followed their own course, and animals and plants were not harmed. 3) Humans lived to their full life span. People had knowledge but there was no use of it. This is called the big One. (Chuang Tzu, Chapter 16)

Thus according to Chuang Tzu, gods and spirits do not interfere with people in primary society. It is consistent with Karen Armstrong's view that both arts and God are the product of human imagination, inspired by the same feeling of wonder. Neither arts nor religions should normally interfere with people. Although Chuang Tzu did not mention the secondary society he was in, he apparently described this happy and peaceful picture of primary society in contrast to secondary society. Thus it is the opposite in secondary society, namely, 1) gods interfere with people, 2) they damage their natural environment, and 3) people's lives are cut short by their own actions. Both arts and religions can give the feeling of awe, but only organized religions can interfere with people with such a power that they are able to make them fearful. Thus they have to obey gods with awe.

In reality, all cultural traditions fall between the two extremes. Nevertheless, we still can tell which tradition is close to which extreme. The early Mesopotamian civilization which started with the advent of cities was nothing but an economic enterprise. They dug canal networks for irrigation and erected huge platforms to build the temples, which were not only far the largest buildings in the cities but were also visible in the landscape miles away and dominated the city's skyline. A scholar offered such a description of their religion:

"The importance of a deity was measured by how well his soldiers performed in battle and how much land they conquered. Not much going on in (Sumerian) heaven unless you were a god... the dead spent eternity in a dreary, poorly lit, depressing shadow world... where they wished they were dead or deader." [2] It was no wonder that archaeology documented shortened life spans associated with the emergence of civilization in the Middle East.

Their neighboring Egyptians started with rural areas and had a united nation a few hundred years before Mesopotamia. Their religion seemed better. The same scholar gave such a description: "Egyptians believed in a continuation of one's earthly condition in one's earthly body after death....The cult of Osiris, which grew rapidly during the Middle Kingdom (c 1900 BC), promised resurrection and eternal life to all, regardless of social status... did not really have a hell..." [2]

The earliest civilization in Europe was created by the Minoans who lived on the island of Crete. They possessed hardly any weapons and had no constructions for defense. They worshiped a goddess. Their shrines were located at home, in caves, and on hilltops. A scholar says, "In Minoan religion, there is a conspicuous lack of anxiety about death. A hymn to Nature as a Goddess seems to be heard from everywhere, a hymn of joy and life."[3]

At one time, Chinese civilization was close to a Taoist ideal society. Their society was quasi-primary society, a society similar to primary society. Their countryside consumed what they produced, and only rarely bought something from outside. When I was a child in the early 1950s, the gods Chinese peasants worshiped were all natural deities. The only temple for villagers to pay respect to the gods was for the god of earth. Since it was considered as representative of a local god like a tribal leader, a village may have several such temples, each for a clan or a cluster of households. They were usually the size of a room, much smaller than a farmer house. Even though only a single room, peasants never forgot to use it for something else. They could be used as gristmills, a public place for meetings, or a playing ground for children during rainy days. In my village, all the temples for the god of earth had no image of the god. Each household of peasants usually worshiped three additional gods:

the kitchen god, the fortune god, and the god of heaven and earth. Except for the kitchen god who had a paper portrait hung on the wall, the other two had only specific locations, the storage room for the fortune god, and the yard for the god of heaven and earth. The god of heaven and earth was really a god of nature and had thus no image, but the fortune god was a male deity. A Chinese calendar was often printed below the portrait of the kitchen god to increase its sale. As a child, I saw clearly that Chuang Tzu was right: Gods do not interfere with people, and they do not have the power to do so. The Chinese countryside also had temples of Buddhism, Taoism, and even Catholic churches. The power of their gods usually stayed inside their buildings. Most Chinese people worshiped them all, disregarding their difference.

But things changed with the advent of Mao's Communism, which was in fact a powerful religion in all aspects. When I joined a Sunday service in a Church for the first time at Cambridge in 1980, I was amazed to find out all the formality exactly the same as I went through a hundred times in China to worship nobody else but Mao. The only noticeable difference was the color of the book we held to our chest while chanting and singing. Mao's book was red but the bible was blue. A Chinese palmist usually reads the face and the palm to tell one's future. When Chinese peasants saw the awe-inspiring portrait of Mao, with the unusual mole on his chain, they claimed that this man was born a God like Jesus. To be precise, they saw him as another emperor, since they judged emperors as godlike. However, Mao was not an ordinary emperor, and he was much more powerful than any Chinese emperor. He had a much larger bureaucratic machine facilitated by modern communication technology. For the first time in Chinese history, he organized five hundred million peasants to shout with one voice and move in one direction. They did achieve miracles but their miracles were nothing but harmful.

My junior high school (grade 7-9) was ten miles away, and I walked home on weekends. I still remember the beauty of the isolated Chinese countryside: orchards of flowers and fruits one after another beside the road. The peasants were so happy to see someone passing by their fields. They often stop working to show their hospitality to me. They even offered me the produce of their farms. Once Mao's order came down, the landscape changed overnight. The flowers and orchards were all gone. I had to cross several canals without even a drop of water in them. One half finished reservoir could be seen miles away. I was enticed to climb up its banks, more than a dozen meter high, and saw hardly any water inside. It was like a huge bowel or open mouth trying to suck water from the blue sky. We did not know how dreadful the hell Mao devised for his people, because he put them all in hell when they were still alive. One thing is certain that they could no longer live to their full life span, because many of them had to die of starvation. Mao's communist religion pressed its people so hard that a lot committed suicide.

I heard suicide again many years later in a recent visit. A young lady told me, "It is better than dying of cancer!". They think all cancers in the village are caused by water pollution. The most instrumental is, however, the so-called spiritual pollution: Corruption is everywhere, and 90% of Chinese billionaires are believed to be from government official families. It is no longer an easy job to feel happy. If those peasants have the power to devise a hell, they will certainly make one for those corrupted billionaire officials. [4]

* * *

Afterword: Oceans, Continents, and Religion

Both the ancient Chinese and Mediterranean people thought they were at the centre of their world. Ancient Mediterranean people thought their world was the Mediterranean sea surrounded by endless lands. The Greeks regarded their Apollo Temple at Delphi as the centre of the world. Ancient Chinese people thought their world was the land of China surrounded by endless lands. It was only during the third century BC when a scholar (Zou Yan, 340-260 BC) speculated that there were a total of nine continents surrounded by water, and

China was located on one of them. His theory remained as a wild unpopular speculation through Chinese history.

In his sixth edition of the book *Human Evolution and Prehistory*, William A. Haviland includes a map of the major early civilizations: Mesopotamia, Egypt, India, China, Mesoamerica, and Peru. China was the only inland civilization while the five others all had their coasts. [5] The first Chinese dynasty, Hsia (2200-1766 BC), was indeed an inland country without any coast.

The *Book of Mountains and Seas* was traditionally credited to Yu the Great and his minister Yi. Most scholars believe that it was compiled during the Warring States Period (476-221 BC) but it used previous material. This book has 18 chapters with each chapter dedicated to a geographical area. One chapter is for the Middle Mountains, and another for Within the Seas. The remaining 16 chapters are for the four directions, the north, the south, the west, and the east. Each direction has four chapters, and for the east, they are *The Eastern Mountains, The East Beyond the Seas, The East Within the Seas,* and *The Eastern Wasteland.* Since each direction is the same and all ended with the Wasteland zone, the authors of the *Book of Mountains and Seas* clearly had no knowledge that China was bordering seas and oceans in the east but lands in the north and the west. It further supports that the Hsia were inland people who had no knowledge of seas and oceans.

The *Classic of Poetry* has a collection of 305 ancient Chinese poems from the Chou dynasty (1122-256 BC). In this book, the Chinese character for "sea" (hai) appeared only seven times (0.02%). It is not surprising that the folk songs (feng), which make up the major part, does not use the Chinese character for the sea at all as their authors had no experience of the sea. The intellectual officials seemed to have knowledge about the sea, since one of the seven lines in the *Classic of Poetry* that have the Chinese character for sea reads, *all rivers will flow into the sea.* But the remaining six only use the word "sea" to indicate the remote peripheral areas of their world. Furthermore, the ancient Chinese called any large lake a sea. Therefore, those 305 poems provided no evidence that their authors had any experience with the sea. Although the authoritative historical maps always ascribe a substantial length of coast to the Chou dynasty, their authority might have never reached the coast though their cultural influence might have. Thus Chinese people called their country the middle country, a country surrounded by many other countries.

That may be why some scholars labeled Western culture as an oceanic culture, and the Chinese, as a continental culture. The former had an open mind to curiosity while the latter did not, since the endless blue water of seas and oceans was always mysterious to the human mind while the solid land was much less so.

When I first came to the idea of primary and secondary societies, I thought that the people who live in a primary society stand on the ground while the people who live in a secondary society live their lives as if they are on the sea. When you are in a ship on the sea, you are always going somewhere, and the destiny is not up to everybody's choice as there is only one for all people on board. If the ship wants to stay where it is, the ship needs to cast an anchor. The people who live in a secondary society, therefore, need a reference point outside their ship of society, either a destiny or an anchor. Life on the sea harbors much more uncertainty than life on land.

The Greek historian Thucydides (?460-395 BC) wrote:

For in ancient times both the Hellenes, and those Barbarians, whose homes were on the coast of the mainland or in islands, when they began to find their way to one another by sea had recourse to piracy. They were commanded by powerful chiefs, who took this means of increasing their wealth and providing for their poorer followers. They would fall upon the unwalled and straggling towns, or rather villages, which they plundered, and maintained themselves chiefly by the plunder of them; for, as yet, such an occupation was held to be honourable and not disgraceful. [6]

Thus, it is not pure coincidental that Mediterranean civilizations started with a typical secondary society while Chinese civilization started with a super state of primary societies.

Thanks to modern science, the seas and oceans have lost their mysterious quality. But they still stimulate our feelings and aspirations. When you are facing the turbulent sea waves of the ocean at the shore, you feel the tremendous power of this vast water. Our land does not give us such feelings. Growing up in an inland province of China, I had never seen a sea before I read a poem about the sea when I was a university student. A line of the poem reads, "I was born to love the great sea with my whole heart." It struck me as part of my makeup. The following lines are from a Chinese warlord and poet who lived in the second century AD (Cao Cao, 155-220):

> *I travel to the Rocky Shore,*
> *I come to watch the ocean…*
> *The sun and the moon rise and set,*
> *Both seem to come from this ocean.*
> *The glittering stars cover the whole black skies,*
> *They seem to be all inside this vast water of ocean.*

Whenever I am at a sea shore, the far reaching ocean transforms my mind into a state of grandeur and nobility. But I am again in a business frame of mind when I face my daily routine soon after I leave the sea shore. This might not be the case for the ancient people who lived an idle life in primary society. Confucius once listened to the lofty music Shao, and he lost his taste for delicious food for three months. No doubt the sight of ocean affected ancient people's behavior.

The prehistoric megalithic monuments seemed to spread along the coast, especially in Europe (Figure 3), where several thousands of such megalithic constructions have been found. A remarkable example was the Stonehenge on the British islands: Several pieces of huge stones were erected to form a circle. The first Stonehenge which consisted of huge tree trunks dates back to 8000 BC. You need hundreds or even thousands of people to cooperate in their efforts for months to build those huge constructions. Since they did not have any practical value, it was not easily understandable to those who participated in the construction. They needed a god, or a leader, or a uniform belief which was powerful enough to motivate those people. They lived in primary society, but they must have formed a temporary secondary society to carry out those huge projects.

Chinese civilization started from the inland area along the Yellow River, where there was no such monumental constructions excavated except for walled towns. City walls or the moat around a village had their practical value even to a primitive mind. Megalithic monuments were, however, found in the areas east of the birthplace of Chinese civilization and therefore near the sea. One such area was in what is nowadays' Shandong and Liaoning provinces. The Shang people originated from this area while the Hsia and Chou people were from the inland areas. The Shang people worshiped many more gods and spirits while the Hsia and Chou people seemed more practical.

Furthermore, the Shang people were good at trade and commercial activities. So were the ancient Mediterranean people including the Mesopotamian and the Egyptian people. By sea, their commercial trade went as far as the Indus Valley and left many artifacts there. The Indian civilization was classless, and they did not import any luxury goods. Thus it is not surprising that the Indian civilization did not feature notable megalithic monuments, though the Indians did not appear less religious.

If the prehistoric megalithic monuments spread along the coast, some early civilizations might have well developed along coasts. This is indeed the case. The Mesoamerican civilizations and the South American Andean civilizations all developed along the coast and were all characterized by megalithic monuments. Megalithic monuments were, however, most notable on the pacific islands. Hundreds of human shaped statues were found on Easter Island, and the largest is ten meters high and 80 tons in weight. Both the sea and those colossal figures might stimulate the same feelings in their ancient viewers. [4]

When I was in Cambridge, England in the early 1980s, my landlady who had lived most of her life in continental Europe once described the landscape of the European countryside: Magnificent church buildings here and there dominated the horizon in contrast to the simple and crude farm houses. The execution of Socrates in the fourth century BC heralded the widely spread religious persecution in European history. That may be why the European rural scenery, according to my landlady, was different from my hometown in the early 1950s, where one could, once outside the village, hardly see any human artifacts except for trees and crops. Thus the rural scenery in the 1950s still carried their different traditions from prehistoric times. It all depends whether their remote ancestors lived near the sea or not. China has caught up to the West in the last few decades. Now you can see many more human artifacts such as wire poles, factory chimneys, and high buildings in the Chinese countryside than in the West, since China is so densely populated.

References

[1.] K. Armstrong (1994): A History of God. New York: Alfred A. Knopf, p5.

[2.] G. Stebben (1999): Everything You Need to Know About Religion. New York: Pocket Book.

[3.] Arthur Cotterell (1979): The Minoan World. New York: Charles Scribner's Sons, 1979. p162.

[4.] The above part of this essay was published in Humanist Perspective. Spring 2009, Issue 168, p34-36.

[5.] William A. Haviland (2003): *Human Evolution and Prehistory*. Belmont, USA: Wadsworth/Thomson. P303.

[6.] Benjamin Jowett (1900): Thucydedes. Second edition. Oxford, Clarendon Press, 1900.

Figure 3 . The distribution of monumental megalithic constructions in Europe. Densely dotted areas: 4800-3000 BC; sparsely dotted areas: 3000-1200 BC.

Figure 4. Those huge stone stattues stand on the north coast of Easter Island. Scattered pieces of white stone found beneath those statues have been identified as the remains of their eyes.

3

Evidence that Chinese People Lived Essentially in Primary Society Until the Warring States Period (476-221 BC)

Summary: The difference between primary and secondary societies was further characterized by analyzing the ways and directions in which, spare time was spent. In support of the conclusion that Chinese people lived in primary or quasi- primary societies well into the civilized stage until the Warring States Period (476-221 BC), evidence is presented along the following six lines: 1) the early Chinese scholars showed no knowledge and experience of secondary society; 2) both Taoism and Confucianism take primary society as their ideal society; 3) ancient China lacked the necessary social apparatus to operate a secondary society for a national or local goal other than survival and security; 4) ancient Chinese military expeditions were more like violent conflicts among primitive primary societies; 5) benevolence/righteousness and ritual/music practice advocated by Confucianism are an extension of primary society culture rather than an indication of the emergence of secondary society; 6) consistent with the above conclusion, many Chinese scholars call the ancient Chinese society the primitive society when they apply the Marxist classification of society to Chinese history.

*   *   *

Chinese civilization started with a super state that functioned in many ways like the United Nations does in the modern world. This relatively peaceful environment allowed Chinese people to continue their primitive lifestyle in the primary society.

Historians often ask why Chinese civilization remains the only one that was continuous in history while other civilizations went through cycles of rise and collapse. This super state of primary societies is no doubt the underlying reason, since only a secondary society is open to diversification and evolution while a primary society is stabilized by human genetics. For the same reason, ancient Chinese civilization showed a remarkable capacity for embracing and tolerating its surrounding cultures and ethnic populations and then integrating them into the mainstream of Chinese culture.

Since I conceived the idea of primary and secondary societies, I have been amazed that evidence to support this theory is readily seen everywhere when one reads Chinese history. But I will first show you the different ways to spend our spare time in relation to different pathways in human history.

(1) How to Spend Spare Time and the Different Pathways of Human Civilizations

Many historians and anthropologists tried to set up some criteria that would show when an emerging civilization was passing through the threshold from a primitive culture. V. Gordon Childe (1892-1957) raised the so-called ten hallmarks of civilization: density of settlement, specialization of labor, management of surplus goods, emergence of a ruling class, state organization based on residence rather than kinship, long distance trade in luxury goods, construction of monumental buildings, standardized art style, writing, and science and mathematics. [1] Such hallmarks or criteria failed to notice that human civilizations could take different pathways. It becomes extremely complex if we try to measure different civilizations that have gone in different directions by the same standard. The above hallmarks and criteria are influenced by European-centralism. Generally speaking, a writing system is critical to a civilization, but the Inca Empire, though with a large territory, long history, and complex social structure, did not have a writing system. The Inca Empire used knots to keep records, and a fast-running messenger system to facilitate an extensive and accurate communication system inside the Empire.

An increasing number of anthropologists have adapted the notion that a culture's emergence as a new civilization can only be determined by analysis based on its own history. According to its historical records and archaeological findings, the culture in question can be divided into several historical phases. A detailed comparison and analysis are carried out with those different phases, and new features which have emerged to execute dramatic influence on the subsequent history are identified to determine whether a new civilization has emerged. [2] To understand the different pathways of different civilizations, spare time spending provides a vantage point to get a bird's-eye view over this issue.

One way to tell a primary society from a secondary society is to see how that society spends its spare time. Spare time is the time left over when one's basic biological needs such as food and shelter are fulfilled, and one faces no immediate danger. It should not be confused with the time left over after work. A primary society devotes its spare time to self-enjoyment while a secondary society uses its spare time to reach some goal. Thus civilization is built on spare time. If humans lived like certain animals bred by man, such as fast growing silk worms and force-fed ducks that have no spare time except for eating and sleeping, humans would never develop any civilization. This is one of the central claims of this book: The development of civilization has nothing to do with our biological needs. The modern world has long been on the road of material civilization. This does not mean that material civilization is the only choice for a secondary society or is the best way of life. The domination of material civilization in the world is largely the result of war, and ancient peaceful cultures like the ones in the Indus Valley and on the Island of Crete must have been assimilated by force in early human history.

The forms of self-enjoyment that a primary society pursues in its spare time include the practice of religion and spirituality, philosophical study and aesthetic creation. Philosophical pursuits cover all knowledge in its depth and breadth. It is part of human nature to feel joy at obtaining new knowledge. Philosophy and aesthetics are the essence of civilization. From pure theoretical deduction, civilization can be developed in pure academic and aesthetic fashion. The development of such a civilization is itself a process of self-enjoyment. It does not need war to hasten its delivery, and it does not need an idle class to supervise it from above.

Civilized humans spend their spare time at either the spiritual level or the material level but for goals that are dictated by their secondary society. If we use the word "pursuit" to describe humans' spare time activity, these fall into one of three levels that are identified according to the extent of deviation of those activities from human nature: 1) within the range of normal spare time activity dictated by human nature, namely relaxing and self-enjoyment; 2) any pursuit for future well-being such as work or labor; 3) any activity that runs against human nature and is harmful to our physical or spiritual well being.

Human activities at 3) or the third level were rare and isolated in a primary society but are often institutionalized in a secondary society. War and wealth accumulation are both pursuits at the material level, and they reinforce each other. But they may also be separated from each other. The Indus Valley and Minoan civilizations both had considerable wealth accumulation but exhibited no sign of war. The rapid expansion of wealth after the Second World War is not associated with any acceleration of war. The ancient Greek city states once grouped around two hostile city states, Athens and Sparta. Sparta was the warring state while Athens was the rich one.

There are about 180 thousand Amish people who lived in the United States and Canada. They refuse to use modern technology and keep the traditional way of life: They are simple, hardworking, happy, healthy, peace-loving folk living in harmony with nature. Their rates of suicide and mental disorder seem to be half of their more civilized neighbors. [3] If they had lived among the warring ancient Mediterranean civilizations, they would not have survived to the present day.

(2) Evidence that Chinese People Lived Essentially in a Primary Society Until the Warring States Period (476-221 BC)

Our solar system has nine planets including the Earth circling around the sun. The sun is many times bigger than even the largest planet, Jupiter. Similarly, many provinces or states surround a much larger central government. But there is no such super center in the Milk Way galaxy where billions of stars surround each other. Scholars call the ancient Southeast Asia political organizations the galactic polity. There were many local powers and their surrounding affiliated towns and villages but there was no super power as the centre for those local powers. In fact, all ancient civilizations developed like the galaxy without a super centre. Even the Roman Empire had to coexist with its neighbors such as the Persian Empire and the Gupta Empire in India.

Ancient China was the only exception. Unlike Central America, the Mediterranean area, India, and Southeast Asia which are all linked to other large lands, Ancient China was isolated by Tibet and the central Asian highland, the cold wasteland of Siberia, and the sea. Yet their land is big enough to feel the need for a super state to keep peace and coordinate efforts against floods. This super state ensured a relatively peaceful social environment, and made it possible for Chinese people to live in a primary and quasi-primary society until the Warring States Period (476-221 BC).

Here I will say a few words about the first three Chinese dynasties, Hsia, Shang, and Chou. According to *The Rites*: *Biaoji*, the Shang dynasty led its people to worship gods and spirits profusely while both the Hsia and Chou dynasties paid due respect to gods and spirits but kept a distance from them. The Chou people were part of the Hsia clans, and they shared the same ancestors from western China while the Shang people were from the East. The Chou dynasty seemed to have waged a major political reform towards a more humanist direction shortly after they overthrew the Shang dynasty. In this book, like many scholars in this field, I will treat the three dynasties Hsia, Shang, Chou as a continuous cultural tradition, but they are not weighed the same in the following discussion.

1. The Early Scholars of Various Schools of Thought had no Knowledge and Experience of Secondary Society:
      During the Chinese Axi al Age, namely the Spring/Autumn and the Warring States Periods (770-221 BC), the scholars of various schools of thought were almost all from the low level of the ruling class, and they concentrated their thoughts on ethical, political, and life issues. No doubt they had a thorough knowledge and understanding of life from both the ruling and the ruled class. Nevertheless, early scholars apparently had no knowledge and experience of secondary society. This clearly indicates that Chinese people mainly lived in a primary or quasi-primary society until the Warring States Period.
      Both Confucius and Meng Tzu said a lot that is not compatible with a secondary society but suits well with the administration of a primary society. While punning on the fact that the Chinese words "government" and "correctness" are the same, Confucius once said to a local lord, "To govern means to behave correctly. If you lead the people by your own correct behavior, who would not behave correctly?" He furthered his point, saying, "When you have straightened out your own life, things will go well without your giving orders. If your own life is not straightened out, even if you give orders, no one will follow them." (*Analects*, 12:17, 13:6) Those words are only appropriate to the headman in a primary society. The leader of a secondary society has to work out a strategy to solve the problem the society is facing and give clear directions to his subordinates and people. It falls far short if the leader only knows how to behave correctly. Without modern communication technology, the exemplary effects could

hardly go beyond the interpersonal level in a primary society. The Chinese peasants in Confucius' time did not have much to do during the long winter. Confucius and his followers did not have any idea how to organize those peasants' spare time to pursue their own well-being. To organize the people's spare time into the development of materialistic civilization is a Western idea. It apparently fell outside of the vision field of ancient Chinese thinkers.

Meng Tzu opposes the strategy to unite China by force, and he thinks that if a government is fully based on benevolent principles and it wins all the hearts of the people, then China will unite automatically under this government. According to a notable Chinese scholar Li Shen, Meng Tzu set up the economical criteria for an ideal society of moderate means. Meng Tzu says, "If the elderly people have meat to eat and silk to wear, and the ordinary people suffer no starvation and are able to clothe themselves properly, there is never such a thing that the leader who has achieved this cannot unite the world under his rule." Such criteria are easily achievable, and many areas of our modern world have reached such levels. But united rules have not emerged everywhere and violent conflicts continue. Only under a primary society system are people satisfied with an idle and lazy way of life after their basic material needs are ensured. They may then live peacefully with each other like in a united country. In a secondary society setting, there are always some people who want to exploit others' labor to achieve their boundless goals, and the social structure of a secondary society does harbor such ambitions. Furthermore, to achieve a united China by benevolent policies, as Meng Tzu advocates, requires the free migration of people to wherever they like. Such free migration was only possible in a primary society setting where neither political borders nor any requirement of resident registration existed.

Lao Tzu's form of governing by doing nothing reflects the social phenomenon that there is no forceful authority in a primary society, and its leadership is based on persuasion and consensus. To follow the natural way and obey the dictates of human nature is what governing by doing nothing really means. Here emphasis should be laid on the often overlooked fact that Confucian exponents advocate the policy of governing by doing nothing as well. *Analects: Taobo* (8:20) admires it, saying, "The Shun Emperor had only five officials to help him but order prevailed all over the land under the heavens." Confucius once said, "Who has achieved governing by doing nothing? It is nobody but Shun. What has he done? He only sat on the throne solemnly facing the south."

In Tao Te Ching, Chapter 29, Lao Tzu says, "The human world is sacred. It is not something to meddle with, and it is not something to be possessed. Those who meddle with it will fail, and those who possess it will lose it." Lao Tzu himself had no experience of a typical secondary society. Nevertheless, living in a tumultuous period when the ancient Chinese super state of primary societies went through crises, Lao Tzu saw clearly with his philosophical mind the fundamental difference between primary and secondary societies. A society that operates on the second society level is uncontrollable by man. Lao Tzu's words also reflect the fact that in the two-level system, the king and vassals did not have the power to possess or control their subordinate people. From time to time, the king and vassals might have the wish to possess their subordinate people and boss them around. Lao Tzu's words indicate that such attempts had always failed before and in Lao Tzu's time.

In *The Rites: Liyun* (ritual trend), Confucius says, "Therefore, through planning and taking actions, military power and war appeared. Yu, Tang, Wen, Wu, King Cheng, Prime Minister Chou were so selected by history. The principles of rites are employed to show their rightness, to examine their trustworthiness, to find out their mistakes, and make sure that they practice benevolence and rites, and that they talk to the people with consistency. Those who fail to do so will be removed from their positions of power. People regard them as the source of disaster. This is what moderate means is." Here Confucius named the Chinese society from the first dynasty that was founded by Yu the Great until Confucius' time as the society of moderate means. This is what the ancient Chinese super state of primary societies described by this book. It shows again that neither the king nor the vassals had absolute power. It was a system of multiple powers at different levels to balance against each other with the people having the final say. In the absence of a legal system, it is only in a primary society system where the people have the final say.

When Duke Jing of State Qi asked Confucius about governing, Confucius said, "The king does what a king does; ministers do what ministers do; fathers do what fathers do; sons do what sons do." (*Analects,* 12:11)This becomes an important Confucian principle: the king/minister relation equals the father/son relation. To manage a harmonious family is the prerequisite to manage state affairs. Family affairs are only similar to those in a primary society where both family and society are operated based on face-to-face interactions but fundamentally different from those in a secondary society. On another occasion, Confucius said, "When the Tao prevails all over the land under the heavens, the ordinary people do not make comments." In Confucius' thought, the Tao prevails only when everyone does what the social ranking system requires him to. In the two-level system with the king and vassals being the upper level and the tribes/villages as the base level, the king and vassals lived in societies that were separated from those of ordinary people. The ordinary people would only learn what was going on in the country so as to make comments after the ranking system had broken down into chaos.

From the Song and Ming dynasties until 1911 when the last dynasty ended, Chinese children started their education by memorizing the *Analects* and *Meng Tzu*. As a result, all intellectuals were familiar with those two books. It is striking that Confucius and Meng Tzu spoke quite differently. Confucius once said, "If I can become rich and highly respectable, I would be happy even waving a whip to shovel passers away and clear the road for the lords." While Meng Tzu often talked about his lofty ideology of the great man, he said, "I will not be tempted in the face of the rich; I will not bow before the face of the powerful authority; I will not change my faith and lifestyle in the face of the threat of poverty." The reason for their difference is the different social environments they lived in. Confucius lived in the late years when the dominating social life was in a primary or quasi-primary society. So he spoke plainly and unostentatiously as we do today inside our family. Meng Tzu lived when the typical secondary society had just appeared. He had to adopt a set of standard vocabulary and expression to mark his status in the society and ensure the accuracy of communication.

Mo Tzu (372-289 BC) advocates universal love and opposes war. Xu Heng, the farmer school of thought and a contemporary of Meng Tzu, holds that kings had to plough for food and spin for clothes just like other people. Those views reflect their living experience of primary society. Only in the late Warring States Period, Xun Tzu (325-238 BC) and Hanfei Tzu (280-233 BC) had a clear understanding what a secondary society was like. They both realized that it is not enough to advocate only benevolence and rightness and that law and the regulation of rites were also necessary. Nevertheless, they both had the right knowledge about the historical transition from a primary to secondary society. For example, Hanfei Tzu says in his essay *Five Vermin* (wudu) that the Nester (youcaoshi), the Fire-Flint Man (suirenshi), and Yu the Great all solved the problem of subsistence for the people and then became their kings. Tang, Wen, and Wu all practiced benevolence and rightness to overthrow the tyrant rulers for the people and then became their kings. Nowadays, during the Warring States Period, only military power makes a king. So he says, "People competed for power by their morality in the ancient times; people competed for power by their knowledge and wisdom during the middle age; people now compete for power by their military strength."

2. Both Taoism and Confucianism Take Primary Society as the Ideal Society:

Chuang Tzu: Under the Heavens discusses the various schools of thought, saying, "The chaos has taken hold; saints and sages are not well respected; different people hold different moralities and principles; all people under the heavens enjoy their own limited knowledge and understanding. It is like ears, eyes, noses, and mouths all have their sense and perception, but they do not communicate with each other....Sadly, the hundred different schools of thought have gone too far to come back, and they will not come together. The scholars of the coming generations will not be able to see the purity of heaven and earth and see the antique wholeness. Philosophy and arts will disintegrate into fragmentary parts." Taoist traditions advocate the simplicity and purity of the ancient men. Thus Chuang Tzu regards the hundred schools of thought as different academic disciplines that are like separated ears, eyes, noses, and mouths. It indicates that the ancient philosophy and arts, unlike the modern concept of philosophy and arts, were all inclusive: They explained and covered the physical world, the social world, the spiritual inner world, and the life experience from the perspective of all humanity. The first philosophical system to appear was Taoism, and Taoism was directly informed by ancient Chinese philosophy and arts. Since the ancient Chinese primary society lasted long into the civilized phase of Chinese history, Taoist philosophy is really the idealized and philosophized way of life in the primary society.

In contrast, ancient Greek civilization started with typical secondary societies, the city states. Both their material pursuit of wealth and social power and their spiritual pursuit in the fields of philosophy, literature, and the arts were the goals that their society was constructed to attain.

A direct consequence of this is that Taoism takes primary society as its ideal society. This is well known as the hallmark of this ancient philosophy. It is much less known that Confucianism also takes primary society as its most ideal society. Confucius admired the sage kings, Yao, Shun, and Yu. Confucian exponents later took Yao and Shun as their forefathers and held up Kings Wen and Wu of the Chou dynasty as models of wise governance. Confucius once said, "How sublimely Shun and Yu handled the country, without lifting a finger!" "The reign of Yao was so magnificent! He was so sublime that even though there is nothing as great as heaven, he could accord with it. His greatness was boundless and beyond description. His efficacy was amazing, and his writings were enlightening." "Yu was flawless in character. Surviving on the simplest food and drink, yet he was perfect in his piety to the ancestral spirits. Wearing coarse clothing, yet he looked magnificent in his ceremonial cap and gown. Living in a humble abode, yet he exhausted himself in the excavation of drainage ways and canals. I cannot find a flaw in his character!" (*Analects*: 8.18; 8.19; 8.21)

The following is from *The Rites*: *Liyun* (ritual trend):

When the Tao prevailed, the world was publicly owned, virtuous ones were selected and able ones were chosen, and people lived in harmony and honesty was valued. Everyone treated all the others as his own family, and treated all children as his own children. The elderly enjoyed their later years, the middle-aged made their contribution, and the young were nurtured to grow up. All those who had lost his family were taken care of. Males had their share, and females had husbands. Goods were displayed on the ground, and nobody took them as their own. Everybody worked but not for themselves. There was neither plot nor scheme, and there was neither theft nor robbery. The outer doors remained open. It was called the World of Commonwealth.

Thus, the first two philosophical schools of thought in Chinese history, Taoism and Confucianism, both admired primary society as their ideal society. Their founders, Lao Tzu and Confucius, lacked the experience of secondary society. They had no way to envision a secondary society that is fundamentally different from the society they lived in. It provides further evidence that Chinese people lived mainly in primary or quasi- primary societies before the Warring States Period.

3. Ancient China Lacked the Social Mechanism that Operates in a Secondary Society for Overall Plans:

We have discussed that ancient China lacked a clear ideology to guide a secondary society. Now I will show you that ancient China lacked the social mechanism to operate a secondary society for its goals. The goals here are those such as wealth accumulation, territorial expansion and so on other than security and social stability. Security and social stability are the basic requirements for any society before it can exist.

The ancient Chinese super state of primary societies was built essentially on the basis that tribes and vassal states paid tributes and peasants paid a ten percent tax in exchange for protection from this super state system. This protection was proven to be critical for the security and stability of all tribes, vassal states, including this super state itself. According to the authors of Chinese history textbooks, except for guards, there was not a standing army. Peasants were called to form a temporary army for any military operation. As far as military power is concerned, this is a balanced system. The king and his court had their own territory of tribes and villages, just as any vassal states. The king might be more powerful than a vassal state but several vassal states could, in cooperation, easily overpower the king. There was no absolute authority in this system just as in a primary society. Human nature was the main principle to re-just its balance when any destabilization occurred. Therefore, human nature was also the powerful buffer that kept the system balanced and stable. In a primary society, any deviating behavior that hurts harmony and unity of the society will receive condemnation from all members. Similarly, condemnation from all members was a major force for keeping power in check. That's why complaints and condemnation are the main voices in the *Classic of Poetry*. Only those who dared to stand against such popular complaints and condemnation would receive military punishment from the super state. The super state would usually order the neighboring states to punish the guilty state. As to what behavior was wrong, this was determined by human nature, i.e., the popular opinion. Please note that popular opinion does not operate the same way in our secondary society as we have been brought up with a fixed value system. Popular opinion in a primary society system is more close to human nature. As a result, the ancient Chinese super state of primary societies was capable of keeping security and stability. It was not good for any other goals.

The power to control in a secondary society comes mainly from two techniques. One is to control the access to resources such as land, which become the means of production, and thus it is a prerequisite to living. The other is essentially the power to kill, including imprisonment and corporal punishment.

A prerequisite to controlling land for agriculture is so called circumscription. It means that the emigration of dissatisfied factions was blocked in such a way that factions of discontented members of a state cannot escape from their elite overlords without suffering a sharp decline in their standard of living. The earliest states like Mesopotamia, Egypt, and Greece were circumscribed by their dependence on modes of production associated with fertile river valleys surrounded by arid or semiarid plains or mountains. In ancient China, such a circumscription was never available. According to Wang (2004), the locations where the Chinese lived scattered over a vast area interspersed with ethnic minority people until the late Spring Autumn Period (771-476 BC). [4]

Wasteland was everywhere, and Chinese peasants practiced so called mobile agriculture. They moved to a place every a few years after the land was overexploited. Under such circumstances, it was impossible to control the population by controlling access to resources. On the contrary, ancient Chinese peasants were free to move anywhere they wished. As mentioned above, Meng Tzu held the view that anyone who practiced the policies of benevolence and rightness would be able to unite China under his rule, as all Chinese peasants would come to him. It clearly indicates that Chinese peasants would move into the neighboring state if they were not happy with the vassal state they were in. King Li of Chou (877-841 BC) issued a new policy to claim the state ownership of mountains and rivers, which enraged the peasants who lived inside the capital and eventually resulted in King Li's abandoning the throne. Thus King Li of Chou tried to control access to essential resources but failed.

It is widely accepted that *The Rites*: *Great Learning* was written by the Confucian scholar Zengsen, one of Confucius' disciples, who lived in the early Warring States Period. It has the following records: "Therefore, it is of the first importance that gentlemen who are in a leadership position have to be careful about their virtue. After you have virtue, then you have people to come under your leadership; after you have people, then you have land; after you have land, then you have good income; after you have good income, then you can use it for your purpose." This makes it clear that financial income was dependent on a good numbers of peasants. Only the land that was occupied by loyal people could be counted on, whereas the wasteland could be occupied by anybody who wanted it. The same principle of leadership holds true for any primary society where the headman has to have support and consensus from his people to execute any power.

The lack of circumscription also affects military power, as any recalcitrant person could always run away. No standing army lessened military power even further. Peasants may be reluctant to fight a battle which they deemed to be wrong. Ancient China did not have a strong military power but a loose military organization that was balanced and checked at all levels. For example, King You of Chou (781-770 BC) deposed the crown prince. This deposed prince ran to his maternal grandfather, who invited barbarian troops to overrun the capital and killed the king. The authority of the king over his vassals was not absolute. Nevertheless, this amateur army could effectively fend off invasions by barbarians and offer emergency help during a natural disaster. Modern military power is built on strict discipline and blind obedience, and neither is part of human nature. Humans had to go through the hardship of warring states for many generations before the first well disciplined and well organized army appeared on earth.

It must be pointed out that the monopolization of essential resources and the power to kill has the capacity of destabilizing a primary society and forcing people to deviate from the dictates of human nature. In the absence of such monopolized power, human nature favors face-to-face interaction and the principles of equality and reciprocity, and shows remarkable resistance to the emergence of a secondary society and its social structure. It was almost impossible to undertake a major project which needed nationwide participation.

According to Chinese records and recent archaeological findings, China had mastered metallurgy of bronze around 2200 BC when the first dynasty Hsia was founded. While Mesopotamia and Greece introduced bronze tools into their agriculture shortly after they mastered the technique, China used mainly wood, stone, bone, and shell materials for their farm tools up to the Western Chou dynasty (1122-771 BC). China had long mastered the technique of pottery and ceramics before the first dynasty appeared in 2200 BC, but most Chinese peasants lived in mud huts up to the 1950s. They lacked the social apparatus to produce bronze and bricks nationwide on a large scale. Economic backwardness does not necessarily spell an unhappy and dull life for the peasants. Chinese peasants practiced mobile agriculture much later than the Mediterranean people did. It is well established that stationary agriculture brought humans many problems such as poor diet, contagious diseases, over populated land, and, most importantly, peasants had to say goodbye to their familiar primary society.

The only exception was the famous flood control campaign led by Yu the Great around 2200 BC. There was a major earthquake around that time. It is speculated that this major earthquake blocked the original river course but the new one did not establish itself for many years. As a result, floods came every summer but receded during the winter. It affected the areas where the Chinese people lived. This anticipation of devastating floods every year itself motivated the whole population, and justified it as a security and survival issue. A similar situation occurred during the early Eastern Han dynasty (58-75 AD). The government spent a large amount of money to organize a massive project and established a new course for the Yellow River. Both events prevented further flooding and predetermined the course of the Yellow River for many generations to come. [5, 6]

Here I quote from Perry Anderson to support my conclusion. He identifies two pathways leading to the emergence of states: the highly cultural pathway and the tribal pathway. The former was adapted by Mesopotamia, India, Egypt, and China. The latter was exemplified by the kingdoms established by the Germanic and Celtic people. Among the four major ancient civilizations, Mesopotamia, India, Egypt, and China, Anderson thinks that China was an exception, different from the other three. Anderson based his comparison on the data from the Shang and Chou dynasties. According to Anderson, Chinese agricultural technology remained at the level of the New Stone Age. China had neither the irrigation system of India and Mesopotamia nor the yearly flood controls exercised by people who lived along the Nile in Egypt. Chinese urbanization was much less pronounced than the other three, and its commercialization was rudimentary. Ancient China did not seem to be involved in any conquering wars or trade, and diplomatic relationships with other civilized countries but only interacted with barbarian ethics. As a hegemonic power, ancient China waged war only at the level of the Bronze Age, namely the chariot level, which was only on small scale. There were only a few domestic slaves, and ancient Chinese society could not be called a slave society. [7]

Some scholars hold that for a newly emerged state, two criteria have to be met: social stratification and the forceful authority system. In the ancient Chinese super state of primary societies, the authority was hardly forceful since its power was balanced and limited at all levels. It is not surprising that its agriculture, cities, trade and war were all on a small scale. As pointed out before, the backwardness in material development did not hinder a society's spiritual advancement in the fields of culture and philosophy.

In conclusion, ancient China had neither sufficient control of access to essential resources nor a well disciplined and well organized army to monopolize the power to kill. Thus the authority of ancient China was not much different from the authority of a headman to his primary society. Consensus and persuasion remained as the main forces to keep society stable and functional. In other words, human nature was still the basis for ancient Chinese society. China did not have the power to support any large scale projects like the pyramid construction in Egypt.

4. Ancient Chinese Military Conflicts Were More Like the Violent Conflicts Among Ancient Primary Societies:

Parallel to the super state of primary societies, ancient Chinese wars showed characteristics of the violent conflicts of primary societies. When their survival was at risk, prehistoric primitive people might also attack their neighbors for food. They usually took the strategy of ambush in order to reduce the possibility of violence and injuries. When two groups had conflicts that could not be settled any other way, they might also settle the conflict by a fight. Such a fight was usually carried out in a relatively fixed manner according to the local ritual customs. The injuries were not severe, and death occurred rarely. Such violent conflicts remained isolated in early human history. They neither accelerated nor grew in scale but remained at the same level. Thus it was fundamentally different from wars waged by civilized states. Such wars tended to spiral into larger conflagrations as William Eckhardt described. (See Essay 1)

The famous Chinese historian Ray Huang (1918-2000) says, "The chariot war during the Spring Autumn Period (770-476 BC) was really an aristocratic war. Those aristocrats often saw it as a way to compete for skills. There were formalized procedures for the battle formation. There was a widely accepted way to approach each other to start the fight. Thus war was still under the control of rites. The general trend was that no side went too far for its own benefit." [8] We can also say that such wars were still under check by human nature. Only during the Warring States Period (476-221 BC), war became more like the one among secondary societies. They sought hegemonic power and territorial expansion by war. Duke Xiang of State Song fought a war strictly according to the ritual requirements but was defeated during the Warring States Period. He was scorned and laughed at by others.

From the Shang dynasty until the Spring Autumn Period, China had guards to protect the royal house as the only standing army. Peasants who lived inside the national capital and the capitals of vassal states could be called upon to form a temporary army when there was a need. Minority ethnic people did not usually take part in this peasant army even though they received protection from the Chinese government. The toppling of the Hsia by the Shang, and the Shang by the Chou dynasty were both unpopular governments replaced by a popular revolt led by a subordinate state. The unpopularity of the former dynasty has to be understood in the primary society setting where the tolerance of deviation from human nature was very limited. In the Mediterranean traditions, the winning side took all the defeated people as slaves. This was not the case with ancient Chinese wars. According to the *Historical Records*, "King Tang of Shang named all Hsia people a state, and their state became State Qi during the Chou dynasty....When the Chou dynasty replaced the Shang dynasty, the Chou named the son of the former king of Shang as a duke to form a state for the Shang people. The Chou ordered them to continue worshiping their ancestors and following the policies of King Pan-Gen. The Shang people were very pleased."

According to *Historical Records*, the revolt led by the Chou gathered less than 50,000 troops while Shang motivated more than 700,000 to crush the revolt, though those numbers may have been far exaggerated. According to those figures, the latter was more than fourteen times of the size of the former. Most of those 700,000 troops joined the revolt instead of crushing it at their first meeting in the battle field. There was hardly any fight, and the war ended on the same day. Two years earlier, the Chou attracted eight hundred vassal states at a gathering. It shows that the vassal states or tribes were the main social units. Both states, or tribes, and people were relatively free to leave one side and join the other. That may be why those 700,000 troops did not revolt themselves but waited to join the Chou people. They did not have the choice of skipping over their confederation of tribes to join another potential super state.

It is interesting to compare what Lao Tzu and Heraclitus said about war. Lao Tzu said, "Do our best to avoid any battles, do not bare our arms and chests, do not carry weapons, and never have such an idea that we do not have a powerful enemy." Lao Tzu was an extreme pacifist, and he advocated celebrating military victories with funerals because of the deaths of soldiers on both sides. In contrast, Heraclitus said, "War is father of all, king of all. Some it makes gods, some it makes men, some it makes slaves, some free." "We must realize that war is universal, and strife is justice, and that all things come into being and pass away through strife."

Those words by Lao Tzu and Heraclitus in fact summarize the different ideologies behind their different social environments.

5. Benevolence/Righteousness and Ritual/Music Practice Advocated by Confucianism is the Extension of Primary Society Culture Rather Than an Indication of the Emergence of Secondary Society:

If we consider both Taoism and Confucianism as a way of life, neither Taoism nor Confucianism alone is enough to summarize Chinese culture. Only mutually complementary Taoism and Confucianism can represent mainstream culture through Chinese history. As philosophies, both Taoism and Confucianism first appeared in the late Spring Autumn Period. As a way of life and thinking, the rudiments of mutually complementary Taoism and

Confucianism must have started at time when Chinese civilization began. Ancient Chinese society might have often deviated from the standard primary or quasi-primary society, and violent conflicts were the results. The people in authority had to promote virtue and adopt humanist policies and ritual/music practice to stabilize the society against violent conflicts. In confronting violent conflicts, the rudimentary Taoism and Confucianism were different but mutually complementary. Rudimentary Confucianism tried to use sage policies to control the situation while rudimentary Taoism advocated antique simplicity and primary society. Their efforts ended with the same results: The emergence of secondary society from violent conflicts was prevented, and China remained at the level of primary and quasi-primary society. Since the first philosophical system to appear was Taoism, the dominant way of life and thinking was a precursor to Taoism and not Confucianism in ancient China. The benevolence/righteousness and ritual/music practice advocated by Confucianism can however be considered as an extension of primary society culture.

The core theory of Confucianism is the ethical code of benevolence and righteousness (renyi). The core concept of this ethical code is benevolence (ren). Confucius once said, "Benevolence means loving people." In fact, ren (benevolence) and man are interchangeable words in the *Analects*. When a primary society is facing an unwanted division, they call on people to feel their subconscious bond with society and with others, since nobody has the power to force other members to stay. The members of a primary society are linked together emotionally and psychologically.

Confucius came up with a similar way to call on people's subconscious, and remind them: "Please remember, you are human beings and behave like one!"

The Rites: *The Bright Hall Status* records, "Duke Chou... courted vassals in the Bright Hall, introduced the rites and music he had formulated for the vassals and the country, and announced the standard measurements to the nation." Duke Chou ruled the country on behalf of the young king four years after the Shang dynasty was overthrown in 1122. He started the ritual/music traditions to replace the former Shang's worshiping gods and spirits. It represents a humanist political change. Please note, he coupled rites with music. The Chinese character, yue or le, has the connotation of music, joy, and happiness. Thus it incorporates entertainment into the ritual/ music practice, though Duke Chou aimed mainly at keeping the ranking system stable and harmonious. Today we have no way to see what the ritual/music traditions looked like from the Hsia to the early Chou dynasty, since the book *The Rites* contains many new developments of later times. It is however certain that those traditions must have been much more similar to those of a primitive primary society.

In the early stage of primary society, even language was in its rudimentary form and was inadequate to communicate with preciseness. The ritual/music traditions served as an important apparatus to integrate all elements and unify all members into a psychological and emotional wholeness. Here we can speculate that when a group of primitive people were idling and had nothing to do, they expressed their feelings to each other, trying to exchange at the most basic psychological and emotional level, a link to connect them all into a whole. Such exchange and linking activities are positive stimulants to the nervous system, and are good for spiritual and physical health. One way of partaking in such exchange and linking activities is the ritual/music traditions, in the form of dance, singing, and music. It serves as entertainment, a psychological and emotional exchange, and as spiritual uplifting.

Like language, the ritual/music traditions are expressed in a symbolic system of representations at all levels. In comparison with language and law as apparatuses to unify a secondary society, the ritual/music traditions operate at a more psychological and emotional level. All primitive societies have their ritual/music traditions, which play an important role in keeping the society functional and harmonious. Only in modern well developed secondary society, have the ritual/music traditions as well as religious life retreated into a complementary role to the main operating social structure. Confucianism stresses the value of the ritual/music traditions along with benevolence/righteousness. It reflects that both Confucianism and Taoism advocate primary society as their ideal society, and

Confucianism further seeks to ameliorate the worst aspects of a secondary society by using a primary society as the model.

6. Ancient Chinese Super State of Primary Societies in the View of Historians and Sociologists:

Marxists classify all human societies into four stages, the primitive, the slave, the feudal, and the capitalist society, according to their mode of productivity. Although the classification of human society into genetically coded primary society and man-made secondary society does not necessarily fit in this Marxist classification, primitive society roughly corresponds to primary society, and the latter three are secondary societies. Many historians and sociologists see Chinese society before the Warring States Period as a primitive society. This further supports the notion that Chinese people mainly lived in primary society before the Warring States Period.

As mentioned above, according to Anderson, China lagged far behind on the scales of urbanization, trade, war, and political organization. Compared to the other three civilizations, China was apparently on the side of primary society.

According to a notable Chinese historian, Wang Yuzhe, Marx considered ancient Chinese and Indian societies as primitive societies. He calls them oriental rural communes. The majority of those communes' members were not slaves. In their late years, both Marx and Engels modified their view on the social nature of oriental rural communes. They realized that some of those communes were primitive societies while others may be slave societies. Those commune members were not owned by slave masters but belonged to the despotic king. [4]

Such forceful despotic kings did not appear in ancient China until the Warring States Period. Karl A. Wittfogel (1896-1988) expanded the Marxist theory of the so- called Asian mode of production and oriental despotism. Karl A. Wittfogel also thinks such despotism first appeared during the Warring States Period. It is consistent with the view of this book that Chinese society went through a fundamental transformation during the Warring States Period.

Many Chinese scholars also think that Chinese society was a primitive society before the Warring States Period. The following is from the book by Wang Yuzhe:

"During the early phase of this discussion, many scholars from our country held such a view that ancient Chinese society was a primitive society. A few Japanese and Indian scholars shared the same view. After many years of discussion, such a view attracted less attention. But in the 1970s and 1980s, such a view returned and prevailed in the circle of historical forums."[4]

It must be pointed out that calling something a primitive society is a judgment from the economic perspective while calling it a genetically coded primary society is a judgment from the view of genetics and human nature. The two are fundamentally different, though they may be identified in a similar period in human history.

(3) Conclusion: The Far-reaching Influence on Subsequent Chinese History

This primary society system stabilized Chinese civilization's continuous flow in history while all other ancient civilizations were subject to rises and collapses.

Furthermore, the ancient Chinese super state of primary societies left its far-reaching influence on subsequent Chinese history. It remained as an important factor in shaping Chinese culture and society. Having gone through the bloody Warring States Period, Chinese society was modeled as follows until 1911 when the first Chinese republic was founded:

The emperor and his clans   distorted quasi-primary society
|
Bureaucrats and their
     reserved intellectual
        candidates   secondary society
|
Peasants and urban residents   quasi-primary society

The only difference between this model and the former model of the ancient Chinese ancient super state of primary societies (see Essay 1) is the replacement of the former vassals with bureaucrats and their intellectual candidates, who formed a typical secondary society with the capacity of free critical thinking. Chinese urban residents never played an independent role in Chinese history, and remained the same as any peasants. According to John King Fairbank (1907—1991), with a population of no less than four hundred million and a vast territory, the government of the Qing dynasty only employed some twenty thousand bureaucrats but with more than a million intellectual candidates who served as a reserved backup for the bureaucrats. They had all been trained in Confucian ideology: benevolence/righteousness and the ritual/music traditions. The emperor and his government still painted themselves as the super state for all humanity. Although it is really hypocrisy, remote minority ethnic states had no reason to dispute this, as they enjoyed no less independence and suffered no material disadvantage. That's why the Chinese system showed remarkable ability to be magnanimous and accommodating towards the different cultures and ethnicities around the Chinese borders. The replacement of an old dynasty with a new one often only meant that the new emperor and his clans would pick up another twenty some thousand bureaucrats from the same pool of intellectual candidates.

During the so-called classic age (500-323 BC), Athens had only a population of one or two hundred thousand. The well developed social structure of secondary society enabled them to mobilize all levels of people and pool together their wisdom and labor. In a short period of time, they accumulated enormous wealth, established a powerful navy, erected magnificent temples, created a profound philosophical system and outstanding culture. For several thousand years of Chinese history, China never set up a typical social structure to motivate all her people like Athens did. The Chinese imperial power never went very far beyond twenty some thousand bureaucrats. This large reserved pool of intellectual candidates served as a bridge between the Government and the peasants. Chinese peasants mostly lived a life their own except for paying tax (See Essay 2). It was not always an easy job to motivate the peasants for a public project.

If we take primary society as the foundation, what Chinese civilization built were solid one-storey houses with space for development laid in all directions. The chance for any sort of collapse was small. In comparison, the ancient Greeks built skyscrapers with space for further development available in the sky. The risk for such buildings to collapse was high, and once they fell down, it was not an easy job to rebuild them. A big gap exists between the two regarding wealth accumulation and material achievements, but their spiritual creations, philosophy and culture, show little difference. As to the psychological and emotional experience of the average citizens, it is beyond doubt that the ancient Chinese felt much happier than the ancient Greek though they might be less excited.

As mentioned above, Anderson says, "There were not many slaves, and those slaves were domestic. Ancient Chinese society cannot be considered a slave society." I agree with Anderson though many Chinese textbooks still list ancient Chinese society as a slave society. It has been the official view since the Communist Party took over China in 1949 in spite of different views among Chinese scholars in recent years.

There was no social mechanism to drive and monitor a slave class in ancient China. Ancient Greek society was very similar to modern society in the way that it integrates people of all levels and classes into a network to work for the same goals. The driving force and the social direction are built into the social system, and not necessarily the will of any individuals. Ancient China did not construct such a social system, and Medieval Europe lost such a social system. In spite of the readily available technology, material, and slaves, the productive mode of Medieval Europe harkened back to a more primitive way. From 650 to 950 AD, the subsistence was mainly hunting, gathering, and raising free range pigs. They practiced no agriculture as people all lived around forests and wastelands, and the density of population was low. [9]

During the Hsia, Shang, and Chou dynasties, Chinese people and minority ethnic people lived side by side. The Chinese government had no control over those ethnic groups. Under such circumstances, it was almost impossible to prevent slaves from running away. There was also no social mechanism to supervise slaves nationwide and prevent their revolts. The Chinese peasants had little property themselves and couldn't possibly supervise a slave class with even fewer possessions. It was possible that the army of the Shang dynasty captured a few hundred captives and forced them to build city walls or palaces for a short period of time. It was a totally different matter to manage a slave class nationwide. The presence of a slave class contradicts the view of this book that the ancient Chinese lived essentially in a primary society, which was operated based on human nature. Medieval European people lived an enjoyable and poetic life when they were hunting in the forest and picking up wild fruits to eat from time to time. Finding a way to attract those people into a life of wealth accumulation and let them supervise slaves was never a simple social process. That's why Europe went through so many revolutions and so much social turmoil in modern history.

One difference between a primary and a secondary society is the different functions of language. In a primary society, language is mingled with emotional and psychological exchange, and it has an aesthetic value. In a secondary society, language becomes a way of communicating and exchanging information, a social apparatus to unify all the wills of people and coordinate all efforts into the pursuit of goals that the society is built for.

Anthropologists believe that primates groom each other as a way to solidify their social bond while naked humans chat with each other for the same purpose. In a primary society, language has the same function as a ritual/music performance that integrates all members into a whole at the psychological and emotional level. The ancient Chinese super state of primary societies allowed the secondary society to emerge gradually and smoothly. The result was a united culture and language. The vast area north of the Yangtze River including Sichuan speaks the same language. Even with States Wu, Yue, and Chu, all located south of the Yangtze River, no translators were needed during the frequent interactions in the Spring Autumn and Warring States Periods. This is unique in the world, and it is because the super state assumed the responsibility for all humanity so that the emergence of secondary society synchronized with its language development.

Matrilineal society as a historic stage in human history is a matter for debate. The Western history textbooks do not carry an account to explain how matrilineal society transformed into patriarchal society but most Chinese textbooks do. Most scholars, however, believe that a more peaceful goddess-worshiping culture was widely spread in the world before modern civilizations emerged. Those people might have united around an elderly mother but a male leader might manage the society. Males and females were more equal in their social status. If we call this culture as a motherly culture, the motherly culture might have been conquered by patriarchal society in Europe and the Mediterranean world while in China, the motherly culture and patriarchal culture might have coexisted side by side before the patriarchal culture prevailed. [10] As mentioned in Essay 1, James DeMeo thinks that the harsh living environment of widely desertification gave rise to a patriarchal society. Those patriarchal cultures invaded India, Persia, and Europe. But they did not invade ancient Chinese society. The Huns never entered the core area of China. DeMeo thinks the Shang people were from a patriarchal culture and the Hsia people were Chinese aboriginal people. Even if DeMeo is right, the Chou people were a branch of the Hsia people and they laid down the philosophical foundation for Chinese culture. In the model of this two level system, the village/tribal societies represent the motherly culture while the vassals and the king represent the patriarchal culture. In contrast to the West, Chinese patriarchal culture only played the role of police to keep peace and maintain the stability of society.

The ancient Chinese super state of primary societies also had its negative consequences. It hindered the proper development of an effective and controllable social structure at the secondary society level. After the Warring States Period, the vassals were gradually replaced by intellectual bureaucrats. The emperor's power was increased enormously but a social mechanism to check the emperor's power had never been well developed. For example, the constructions of the Great Wall and the Great Canal were totally motivated and organized by orders from the government, lacking any internal checking apparatus. If a more modern commercial mechanism had been used, the government had hired peasants to complete those projects, there would have been self- limiting factors such as the availability of money and the willingness of the peasants. Those projects would not have gone beyond the capacity of the society to support. The lack of such social mechanisms resulted in the sudden collapse of the two powerful dynasties, Qin and Sui.

According to government records, the Chinese population decreased by half during the reign of Emperor Wu of the Han dynasty(140-87 BC) and during the reign of Empress Wu Zetian of the Tang dynasty (684-704). We do not know whether half of the populations died of starvation or escaped into the mountains, but either way a society that could stand losing half of its population and did not collapse is far from normal. Such things would have never happened in a primary society. In 841 BC, the angry residents inside the capital swarmed into the palace, and the king ran away and never dared to return. The king did not order his army to surround the capital and crush down the revolt. It is apparent that the army was still under the influence of human nature, unwilling to follow the king to do something obviously against human nature. In contrast, the Taiping revolt lasted more than ten years and occupied half of China but eventually ended in failure (1851-1863). It claimed twenty million lives. Modern scholars all believe that the policies of the revolt were more humanist than the Ching dynasty. Even the powerful general, Zeng Guofan, who emerged as the new political star with military power, was much better than the Emperor and the Dowageer, who were on the throne during that time. China lacked the apparatus to select the best one among the opportunities offered up during the chaotic periods, let alone when the government was stable.

References

[1] a: Martha Lamberg-Karlovsky, "Introduction: In the Beginning", in Martha Lamberg- Karlovsky, eds., The Breakout: the Origins of Civilization, Cambridge, MA: Preabody Museum of Archaeology and Ethnology, Harvard University, 2000, pXIII. b: Vere Gordon Childe ，"The Urban Revolution," The Town Planning Review, 21:3-17, (1950).)

[2] Chang, Kwang-chi (2004): On the Origin of Chinese Civilization. Cultural Relic (wenwu), 2004, No. 1, p73-82. (In Chinese)

[3] Susan Rensberger, Understanding the Amish, New York: Alpha Books, 2003, p153- 154.)

[4] Wang Yuzhe (2004): Ancient Chinese History. Shanghai: Shanghai People's Publishing House. (In Chinese)

[5] Zhang Renzhong (2006): Ancient Chinese History. Beijing: Beijing University Press. P138. (In Chinese)

[6] You-Sheng Li: A New Interpretation of Chinese Taoist Philosophy. London, Canada: Taoist Recovery Centre. P86. (In Chinese)

[7] Perry Anderson (2000): The Origin of Ancient Chinese Civilization. Twenty First Century. 58, 2000, 4. (In Chinese)

[8] Ray Huang(1989): Talks About History Beside the Hudson River. Taibei: The Times (shibao). (In Chinese)

[9] F. Delouche (ed): Illustrated History of Europe. New York: Henry Holt and Company, 1993, p137.

[10] You-Sheng Li: A New Interpretation of Chinese Taoist Philosophy. London, Canada: Taoist Recovery Centre. P8-89. (In Chinese)

4

The Vulnerability of Primary Society in Front of Secondary Society

Humans had been living in primary society for thousands of years and showed remarkable resistance to the emergence of secondary society. Surprisingly, once a secondary society well established itself and comes to assimilate or conquer its neighboring primary societies, the vulnerability of primary society is more than obvious: It is literally defenseless.

Of course, there had been no typical primary society any more once all sorts of secondary societies appeared in human history. But some lands were closer to the ancient system of primary society while others may be a typical secondary society. During the numerous conflicts and violent confrontations in human history, the more traditional societies were always the defeated side, and they showed very little resistance.

A typical example was the colonization of Latin and South America by Spanish adventurers. Hermando Cortés and Francisco Pizarro, each led only a few hundred men miraculously conquered vast lands of the powerful Aztecs empire and the Inca empire respectively. The following is a brief account of how Hermando Cortés defeated the Aztecs.

When Hermando Cortés first met the Aztec king, he was received with great respect. The king sent presents of gold to Cortés, since the king believed that Cortés was an ancient Aztec god that was supposed to return one day. The king had thousands of armed warriors at his command, he could easily have Cortés and his men all killed if he had chosen to treat them as his enemy. Instead, he decided to welcome those Spanish invaders to his capital. Once inside the capital, Cortés took the king as a hostage and killed him later, and Cortés' followers invited Aztec nobles to a feast and murdered them all. As there were hardly any leaders left, the Aztecs surrendered in 1521. If the Aztecs had had a clear idea what a miserable life was waiting for them for the next few hundred years, they would have certainly not given up so easily. The Spaniards had mutated to adapt an aggressive culture but still wore the same human appearance. That was what misled those innocent people.

During the Opium War in 1840, the Great Britain only sent 5,000 soldiers to invade China. Their warships traveled in thousands of miles along the Chinese coast to find a defenseless site, and they eventually entered a northern Chinese river. The Chinese government could have easily cut off their retreating path and annihilated them all, if they had sent many more Chinese soldiers. On contrary, the Chinese accepted defeat and signed the humiliating treaty. When a massive peasant revolt occurred eleven year later, the Chinese government was so determined to crack it down that it spent more than a dozen years and resulted in more than twenty million deaths. According to some Chinese scholars, it is simply because the Chinese government saw the British as its honorable guests, or gods in the Aztecs king's mind, and Chinese peasants as their slaves.

In comparison with Western urban life, the Chinese rural areas are much closer to Taoist ideal, and similar to the primary society. Many Chinese peasants, especially the old generations, are still living their isolated life unaware of what going on in the world and in the Chinese government above them. The following is my experience showing how vulnerable those Chinese peasants are in front of the unfriendly secondary society.

Having brushed all criticism aside and dismissed the Minister of Agriculture, Mao Zedong (1893-1976) pushed forward the Agricultural Collectivization Campaign nationwide in 1956. My village formed the first agricultural cooperative in early winter that year. Since there was not much farming work to do in winter, peasants had time to discuss their concerns. They all worried a little but felt excited too. Young people were so happy as if they were watching an interesting drama unfolding in front of them. As a child, I overheard many of their private discussions, since several peasants often stayed in my bedroom until midnight. Their minds were occupied by the uncertainties in the coming years. Nevertheless, all their words and calculations were limited to the difference in the coming wheat harvest next summer, or even in the annual income for their families. They did not have the slightest idea what a disaster would happen to them a few years later.

Marx was said to have such comments on peasants: They are like the potatoes buried underground, and only through others such as leaves and stems, they received the sunlight and rain. The Communist collectivization of agriculture is a form of secondary society, and the peasants were brought onto the ground from their underground potato positions. Of course they felt at loss.

It must be pointed out that it went pretty well at the beginning. My village was divided into a dozen of so-called productive teams, each team had roughly 150 peasants including children. It was like they were once again in the primitive egalitarian society. Peasants were jubilant at their enlarged family life: Cheers and laughter filled up all their productive activities. Everybody worked hard with high ardour. They all let the fine quality of human nature emerge from them: They showed selfless concern for the ones in need; they showed enthusiasm toward collective affairs; they showed fine propriety and high style of self-discipline and self-refrain. Though there were no big events but everything was going smoothly. Whenever I remember those days in my village life, I feel certain that humans have the ability to manage themselves.

As Lao Tzu worried, the disaster came from the secondary society and their interference. In spite of tremendous political pressure, the Communist Government kept saying, "The agricultural cooperative is formed at peasants' free will, and they will see this is the best for them." As a result, some 10 percent peasants did not join in, and those were all able men. Their farms were cared better, and yielded better harvests. Peasants felt quite okay about this, since it did not mean much difference to them. Every peasant had to admit that the collective peasants had much more laughter when they were working. Nevertheless, politics felt humiliated by this and could not condescend to admit it either. Politics was inseparable part of secondary society, and peasants had no such brains to understand it. All those non-collectivized peasants were beaten up by whips, and they needed days in bed to recover. Some were even tied up and pulled by horses half a mile on a rocky ground. Then they all shouted at top of their voices, "Agricultural collectivization is the best for us, and we all want to join in".

You may say, what about if those peasants had stood up for themselves? We have lived in secondary society for so long, and we cannot judge those isolated peasants from our view. An old man in his late sixties or early seventies once picked up a bundle of green onion from the collective field but was accidentally seen by others. He hanged himself a few hours later. In the countryside setting of China in the 1950s, people would not call such an act as stealing. On contrary, people would say those who went so far to take a few green onions must really need them, and it served the onions a better use. But this bundle of green onion did not belong to anyone he was familiar with, but belonged to an unknown world with godly power, the secondary society. With shame and fear, he gave up his life to redeem his sin. For the same reason, those peasants were beaten by the power from an unknown world, and they did not dare to fight back. The few ones who did stand up against this crazy agricultural collectivization were usually intellectuals or even government officials, who either lost their jobs or ended in prison.

Once corporal punishment started and dissidents were eliminated, all bizarre orders were carried out without much resistance such as cutting off the young crops off ground and then planting sweet potatoes and so on. In a secondary society, ideas can become a leading ideology that has its own life, and an action can trigger a chain of actions like an explosion beyond man's control. Nobody understands this new world completely, though it is a creation by man.

The productive team was no longer farming but dealing all those bizarre orders. I still remember one summer evening in 1957, it was almost bedtime when an order came from above saying everyone had to work in the farm field overnight. In dark, the team leader lowered his voice to tell each of us in turn, "You can sleep on the ground once you are in the field but keep your lanterns high. You may come back stealthily after midnight." I did sleep on my hand tools as he told me. The government officials were supposed to check us by looking at our lanterns from distance on the motor road. When we groped back drowsily, our clothes were heavy with dew.

Such a chaotic leadership eventually stirred up the countryside life and caused trouble everywhere. When the autumn came in 1958, the local leaders were not good enough to coordinate the harvest but strong enough to keep peasants away from it. As the result, a major part of the crops was left in the field being rotten away while the government exported enormous amount of grains in exchange for industrial equipments. There was nothing left to eat in the winter, and all oxen and horses were eaten up. For years to come, the lucky peasants exhausted themselves in the place of oxen and horses to pull loaded carts, ploughs, and grind mills while the unlucky ones were dying off with empty stomachs. Pigs are friendly to each other and played with each other when there are a few but they become all motionless when there are hundreds of them. The Chinese peasants all now wore a lethargic face, apathetic to everything happening to them. Thus, they had finally entered the secondary society created by man.

It is remarkable that females were much less crazy than men, rural residents were much less crazy than their urban citizens during Mao'era. It is equally remarkable that many famous public preachers who gave speeches from place to place about how they applied Mao's teachings to reform their minds were females both in cities and in the countryside. I guess females were more religiously loyal while men were more fanatically absurd.

*　　*　　*

Afterword: From Motherly Culture to Patriarchal Society

As mentioned in Essay 1, a dramatic climate change around 4,000 -3,000 BC led to desertification in vast areas along central Asia, Arabia, and northern Africa. According to James DeMeo, this harsh environment hatched a new culture, hallmarked by patriarchal warfare. They soon conquered and replaced the previous peaceful culture in the Old World. DeMeo calls the former peaceful culture, the unarmoured matrist and the latter, the armoured patrist. DeMeo lists out all the characteristics for the two cultures. [1] In many ways, the patrist is a secondary society while the matrist is a primary society.

Typically, the ancient Aryan or Indo-European people conquered the Indus River valley, Iran, and Europe. For example, the Mycenaean civilization of Indo-European origin replaced the Minoan civilization of Asian origin in ancient Greece. Norman Davies writes, "Whilst they (the Minoans) basked in the Bronze Age, the northern lands lingered in the later stages of the Neolithic. The westward march of the Indo-Europeans had undoubtedly begun. It is sometimes associated with the advent of a male-dominated warrior culture, which subdued both its peaceful predecessors and its own women."[2]

DeMeo is right in India and Europe but is not right in China, which went through a quite different pathway for the transition from a matrist primary society to a patrist secondary society, or in other words, from a motherly culture to a patriarchal society.

In China, the Chinese version of "Minoan civilization" emerged as a military power headed by the Yellow Emperor. In stead of being conquered and replaced, the Chinese "Minoan civilization" defeated the peace-violators and formed a super state to function as police to keep peace in the vast areas of China.

To understand how this happened in China, we need to know the power struggle between the two sexes. André Bé teille reviewed the issue thoroughly and concluded that power lay generally in the hands of men, especially in the politico-jural domain, irrespective of the form of descent but in even the most strongly patriarchal societies, women play an important role in domestic affairs. They may play a major part in everything concerned with food, health, and nurture. [3]

Many Chinese records from different lines indicate clearly a prehistoric matrilineal society in China. For example, the Chinese character for surname (xing) has a radical element, "female". All members of a matrilineal society had the same surname. Men were not allowed to have sexual relationship with the females who had the same surname. Men had to go to a different matrilineal society to live with their female partners at night but came back during the day. Since ancient Chinese people practiced mobile agriculture and had to move around a lot, two tribes with different surnames formed a special bond for sexual relationship among their members. To make their relation stable, they always moved together. With such a relationship, the matrilineal line stayed in the same tribe while the patrilineal line zigzagged between the two tribes. During the Chou dynasty, the shrines of the deceased kings were arranged in two lines with the father and son in different lines. It was apparently the heritage of the twin tribal sexual relationship. Wang went into detail to list evidence from seven lines to indicate a matrilineal system in ancient China. [4]

We assume, Chinese community at the level of bands or tribes was probably headed by a lady who relied on her brothers for any affairs in relation with other bands or tribes. When her husband became a king or a vassal or made a fortune by new farming techniques, the lady gave up her position as the head of the community and decided to stay within the family headed by her husband. After a few generations, this family eventually became a large clan of patriarchal society with a new surname system, shi. The Chinese records say that ordinary people had only the old surname system, xing, but prominent people had both xing and shi.

Chinese scholars believe that the Yellow Emperor and his successors represent the time when a patrilineal system first appeared in Chinese history. Therefore, the Chinese super state represents the newly emerged patrilineal society while the village/tribal society represents the original matrilineal society. Thus this motherly peaceful society was paralleled with the newly emerged patriarchal society for a long time before the former was integrated into the latter system. According to the *Historical Records*, the Yellow Emperor had 25 sons but only two inherited his surname, xing. Furthermore, none of those 25 sons accessed to the throne but his grandson did. It indicates that his sons and grandsons belonged to different clans. It is evident that during the Yellow Emperor's time, the Emperor's clans were still in a matrilineal society, though the social power was in the hands of men. It was literally a patriarchal but matrilineal society.

As mentioned in Essay 1, multiple cultures and multiple cultural centres developed all over China in the New Stone Age without a dominant one. Only two cultures showed clearly a female-centred nature, the Yangshao culture and the Hongshan culture. In the Yangshao culture, young females tended to have more burial goods, and mothers were often buried with her sons. In some cases, many long deceased skeletons moved to a newly buried female, which is interpreted as descendents being reburied with their grandmother. In the late years of the Yangshao culture, elderly males also tended to have more burial goods. Geographically the Yangshao culture corresponds to the Yellow Emperor and his people in Chinese records. Those records of the ancient matrilineal society were thus confirmed by archaeological findings of the Yangshao culture.

In the Hongshan culture, a remarkable goddess temple was excavated. It was the largest in the New Stone Age China. Several naked goddesses showing their breasts were found. The largest one was five meters high. According to a recent popular interpretation of Chinese records, the Hongshan people joined the Yellow Emperor to defeat the more patriarchal people from the east, the peace-violators.

Wang gives a very sound explanation how matrilineal society changed into patriarchal society. With the matrilineal society, women were gatherers and farmers while men were hunters. Women brought home more food than men. When agriculture became intensified and needed much more strength and skills, men became farmers while women became spinners and weavers who stayed at home. Thus properties were accumulated by men's labour, and men wanted their children to inherit their possessions, and a patrilineal nuclear family emerged without causing any conflicts. To support this transition, archaeological study has found that buried couples first appeared with the subsequent Longshan culture (2600-1900 BC). [4, p94]

The vulnerability of primary society in front of secondary society was reflected in the traceless conquest or replacement in cases of India and Greece but in the smooth transformation from a matrilineal society to a patriarchal society in China. Since such a smooth transformation required consensus of all groups of the society, it took a much longer time and it might have taken hundreds of years to complete.

As a classic, *Classic of Poetry* has been studied by scholars at all levels for more than two thousand years. One of their apparent goals was to find out who was the author. Their conclusion was based on history, records, and the voice of the poem. Nowadays' edition has a brief introduction in front of each of the 305 poems. As shown in the model of Chinese society between 2600 and 476 BC in Essay 1, the village/tribes were mainly primary societies while the king, vassals, and their clans were quasi-primary society. Furthermore, the village/tribes maintained more matrilineal traditions while the king, vassals, and their clans were exclusively patriarchal societies. The *Classic of Poetry* has four sections, *Feng, Xiaoya, Daya,* and *Song*, which represent a different authorship from the village/tribes, low ranking officials, high ranking officials, the king and his court respectively. The following table shows the authorship shifting from females to males among those four sections:

Table 4.1 The Ratio Male/Female Poets in *Classic of Poetry*

	Numbers of male authors	Numbers of female authors	Ratio males/females
Feng	32	51	0.63
Xiaoya	16	6	2.67
Daya	3		∞
Song	4		∞

After the dramatic transformation of Chinese society during the Warring Period (476-221 BC), poem writing became essentially a male thing. Although one or two female poets appeared from time to time during Chinese history, more than ninety percent of Chinese poets were men. I have an anthology of Chinese poetry from the Tang and Song dynasties, in which, eleven out of 125 (8.8%) poets were female and 45 out of 589 (7.6%) poems were by female authors. Out of the eleven female poets, only four had names, and the rest were identified as whose daughter or whose wife or a woman from which province. Some of the female poets even received the name as a prostitute. It must be pointed that the female poets were over represented in this anthropology as modern editors tend to select the overlooked female authors, though they claim to be neutral. As far as poem writing as a way of self expression, female voice seemed to fade away willingly.

Apart from poem writing, Chinese women were active publicly and politically during the Han and the Tang dynasty (618-907). Many women held the highest power by marrying into the royal family. Women even played polo in the Tang dynasty. Without any order or even encourage from the government, why millions of Chinese women adapted to the painful and humiliating foot-binding during the Song dynasty (960-1279) is still a mystery.

The Song dynasty was far different from other Chinese dynasties in several aspects. The Song dynasty faced several more powerful hostile countries in the north and was eventually conquered by one of them, the Mongolian empire. The Song dynasty was also the most advanced one in science and technology, in urbanization, and in commercialization. The men during the Song dynasty traveled more and more from their homes, either on business or on military expedition. The bustle urban life posed apparently more sexual attraction to those wives at home. We assume, those women took the foot-binding willingly to ensure their husbands about their loyalty. We thus see how easily the secondary society damages the primary society so deeply and so painfully.

In conclusion, the tragic nature of the primary society in front of a secondary society is that those who live in a primary society are still in the control of human nature while those in secondary society are not. Human nature gives too easily to social power, and primary society is, therefore, defenseless and vulnerable.

*   *   *

References

[1] J. DeMeo(2004): Saharasia. Orgone: Orgone Biophysical Research Lab.

[2] Norman Davies (1997): Europe: A History. London: Pimlico. p92-93.

[3] André Béteille (2002): Inequality and Equality. In Tim Ingold eds: Companion Encyclopedia of Anthropology. London: Routledge. P1022-1023.

[4] Wang Yuzhe (2004): The Ancient Chinese History. Shanghai: Shanghai People's Publishing House. P73-80. (In Chinese)

5

Julian Jaynes' Theory of the Bicameral Mind and Different Pathways Leading to Subjective Consciousness in Human History

Summary: That the man-made secondary society is foreign to humans is once more illustrated by the phenomenon of bicameral minds, first described by Julian Jaynes. According to Jaynes, people with bicameral minds followed auditory hallucination, the divine voice, in response to an enlarged community from 9000 to 1000 BC, and subjective consciousness appeared around 1000 BC. Unlike the Mediterranean civilizations on which Jaynes' theory is based, Chinese civilization started with genetically coded primary society and therefore, went through a different pathway in the evolution of human minds to subjective consciousness. This essay presents overwhelming evidence for the presence of subjective consciousness around 1400 BC in China, and therefore, subjective consciousness may have appeared in a primary society setting. The bicameral mind pervasive among the Mediterranean civilizations was likely a response to the sudden appearance of secondary society. The author believes that subjective consciousness might have first appeared with the tool explosion around forty thousand years ago and switched to the bicameral mind in early Mediterranean civilizations but not in early Chinese civilization. The left and right hemispheres of our brain and their connection provide a good neuropsychological explanation for the emergence of a complex secondary society five or six thousand years ago after humans had lived in primary society for millions of years. As the processor of visuospatial images and holistic or intuitive awareness, the right brain may be responsible for the primary society while as the processor of language and rational thought, the left brain may be responsible for the secondary society.

*   *   *

When I was once searching on the internet about poetic thought last year, a peculiar term came into my vision field and caught my full attention immediately: the bicameral mind. I literally forgot everything that had so far engaged me and spent the next two weeks reading about the theory of bicameral mentality and its author, American psychologist Julian Jaynes (1920-1997). According to Jaynes, humans once lacked consciousness but followed auditory hallucination, the divine voice, in response to an enlarged community and the subsequent hierarchal theocracy. Human consciousness is only a cultural artefact based on language, and it first appeared around 1000 BC.

Thus both the division of human society into primary and secondary societies and the theory of the bicameral mind hold the insight that a fundamental culturally constructed change took place in recent human history due to a bigger society. As the theory of primary and secondary societies holds that Chinese civilization started with primary society while the Western civilization started with a typical secondary society. One may expect that the Chinese history of bicameral mentality may be fundamentally different from the Western one. Julian Jaynes based his theory mainly on analysis of the Western history, including that of Mesopotamia, Egypt, Israel, and Greece. Very little study has been done regarding the application of Julian Jaynes' theory to Chinese history.

A preliminary analysis of available literature confirms that the phenomenon of the bicameral mind was much less visible in Chinese history. Divination by oracle bones appeared around 4000 BC in China, and the earliest records that are detailed enough for assessment yield overwhelming evidence for the presence of subjective consciousness around 1400 BC in the ruling class, but the bicameral mind seemed to prevail among the peasants. Records from around 2356 to 1400 BC also suggest subjective consciousness, though it is inconclusive whether those records are absolutely reliable. The idea of a morality apart from legality only began to appear in Greece in the 5th century BC while Chinese civilization started with a strong emphasis on morality. Therefore, Chinese history is more consistent with the weak form of Jaynes' theory that consciousness could have begun shortly after the beginning of language and co-existed with the bicameral mind before the latter was sloughed off. It is a striking contrast to the full-blown bicameral minds in the early Mediterranean civilizations.

I will introduce Julian Jaynes' theory, the definition of subjective consciousness, and then concentrated on the documentation of the presence of subjective consciousness in China around 1400 BC followed by a short discussion.

(1) Juilian Jaynes and his Theory of the Bicameal Mind

Julian Jaynes was born in 1920 to a highly educated mother of 30 and a priest father of 66. His father died two years later of heart attacks and left him a fatherless childhood. Julian Jaynes attended Harvard University and was an undergraduate in McGill University. He received both his master and doctorate degrees from Yale University. He made significant contributions in the fields of animal behavior and ethology. After Yale, Jaynes spent several years in England working as an actor and playwright. Jaynes later returned to the states, and lectured in psychology at Princeton University from 1966 to 1990, teaching a popular class on consciousness for much of the time. He was in high demand as a lecturer, and was frequently invited to lecture at conferences and as a guest lecturer at other universities. He spent much of his summers at his home in Prince Edward Island, Canada while teaching at Princeton University. After he retired, he lived in Prince Edward Island and died in 1997.

Julian Jaynes was best known for his book *The Origin of Consciousness in the Breakdown of the Bicameral Mind* (1976)[1], in which he advanced his theory of the bicameral mind. Jaynes uses the word "consciousness" but does occasionally use the term "subjective consciousness" to talk about his theory on human consciousness. Since Jaynes's theory remains highly controversial and consciousness is a common word, the term "subjective consciousness" seems to be the preferred one for the "consciousness" in Julian Jaynes' terms.

To help students master his concept of consciousness precisely, Julian Jaynes usually started his lecture by talking what consciousness is not. First, consciousness is not all of mentality, as so many things that the nervous system does for us automatically without our consciousness. For example, a large class of activities is termed as preoptive such as how we sit, walk, move. All those activities are done without consciousness, unless we decide to be conscious of them, the preoptive nature of consciousness. Even when we are speaking, the nervous system automatically picks up the right word from the lexical storehouse in the brain and adds it to a string of words framed in the grammar structure. What we are conscious of the actual speaking can only be best described as intentions of certain meanings. Consciousness should not be confused with simple sense perception. All worms have sense perception, and we cannot say worms have consciousness.

Secondly, Consciousness does not copy experience, as we do not always remember what we have experienced. Our memories are even constructed differently from what we have experienced. Our memories of swimming tend to see ourselves from another point of view, a bird's eye view, which we have never experienced.

Thirdly, consciousness is not necessary for learning. For example, learning motor skills seems to happen without much consciousness. When we are first to learn how to ride a bicycle, it requires our consciousness to plan and start the process of learning and practicing. The nervous system takes care of a major part of the learning process by the so-called automatization of habit: Our feet are paddling for most of the time without our consciousness, and we are even surprised to find out that our skills have improved more than we have expected.

Fourthly, consciousness is not necessarily for thinking or reasoning. Here I introduce a Julian Jaynes' term, the struction. Structions are like instructions given to the nervous system, that, when presented with the materials to work on, result in the answer automatically without conscious thinking or reasoning. Such phenomenon applies to most of our activities, from simple judging, solving problems, and to scientific and philosophical activity. Consciousness studies a problem and prepares it as a struction, a process may result in a sudden appearance of the solution as if out of nowhere. During World War II, British physicists used to say that they no longer made their discoveries in the laboratory, they had their three B's where discoveries were made, the bath, the bed, and the bus. It illustrates well that discoveries as an important process of thinking and reasoning can be achieved without much consciousness except for the consciousness starts the automatic process.

Finally, most people would say consciousness is in our heads, but since we cannot say the location of bicycle riding is inside our heads, Julian Jayness thinks the phenomenal location of consciousness is arbitrary.

Jaynes also lists several features of consciousness such as a mind space for introspecting, narratization or self-talk, an analog ' I' acts as the agency for the introspection and narration, and consilience. Consilience is the mental process to make things compatible with each other, or to narratize and consiliate all together into a story.

Only after we get rid of all common misconceptions about consciousness, may we be in a position to understand Jaynes' theory of the bicameral mind. Jayness summarizes his theory in four ideas: 1) consciousness is based on language; 2) a different mentality, the bicameral mind, existed based on verbal hallucination before the development of consciousness; 3) consciousness appeared around 1000 BC; 4) the right hemisphere of the brain hears the auditory hallucination, a divine voice, and the left hemisphere carries out the order from the hallucinated devine voice.

The three phases:

Phase 1: Primitive Mentality, Homo Sapiens

200,000 BC	language evolves
40,000 BC	tool explosion
10,000 BC	first gods

Phase 2: Bicameral

9,000 BC	first towns 3,000
BC	writing begins

Phase 3: Conscious

1,000 BC	divination, prophets, oracles
0	
1,000 AD	
2,000 AD	

Jaynes termed the first phase as Neanderthals, and I changed it to primitive mentality and home sapiens. Now it is well established that Neanderthals are not our direct ancestors.

Thus the West went through a bicameral phase from 9000 to 1000 BC, which was characterized by a forceful theocracy. They organized their complex city states under the name of gods, and people developed bicameral minds to hear the divine voice and obey those gods. The subjective consciousness emerged after the bicameral mind broke down. As pointed above, the early Chinese social environment allowed them to still live in primary and quasi-primary society, which was based on human nature. The ancient Chinese did not go through this bicameral phase though to a certain degree, they might still have the bicameral mind in a different context.

(2) The Definition of Subjective Consciousness

What constitutes the subjective conscious mind may be a matter for debate. In his essay entitled *Consciousness and the Voices of the Mind* [2], Julian Jaynes attempts to clarify what subjective consciousness is, "Subjective conscious mind is an analog of what we call the real world. It is built up with a vocabulary or lexical field whose terms are all metaphors or analogs of behaviour in the physical world ... And it is intimately bound with volition and decision."

From the view of a society, this real world consists of many minds of the members of the society, and those minds communicate with each other by the vocabulary of metaphor. Thus impressions, feelings, emotions, concepts, imagery and other elements, which are available for introspection but may or may not be represented by words, are the building blocks of this real world or the subjective conscious mind. Each individual mind though may be different is greatly influenced by other minds and by the vocabulary they share. If we consider the analog of the real world as a perspective and consider volition and decision as free will, subjective consciousness essentially equals perspective plus free will.

A fundamental question is why humans are able to build secondary society while animals are not. The answer is that humans have the ability of self-transcendence: They are continuously looking for something higher than themselves and their real life. This eventually let them create new worlds for themselves. Under certain circumstances, people with primitive mentality and bicameral minds may be able to use rudimentary language in a creative way, but they use language just as other tools only to enrich their lives. Humans with subjective conscious minds use language to create totally new worlds such as many novels, especially scientific fictions. Each novel literally represents a new world created by man. Our secondary society is also one of those worlds created by humans. But this one is a real one, created not by one person but by numerous people over thousands of years. Such new worlds themselves are a result of free will, and those new worlds in turn show individuals how to execute free will to create unique lives for themselves.

As mentioned above, one feature of subjective consciousness is narratization or self-talk and an analog ' I' acts as the agency for the narration. Our life may be considered as a novel or fiction narrated in multiple media, words, images, concepts, feelings, and so on for a life long time. As the narrator of this novel of life, we exercise free will all the time in our inner world. Neither primates nor early human beings could achieve such a life experience. What is the minimum requirement of vocabulary for subjective consciousness to appear? The number of words has to be enough for the members of society to create a new world or a new life in their minds first before a world or a new life is created in reality. A few hundred words may be enough for a modern writer to create a fiction, but I tend to think many more words may be needed for subjective consciousness to appear among ancient people.

Each secondary society is a creation by man but primary society is the society humans are born with. With the above mentioned Chinese super state of primary societies, the ruling class of the king and vassals might not be able to change the overall social structure to create a new sub-society but as an idle class, they might be able to develop sophisticated vocabulary and form a subgroup with a distinct culture, which might not suit the definition of secondary society but was certainly a creation of their own. When a particular social issue was elaborated and debated for a long time even in a primary society setting, it might have created free will and led to the emergence of the subjective conscious mind.

(3) Evidence for Subjective Consciousness Around 1400 BC: The Oracle Bones

From the late Shang dynasty between 1400 and 1122 BC, some fifteen thousand pieces of oracle bone inscriptions have so far been excavated. It was in 1400 BC when King Pan-Geng gave his three speeches that are available for analysis. The reader should be reminded that the dating of Chinese history before 841 BC is only approximate.

From 1400 to 1122 BC, the kings of the Shang dynasty, the ministers, and the diviner officials developed an extraordinary enthusiasm towards divination by oracle bones. It is very much like the Egyptian pyramids that stand out without any match in human history. They certainly created a life of their own, a life of divination by oracle bones.

In the West, especially in Mesopotamia and Greece, civilizations started with city states where primary society was broken to form a typical secondary society with free individuals. In its early stage, there were no well established laws and social structures to provide the cohesive force to stabilize the society. A forceful religious faith was a must, and the execution of Socrates shows how forceful the religious faith could be. Such social circumstances provided the cultural environment to hatch the bicameral mind. Thus, people heard divine voices, and they sought divine voices by divination when they could no longer hear the voice clearly.

Chinese civilization started with primary society, and there was no forceful authority in primary society. The gods they imagined were just like their headmen, not forceful either. According to the belief system of the Shang dynasty, there was a natural deity for each of the natural forces they could perceive such as the sun, the moon, the wind, the rain, the snow, the cloud and so on. There was a super god, but their deceased ancestors seemed to be the most important ones. Those ancestors and gods had the power to influence the human world and their lives, but they represented a different world. People could seek favour but could not seek orders to organize their lives from those ancestors and gods, just as the members of a primary society cannot expect their headman to organize their lives. As a result, they had endless questions to ask and to ponder, which, facilitated by language development, eventually led to the emergence of subjective consciousness.

1. The Divination by Oracle Bones was Sophisticated Enough to Hatch Subjective Consciousness in the Late Shang Dynasty:

As mentioned above, more than 150,000 oracle bones were found for the two hundred and seventy eight years from 1400 to 1122 BC. Considering that many may still lay underground and even more might have been lost during the last three thousand years, and that a piece of bone could be used repeatedly and one session of divination might contain several questions, the number of questions subjected to oracle bones may be several times of those discovered oracle bones. Curiosity and the idle lifestyle of the ruling class were apparently the major factors behind those questions. Those oracle bone inscriptions contain more than 5000 Chinese characters but only a third was deciphered. Nowadays, one needs only to master 1000 Chinese characters to be able to read newspapers, and university graduates only mastered some 4000 Chinese characters on average.

A wide variety of topics were asked, essentially anything of concern to the royal house of Shang, from illness, birth and death, to weather, warfare, agriculture, tribute and so on. One of the most common topics was whether an illness of any member of the royal house and any member of the court officials was curable or not. As a topic of divination, the illness was often a minor one such as toothache.

Each oracle bone inscription normally consists of four sections, preface, topic, reading, and verification. During a divination session, the shell or bone was anointed with blood, and an inscription starts with the date that was recorded using the Chinese system of Heavenly Stems and Earthly Branches, the diviner's name was also noted. Next, the topic of divination was posed, such as whether a particular ancestor was causing a king's toothache. Then the bone was subjected to heat until it cracked. The diviner in charge of the ceremony read the cracks to learn the answer to the divination. The divined answer was sometimes marked either "auspicious" or "ominous". The king occasionally added a "prognostication" and his reading on the nature of the omen. On rare occasions, the actual outcome was later added to the bone in what is known as a "verification". A complete record of all the above elements is rare; most bones contain just the date, the diviner, and topic of divination, and many remained uninscribed after the divination. There is some evidence that the divination was made on brush-written words, and those written words were inscribed later by a workshop.

From the different names of diviners on the oracle bones, we know that the king had many diviner officials. Those officials prepared the oracle bones and kept them for late reference. One topic of divination could be raised multiple times, and often in different ways or by changing the date being divined about. This indicates that they concentrated their minds on one question for a period of time.

2. Two Examples of the Oracle Bone Inscriptions Show the Mind Space of the People Who Were Involved in the Divination:

The following is a typical oracle bone inscription:

It will rain today? Rain will come from the west? Rain will come from the east? Rain will come from the north? Rain will come from the south? (郭沫若: 《卜辭通纂 The General Compilation of Oracle Bone Inscriptions》, 375)

This oracle bone inscription shows that those people had a clear representation of the physical world and its four directions in their minds to enable them to ask and monitor the outcome of those questions.

It is understandable to ask whether it will rain or not today but what is the point to ask a total of four questions about which direction the rain will come? It shows an essential part of human nature, the curiosity of an idle mind.

The following oracle bone inscription is a completed one with the verification and was read by King Wu-Ding himself. King Wu-Ding ruled approximately from 1350 to 1292 BC.

Divination date: *Kui/Si;* diviner: *Hui;* Topic: *Whether unfortunate events will happen within ten days;* King Wu-Ding read the bone cracks and concluded: *Ominous, and unfortunate events will happen;* Verification: *Unfortunate events came from the west after five days.*

Zhi-Huo reported that Tu babarians invaded our eastern suburb and destroyed two towns, and Shu babarians invaded our farm fields in the western suburb. (《菁》, 2)

Those divining people apparently had a sense of time, the past, the future, and the present. The ancient Chinese people worshiped ancestors, and they often kept the shrines for each of their deceased ancestors in order of time from one generation to the next. This may give the Chinese a sense of time much earlier than in the West. For the same reason, the Chinese kept good records about their ancestors: their deeds and their words from prehistoric time.

Jaynes' concept of the mind space is much broader than the actual represention of time and physical space. Nevertheless it is part of the mind space that enable us to think about the answers to our questions: The subjective 'I' is able to move around in the imagined space of time and the physical world in the mind.

3. Conscious Dreams in Oracle Bone Inscription:

According to Julian Jaynes, there are conscious dreams and bicameral dreams. There are four oracle bones asking the meaning of a particular dream and whether the dream was auspice or ominous. In their dreams, one saw jades, and one (king) saw many sons, and two saw ghosts in several times (《合集》 5649;《合集》 17383;《合集》 17451;《合集》 17450). Those are apparently conscious dreams. The dreamer recalled their dreams and put them on oracle bones to seek the meaning of them. It is apparently self-introspection:

'I' → ['I' saw ghosts or jade or many sons in dream]

Those oracle bones are direct evidence for the presence of subjective consciousness.

4. Bone Inscriptions of Memorable Events:

Some bone inscriptions were records of a particular event. For example, the king once on a hunting tour (?1203 BC) killed a tiger, and he used the tiger bones to make table utensils, and then recorded this event on it (William Charles White: Bone Culture of China, the University Toronto Press, 1945, Plate XV). This clearly shows that the king was proud of what he had done. It is consisted with subjective consciousness.

5. Conflicting Opinions and the Collection of Ancient Texts

After the Shang dynasty was overthrown by the Chou dynasty in 1122 BC, King Wu of the Chou dynasty sought governing experience from a Shang minister, Duke Ji. According to Duke Ji, the Chinese kings had ruled the country based on nine principles since Yu the Great around 2200 BC. The seventh of the nine principles is about divination. It is a reliable source to see how divination was carried out during the Shang dynasty. (《*Collection of Ancient Texts: Great Principles* 尚書：洪範》)

According to Duke Ji, the first thing for the king was to select and appoint the right persons as diviners. For one issue, the king had to ask three diviners to perform divination and take the two identical readings as the final result, which is consisted with the archaeological finding that divination was often repeated for a single issue.

According to Duke Ji, the king, when facing a difficult issue, had to think it over himself first, and then consult with his ministers, his people, and finally consult with divination. There were six possible ways of conflicting opinions among divination by oracle bones, divination by milfoil stalks, the king, the ministers, and the people (Table 5.1). It clearly indicates that the Chinese super state had no forceful authority. The ruling class had to learn how to deal with different opinions, and it might well have facilitated the development of subjective consciousness.

Table 5.1 The Six Different Ways of Conflicting Opinions and Their Predicted Outcomes

	The king	Ministers	The people	Oracle bones	Milfoil stalkst	Predicted out come when being carried out
1	Yes	yes	yes	yes	yes	Grand concord, best for the king and his family
2	Yes	no	no	yes	yes	fortunate
3	No	yes	no	yes	yes	fortunate
4	No	no	yes	yes	yes	fortunate

5	Yes	no	no	yes	no	fortunate for internal operations but unlucky for external undertakings
6	Yes	yes	yes	no	no	fortunate for being still but un
	No	no	no	yes	yes	lucky for active operations

The different opinions held by the king, the ministers, and the people show that even the ordinary people had their own perspective and free will expressed in words. The following *King Pan-Geng's three speeches* provide detailed records of a real situation of such conflicting opinions.

(4) Evidence for Subjective Consciousness Around 1400 BC: King Pan-Geng's Three Speeches

A notable Chinese historian considers Chinese society as classless primitive society before 1400 BC when the king took part in physical labour among other peasants. According to his study, the capital moved at least seven or more times from 1766 to 1400 BC as required by so-called mobile agriculture. [3]

After 1400 BC, the king or emperor became a full time administrator and the capital did not move unless forced by war. King Pan-Geng used strong words to condemn the interest in gathering and accumulating wealth by his officials, ministers and local lords, because those officials felt it hard to abandon the wealth and move to a new place. It is likely that more accumulated wealth eventually enabled the capital to have a permanent location after 1400 BC.

As the last move of this kind in 1400 BC, the King Pan-Geng met strong resistance from all levels of people. King Pan-Geng gave three speeches to persuade and motivate his officials and people for this move.

Through Chinese history and up to today, Chinese scholars almost unanimously viewed the three speeches as genuine ones by King Pan-Geng himself. They were written down either when King Pan-Geng was alive or shortly after his death. Whether the text of the three speeches was edited by others in its early surviving years remains a matter for debate, though there is no evidence to support either view.

The three speeches have 1400 Chinese characters, which equal about 4000 words in modern English translation. For a king to speak at such a length on a single issue but to different people and on different occasions is unique in early Chinese records: *Collection of Ancient Texts* (Shangshu, 尚書).

1. They Were Trying Hard to Persuade Each Other and Change Each Other's Mind:

As pointed out by Ted Remington [4], "Persuasion, in any true sense of the term, could not exist without the type of consciousness Jaynes describes as only developing toward the end of the second millennium BC. One cannot persuade without the ability to see the world from the point of view of the one to be persuaded. Only by imaginatively inhabiting the mind-space of the other can persuasion be effected."

The three speeches by King Pan-Geng were the records of a long complex process of persuasion during which, the king was trying to persuade his officials and people who were, on the other hand, trying to persuade the king to change his mind. They all showed the vision of the world from the point view of the others, and claiming for the good of the others.

The first speech was delivered to the officials including ministers, local lords, and tribal chiefs. The second speech was delivered to the ordinary people. The third was after the move and was for the officials. The following is from the speech to the people:

"My present undertaking to move you to the new place, is for the long-lasting stability to our country. You, however, show no sympathy with the anxieties of my mind; but you all keep a great reserve in declaring your minds, trying respectfully by your sincerity

to change my mind. You only exhaust and distress yourselves. The case is like sailing in a boat: If you do not cross the river in time, you will ruin the whole cargo. Your sincerity does not respond to mine, and we are in danger of going together to destruction. You do not examine the matter but anger yourselves, what cure will that bring? You do not plan for the future, nor think of the calamity that will come to you. You greatly encourage one another in what must prove to your sorrow. Now you have the present, but you will not have the future; what life can you look for from above? ...Do I force you by the terrors of my power? My objective is to support and nourish you all."

Using the sailing boat for the political situation as an analogy is itself a very abstract concept, a sign of the subjective conscious mind. Persuasion also relies on a conception of time that, according to Jaynes, is only possible after the development of consciousness. The above quotation shows well that King Pan-Geng had a sense of time, since he talked about "future" and "long-lasting stability".

2. The Words Used by King Pan-Geng That Indicate Subjective Consciousness:

Here I only list out three Chinese characters that indicate the presence of subjective consciousness in the speaker. They are plan (mou 謀), volition (zhi 志), and heart (xin 心). They appeared four, ten, and four times respectively.

The Chinese character mou 謀 usually means plan, design or stratagem but can also be used as a noun with the meaning, strategy plans. Since the left half of the character is the radical yan 言, speaking, there are usually a few people who are involved in the activity of mou 謀 like the king designing a path for the country with his ministers, but there can also be only one person in the activity of mou 謀. The Chinese character mou 謀 indicates free will.

One example of Pan-Geng's words with the Chinese character mou 謀 are as follows in English translation:

"As I see as clearly as one sees a fire, if I lack <u>planning and strategy</u>, it will be my fault." (The underlined words are the English translation of the Chinese character in discussion, same below.)

The Chinese character xin 心 equals heart, mind, feeling, moral nature or character, and intention:

1. I have now brought forward and announced to you my <u>mind</u>, whom I approve and whom I disallow; let none of you but reverence my will.
2. Let every one of you set up the true rule of conduct in his <u>heart</u>.
3. If you can put away your (selfish) <u>thoughts</u>,
4. Take counsel how to put away your (selfish) <u>thoughts</u>.

The English equivalents of the Chinese character zhi 志 are will, aspiration, ambition, ideal. Two examples of the words with the Chinese characters zhi 志 are translated as follows:

1. I have now brought forward and announced to you my aspiration, whom I approve and whom I disallow; let none of you but reverence my <u>will</u>.
2. Now I have disclosed my heart and belly, my reins and bowels, and fully declared to you, my people, all my <u>mind and ideal</u>.

In the second example, the king spoke such words: "heart", "belly", "reins", and bowels. It indicates the close relationship that was consistent with the historical fact: The king and his officials lived in a primary society.

3. The Voice of Human Nature vs. Divine Voice: Comparison of Pan-Geng's Move to a New Capital with Moses' Move Out of Egypt:
All the difference between Pan-Geng's move to the new capital and Moses' move out of Egypt may be accounted for by the fact that China was modeled after primary society while Moses' people lived in a secondary society, or in other words, the voice of human nature vs. the divine voice.
Moses led the Israelites, 600,000 men plus women and children and a mixed multitude, with their flocks and herds from Egypt into

the wilderness of the desert for a few decades surrounded by hostile neighbouring states. In fact, they often battled through the way they were taking. Human nature was not enough to provide the needed cohesive force for such a goal. It was not surprising that the divine voice was heard all through the whole process of Moses' move out of Egypt. If we believe the bible, it was God not Moses who led the Israelites out of Egypt. It suits well with the theory of the bicameral mind.

In comparison with Moses and his people, Pan-Geng apparently had a better developed government: He was the king with several ministers to help him, and he also had a hereditary system to ensure the peaceful transition of power to the next generation. As a result of the limitation of primary society, Pan-Geng's move was much easier and simpler than Moses'. Pan-Geng's move took only a month or so, and it was a peaceful journey of some 150 miles. Pan-Geng also had much less people to move, as he called them to his palace to persuade them. For the ordinary people, they might not have the ability to see clearly the advantage this move would bring to them. For the officials, they might understand the political situation but did not want to lose their privileges and wealth. Pan-Geng's persuasion seemed to be much harder than Moses', and he had called both officials and people to his palace, and being friendly to them. He literally had to take his whole heart out to prove that he was sincerely dedicated to them, and his distressed heart also needed sympathy. It clearly shows that the social bond was emotional and psychological one in the primary society.

Pan-Geng warned both the officials and people that they might face execution if they refused to co-operate with the king. Execution sounds harsh but it was almost the only way of punishment available to the king. This punishment could not be taken lightly, as the king's power was well balanced against by ministers, vassal lords, tribal chiefs, and the people. Chinese people lived in numerous colonies that scattered over a vast area with waste land and minority people of different ethical origins between. Unhappy individuals could easily run away, and dissident chiefs could lead their peasants to live among those minority people.

One may expect that a few must be executed before the whole population gave up their resistance. Pan-Geng said in his third speech, "I have not punished any of you." So he did not punish anyone for this controversial move, even some officials had instigated peasants to act against the king.

What happened to those who resisted Moses' leadership? They were much less lucky than the ones who resisted Pan-Geng, since they were in a secondary society where the cohesive force was generated by reward and punishment expressed as divine will.

Nobody gave them a clear warning before hand as Pan-Geng did to his officials and people. According to the Bible (Numbers 16:2-20-32-35), "Two hundred and fifty men of the son of Israel, chieftains of the assembly, summoned ones of the meeting, men of fame. So they congregated against Moses…Jehovah now spoke to Moses and Aaron, saying 'Separate yourselves from the midst of the assembly, that I may exterminate them in an instant'…And the earth proceeded to open its mouth and to swallow up them…And a fire came out from Jehovah and proceeded to consume the two hundred and fifty men offering the incense."

Moses was apparently much more powerful than King Pan-Geng. Moses' power was not from a well developed law system and corresponding social structure but from religious faith and bicameral mentality. In contrast, Pan-Geng had a much more advanced government but much less power as the bicameral mind played only a minor role in Chinese social life. The social order of Chinese society was still based on human nature while the Western social order was pretty much man-made in the divine name.

(5) The Different Social Environments Hatched Different Ideologies

Julian Jaynes says, "It can easily be inferred that human beings with such a (bicameral) mentality had to exist in a special kind of society, one rigidly ordered in strict hierarchies with strict expectancies organized into the mind so that hallucinations preserved the social fabric. And such was definitely the case. Bicameral kingdoms were all hierarchical theocracies, with a god, often an idol, at their head from whom hallucinations seemed to come, or, more rarely, with a human being who was divine and whose actual voice was heard in hallucinations." [2]

I will explain why social conditions for such rigidly ordered hierarchical theocracies were not available in ancient China, and then I will present evidence that China was much less religious compared to the West.

It is well documented that primitive hunters and gatherers lived an idle life as other animals do, and only infrequently did they have violent conflicts. Thus they lived in a relatively peaceful environment as ancient Chinese people did.

The renowned American anthropologist, Marvin Harris, listed many evidences to support his conclusion: "Archaeological evidence from the upper paleolithic period— about 30,000 BC to 10,000 BC— makes it perfectly clear that hunters who lived during those times enjoyed relatively high standards of comfort and security. They were no bumbling amateurs."[5] According to Marvin Harris, those ancient hunters even knew how to control their population. Like other animals, early humans were motivated to intensify production only when they were in trouble. As pointed out in Essay 1, their insolvable trouble was caused by warring states.

Anthropologists believe that the separation of work from entertainment started with the invention of agriculture which requires intensive invest in the future, but humans only worked in modern sense of work when the governments of states provided an idle class to supervise others' work. The transformation from a primitive peaceful idle life to a rigidly ordered hierarchical society in which most people were working day and night like ants is apparently not a natural and simple process. It requires special conditions and special circumstances which appeared in the Mediterranean civilizations but were absent in the ancient China.

Marvin Harris lists three factors as the essential requirement for states to appear, namely population increase, intensive agriculture to produce enough plus food, and the so called circumscription. [6] Circumscription means the emigration of dissatisfied factions was blocked in such a way that factions of discontented members of a state cannot escape from their elite overlords without suffering a sharp decline in their standard of living. The earliest states like Mesopotamia, Egypt, and Greece were circumscribed by their dependence on modes of production associated with fertile river valleys surrounded by arid or semiarid plains or mountains. Circumscription was the critical factor for the three civilizations, as it generated the first genuine rulers in human history who were able to control access to basic resources. To control access to basic resources enabled the rulers to control people and set up a military power to monopolize violence or the power to kill other people. Once the rulers have the power to kill, and the first forceful authority of secondary society is established. Slavery for massive scales of productive and constructive activities was then possible.

In ancient China, such a circumscription was never available to set up any similar states. According to Wang [3], the locations Chinese lived scattered over a vast area but were mingled with minority ethical people until the Spring Autumn Period (771-476 BC). The royal clans and the peasants who lived in the capital practiced mobile agriculture at least until 1400 BC, and peasants were no doubt to practice mobile agriculture much later. As a result, it was almost impossible for the ruling class to execute strict control over its people, since the escape of dissatisfied factions was always possible. Without circumscription and the control of basic resources, the military power to kill was well balanced against each other by this super state structure of primary societies. The king and his court, as the ultimate power of this super state, were the major check for any local power, but the power of the king and his court was in turn checked by the power of various vassal states. The cooperation of a few vassal states would easily overpower the king and his court.

The first social implication of the above mentioned Chinese super state of primary societies was that this super state saw itself as the only government for all humanity. The second social implication of this Chinese super state of primary societies was that the people were left on their own. In a primary society, people cannot expect very much from their powerless leader, the headman. Similarly ancient

Chinese people could not expect very much from gods. Gods were an essential part of ancient Western society, and people expected gods to play a vital role in their lives. Gods and heaven played only a peripheral role in ancient Chinese life.

According to *Collection of Ancient Texts* (尚書), the famous minister Gao-Tao once said (?2300 BC): "Heaven (God) hears and sees, but it hears and sees through our people. Heaven (God) delivers reward and punishment, but it delivers reward and punishment through our people." This was a fundamental belief of ancient Chinese people. For the ruling class, the people were the God, and therefore, the ruling class had to fulfil the people's need to please God. The expression of the same belief became more clearly stated in 706 BC: "The people are the master of gods" (*Zuozhuan*, 左傳). The headman's leadership was based on persuasion and consensus, and so Chinese gods had to please the people to survive.

According to Julian Jaynes, the bicameral mind hears the voice of gods only in stressful situation when a decision has to be made. It is understandable that ancient Chinese people heard less such voices, since they lived in a relatively peaceful environment. This was exactly the case. According to Julian Jaynes' theory, divination appeared only after humans lost their bicameral minds and could no longer hear the voice of gods. Archaeological findings found that Chinese people performed divination using turtle and other animal bones at least six thousand years ago or 4000 BC. Xia listed three earliest findings of oracle bones, and they are dated 4070 BC, 3800 BC, and 3510 BC and from Henan, Gansu, and Inner Mongolia respectively. The finding of the oracle bones in 3800 BC from Gansu consists of six pieces of animal scapulae, which are all etched with marks and symbols and have been subjected to technical heat. Xia listed further 59 findings of oracle bones from the Longshan culture (2600-1900 BC), and mentioned the custom of burial turtle shells around 6000 BC. Those turtle shells were technically modified and decorated, and were only buried with elderly men and women. Those turtle shells are believed to be the precursor of oracle bones, since ancient Chinese people believed that turtles have spiritual power. [7]

Chinese people also saw many less images of gods, statues and paintings. David N. Keightley says, "Characteristically, there is no visual image or even textual description of any early Chinese ruler or deity to compare with the images and descriptions of particular rulers, heroes, and gods we have from Mesopotamia and Greece. There is no Chinese equivalent to the bronze head, which may depict King Sargon the Great, no Chinese version of a heroic, life size, naked bronze Poseidon." [8]

Since the very beginning, Chinese civilization lacked the giant temples dedicated to gods in the Middle East and in ancient Greece. In the ancient Chinese cities, the first eye-catching building was the palace. The shrines to the ancestors were usually inside the palace, occupying a minor part. The capital, Beijing, from the last dynasty of China, Qing (1644-1911), had four temples each in one of the four directions, the south, the north, the east, and the west for heaven, earth, the sun, and the moon respectively. Those four temples embrace the far larger central palace, which shows exactly that gods are peripheral in Chinese life.

Many Chinese scholars believe that the Chinese character for the super god or God, di 帝, symbolizes an inverted triangle on a table for worshippers. The inverted triangle is the symbol for the female sex organ. From 221 BC, Chinese emperors took the same word to name themselves, which makes the Chinese God, di 帝, a more personated figure. Chinese culture has never created a well-known personal image for the super god, di 帝, which is in line with the interpretation that God is essentially the female sex organ. The national leader was called the son of Heaven since the early Chou dynasty but remarks that depreciate Heaven have never stopped. For details, the reader may read Essay 9.

In summary, peaceful social environment, primary society, a culture based on human nature for all humanity, divination by animal bones, a ruling class who saw the people as the basis of their rule may each have contributed to the appearance of subjective consciousness in China.

(6) The Bicameral Mind in China

Subjective consciousness, a perspective plus free will or in Julian Jaynes' term, the real world plus volition, can be greatly influenced by the different states of mind as discussed in Essay 1 and shown in Figure 2.

One window to see what people really saw in their world is to see what their visual artists created for them in history. Those artists represent their culture and their people. Ancient Chinese artists painted mainly mountains, rivers, birds, flowers and so on, and if there is any figures in their paintings, those figures are tiny in vast landscapes. That's because Chinese people lived in a relatively peaceful environment, and they had a relaxing mind. It is breathtaking to notice that for more than a thousand years, the Western artists created nothing but human figures. Landscape as a subtype of painting first appeared in the 17th century in Holland. It shows clearly that war was the main force to shape the society and life in the West but not in ancient China. When your mind engaged in fighting with other people, you see nothing but people who are either your friends or enemies.

Julian Jaynes used to say "Consciousness is what is going on in the minds of any dozen people now on the street". He talks about the idle mind or self-entertaining mind but not the goal-oriented or war-occupied mind. Even the stream of worries, regrets, hopes, and so on is constantly monitored and modified by a more general perspective which has been formed to reach some goals in the subject's mind. This perspective of goals is relatively stable in the subject's life and is integrated into the general perspectives of goals of the society he lives in.

The human mind has to be rational when facing a war or being pressed to achieve a goal. While being idle, humans just as other animals want to enjoy themselves. When the only thing you care about is enjoyment, there is no point to care about rationality and subjective consciousness. There is even no point to worry about the difference between hallucination and reality.

Levy-Bruhl's book "Primitive Mentality" was influential in Jaynes's thinking about the bicameral mind. Levy-Bruhl writes: "In comparison to modern society, a greater number of individuals in primitive societies experiences hallucinations, experiences them more frequently, and the hallucinations play an important role in their day-to-day lives." Levy-Bruhl states: "To them the things which are unseen cannot be distinguished from the things which are seen. The beings of the unseen world are no less directly present than those of the other; they are more active and more formidable. Consequently that world occupies their minds more entirely than this one, and it diverts their minds from reflecting, even to a slight extent, upon the data which we call objective." [9]

Further, Erika Bourguignon, from a study of almost 500 societies has shown that the frequency, accessibility and quality of religious experiences, correlate inversely with the complexity of social structure. In the simplest and most egalitarian societies, ritual trance states tend to be voluntary, conscious and accessible to most people who desire them. [10]

Both Levy-Bruhl and Erika Bourguignon indicated that hallucination was more common in ancient primitive people. But it was only part of the idle mind in the primary society while it became the divine voice to dictate the people to obey their rulers in the secondary society.

Such prehistoric primary society described by Levy-Bruhl equals Neanderthal from 200,000 to 9,000 BC in Julian Jaynes' term. Here I use the primitive mind to represent the mentality of this period of time before the first towns and the bicameral mind appeared around 9,000 BC. In primary society where the mentality is primitive, gods and people are on the same level, which is the reflection of the egalitarian society. Subsistence endeavour is not enough to shift people from an idle frame of mind to a rational goal-oriented mind. The bicameral mind serves as a transitional phase from the primitive mind to the goal-oriented conscious mind.

As mentioned above, the Chinese super state of primary societies enabled Chinese people to still live in primary or quasi-primary society. This makes the shift from the primitive mind to subjective conscious mind much less dramatic, though the bicameral mind was still visible as Julian Jaynes' theory is universally applicable.

The ruling class, the king and vassals, and the peasants lived in separate societies. I have to address the ruling class and the peasants differently to show how the Julian Jaynes' theory of the bicameral mind and subjective consciousness applies to Chinese history. Contrast to the goal-oriented West where people had to look forward to an uncertain future, the Chinese had to look back to their traditions and ancestors to keep the harmony and unity of their society.

There are no Chinese equivalents for the Iliad and the Bible stories, and gods stayed peripheral in Chinese life. With the ruling class, they heard the voice of human nature and the voice of deceased ancestors instead of the voice of gods. Furthermore, such voice usually appeared as conscience or a model to follow but not in spoken words. Michael Carr illustrates that the drunk corpse/ personators speak in the voice of the deceased ancestors as described in the *Classic of Poetry*. Such descriptions are relatively rare in ancient Chinese literature. Furthermore, the spiritual voice speaks almost identical blessings for the descendants, ten thousand year happy life, in the three poems cited by Michael Carr. Those words seem to have been chosen before hand as part of the formality. They are not divine orders as heard by the bicameral man in the West. On contrary, like other Chinese gods, the ancestor spirits were keen to please the people for their survival: They offered ten thousand year happy life after receiving a simple ritual worship. [11]

The process of changing mentality in the ruling class was described well by the following quotation from Lao Tzu:

When Tao is lost, there remains virtuosity. When virtuosity is lost, there remains benevolence. When benevolence is lost, there remains righteousness. When righteousness is lost, there remains ritual. When ritual is lost, what remains is the thinness of honesty and trustworthiness, and chaos is on its way. (Tao Te Ching, Chapter 38)

The above quotation from Lao Tzu can serve as the description of the mental shift from the primitive mind to the bicameral mind and to subjective conscious mind. When Tao prevailed in ancient primary society, the mentality was primitive. That Tao is lost means that the primitive mind is lost. When a primary society is in trouble, people rely on collective unconsciousness to keep the harmony and unity of the society. It was natural that ancient Chinese called up on people's subconscious by emphasizing virtue, benevolence.

The primitive mind must have been lost long before recorded history in China. The earliest Chinese records, *Collection of Ancient Texts* starts with the Yao Emperor (2356 BC). He was the first Chinese leader who emphasized virtue and set up as an example of virtue for his people to follow. This is the clear indication that the primitive mind had been lost, the society had to be reminded of virtue by the leader and by his example. The leader represents the people who had heard the voice of human nature and called on the society to behave according to the requirement of virtue.

Both virtue and morality are the same word in Chinese, de 德. Such a Chinese concept of morality is based on human nature. According to the Taoist theory, de 德 is essentially the obtainment of Tao, and Tao is nature itself that follows the natural way. We are born with the ability of empathy, an ability to understand the emotions and feelings of others and take on the perspective of others. Modern technology such as functional magnetic resonance imaging allows us to observe the brain when it is fully functional. We can see the same pattern of mental activity from both the brain of the patient who is having a surgical operation and the brain of the patient's wife who is watching beside. The sympathizer feels the pain of the sufferer.

The *Book of Ancient Texts* describes the Yao Emperor as such a good example for the society to look up to: "He was reverential, intelligent, accomplished, and thoughtful - naturally and without effort. He was sincerely courteous, and capable of all complaisance. The bright influence of these qualities was felt through the four quarters of the land, and reached to heaven above and earth beneath. He made the able and virtuous distinguished, and thence proceeded to the love of all in the nine classes of his kindred, who thus became harmonious. He also regulated and polished the people of his domain, who all became brightly intelligent. Finally, he united and harmonized the myriad states; and so the black-haired people were transformed. The result was universal concord."

When the Emerpor Yao chose a man to succeed his position as the emperor of China, he found such a man who was unmarried among the lower class of people, called Shun. The tribal chiefs told the Emperor Yao, "He is the son of a blind man. His father is obstinately unprincipled; his (step-)mother was insincere; his (half-) brother Xiang was arrogant. He has been able, by his filial piety, to live in harmony with them, and to lead them gradually to self-government, so that they no longer proceed to great wickedness."

When the society became more complex and people's self-consciousness was growing, the society had to take further steps to keep the society stable. The Shang people seemed to worship various gods, spirits, ancestors. The Chou dynasty (1122-256 BC) introduced a complex system of rituals that emphasizes the ranking system of the society. This ritual system often requires the ruling class of different ranks and the people to participate in ritual performance with music. In a way, it was a resuscitation of ritual performance of ancient primitive society.

During the so-called Spring Autumn Period (770-476 BC), this ritual system was no longer enough to keep the society stable. Benevolence, righteousness, and ritual are the principle belief of Confucianism. When a primary society is in trouble facing an unwanted division, they called on members' subconscious to feel the emotional and psychological bond they have with the society. Confucian scholars are those who heard such voices and called on the society for benevolence and righteousness. According to Lao Tzu, violence-based legal system was invented only after chaos set in. Legal system represents the rational thinking, and therefore, the subjective conscious mind.

As to the peasants, they seemed to acquire subjective conscious mind at the time as the ruling class did. This is likely as they communicated with each other and engaged in the same mental process. Of course, peasants might also have acquired their subjective conscious mind by following their leaders like today's children follow their parents. As mentioned above, the peasants had their own opinion that might be different from the king and his officials, and the peasants tried to persuade King Pan-Geng to change his mind.

A few peasants might have a subjective consciousness but the majority of them might still have a bicameral mind while the majority of officials and the king had subjective conscious minds, because Pan-Geng talked to the officials and to the peasants differently. He mentioned ancestors only when he talked to the peasants. The following is what King Pan-Geng said to the peasants:

I think that my king ancestors employed your forefathers, and I will be enabled in the same way to greatly nourish you and cherish you. If I am to err in my government and remain long here, my founder king ancestor sends down on me punishment and scolds me, and says, "Why do you treat my people so bad?" If you myriads of people do not try to perpetuate your lives and do not cherish one mind with me, the One man, in my plans, the former kings will send down on you punishment, and say, "Why do you not agree with my young grandson, but go on to forfeit your virtue?" When they punish you from above, you are unable to escape.

My king ancestors made your ancestors toil in the fields, you are all my people. You cherish wrongful intentions in your hearts. My royal ancestors treated your ancestors and forefather well, and your ancestors and forefather abandon you, and do not save you from death. If some of you try to damage my administration, and think only of hoarding up wealth, your ancestors and forefathers report it to my founder ancestor, saying, "Please execute punishment on our descendants." So my founder ancestor sends great calamities on those men.

The original text does not have a grammar tense, and so many translations use future tense for those remarks by the deceased ancestors. Here I use present tense for those remarks indicating that Pan-Geng not only considered his people as bicameral, so he spoke to them in the deceased ancestors' voice, but he also temporarily reversed to the bicameral mind when he was saying in the deceased ancestors' voice. In other words, he was possessed by the spirits of those deceased ancestors when he spoke in their voices.

Furthermore, Chinese bicameral men regarded their leaders and ancestor as the model to follow. The ancient Chinese corpse/personators were grandchildren, and girls for female ancestors and boys for male ancestors. Acting out as their deceased grandparents in childhood on such a formal occasion might have planted a firm idea in their minds that they were going to model after their deceased grandparents, which was exactly what the society wanted.

When King Wu of the Chou dynasty talked to Duke Ji, he said, "Heaven, working unseen, secures the tranquillity of the lower people, aiding them to be in harmony with their condition. I do not know how the unvarying principles of the Heaven to govern the country. ''

Duke Ji told the king nine principles, and the first is the five elements, water, fire, wood, metal, and earth. This is almost identical with the ancient Greek four elements, water, fire, air, and earth. But only the ancient Chinese regarded the five elements as the first principle of governing the country, which indicates that ancient China modeled after nature. The second principle of governing the country is so called the five personal matters. "The first is the bodily demeanour; the second, speech; the third, seeing; the fourth, hearing; the fifth, thinking. The virtue of the bodily appearance is respectfulness; of speech, accordance with reason; of seeing, clearness; of hearing, distinctness; of thinking, perspicaciousness. The respectfulness becomes manifest in gravity; accordance with reason, in orderliness; the clearness, in wisdom; the distinctness, in deliberation; and the perspicaciousness, in sageness."

Those words show that the model the leaders set up for their people and the ancestors set up for their descendants is not a particular method or ideology to achieve a particular goal but rather a general character or more specifically, a state of mind, as the ultimate goal of this ancient Chinese super state was to let the country remain in its original natural way of unity and harmony forever.

(7) Discussion: Chinese History is More Consistent With the Weak Form of Julian Jaynes' Theory

When I first came to the idea of primary and secondary society a few years ago, I was possessed by the question what was the brain power storage for the sudden development of a complex new life in the man-made secondary society only five or six thousand years ago after humans had lived a simple life in primary society for at least two hundred thousand years? Now it seems clear that the left and the right hemisphere of our brain and their connection may be the neurological basis. When patients have half of their brain cut off in the surgical procedure known as hemispherectomy, they can survive and function pretty well, but they will have some physical disabilities. The patients may even overcome the physical disabilities by reorganization of the left over half of the brain especially when the patients who go through the procedure are young. Intellectually they are doing well in college, and one of them became the champion bowler of her class, and another, the chess champion of his state according to a neurologist John Freeman of Johns Hopkins University. [12] Thus humans might have half of their brain power stored for the emergence of a complex lifestyle created by humans themselves. According to Julian Jaynes, the connection of the two hemispheres is very limited, and the transferring of information through the two hemispheres must be coded. This also applies to the connection of primary and secondary societies. From primary society to secondary society, a coded system is a must, which may include language, value systems, codes for behaviour, law and so on.

Julie Kane reviewed the literature and concluded, "Particularly in the decade of the 1970s, mass market publications popularized the notion of the left brain as the processor of language and rational thought and the right brain as the processor of visuospatial images and holistic or intuitive awareness." [13] Such descriptions fit well with the concept of primary and secondary societies with the right hemisphere responsible for the primary society life and the left hemisphere responsible for the secondary society life.

From the discussion above, we know Chinese civilization took a unique pathway that allowed Chinese people to remain in a primary or quasi-primary society. Because of the similar social environments, the reason for the Chinese to practice divination might have been the same around 4000 BC as in the late Shang dynasty. They did not seek the divine voice to guide their lives but trying to find answers to questions arising in their life, a sign of the subjective conscious mind. To the prehistoric people, the Mediterranean sea may be a much too more treachery physical environment than the isolated yet vast land of China. The latter might have accommodated a relaxing mind of curiosity but the former might not.

Although all Chinese people regard the Yellow Emperor as their earliest common ancestor, the *Collection of Ancient Texts* starts with the Yao Emperor and the Shun Emperor, (?2356-2205 BC). A total of five short texts are from 2356 to 1400 BC, and all those texts provide further evidence for the presence of subjective consciousness.

According to the text, the Emperor Yao ordered his men to use the configuration and movement of the stars at night to calculate the numbers of days in a year, and concluded that there were 366 days. Modern astronomic studies indicate that the special configuration of stars the Emperor Yao and his people observed occurs every 4000 years, and its last appearance was in 1800. Its previous appearance was around 2200 BC [14]. The Taosi archaeological site, Shangxi province, was considered to be the Emperor Yao's capital. A recent excavation reveals more than a dozen earth columns arranged in a half circle, which is apparently an ancient observatory. Those columns were thought to support stone columns five meter high. Therefore the content of the text about the Emperor Yao is essentially true.

The text about the Emperor Yao uses 172 Chinese characters, which equals about six hundred modern English words, to describe how the Emperor Yao sent out people to observe the star pattern at four places, each in the south, the north, the east, and the west respectively, in order to assess the length of a solar year. I think this shows that the Yao Emperor and his people had a sense of space and time.

There are numerous words used in the text suggest of subjective consciousness. During a conversation with his tribal chiefs, every time the tribal chiefs mentioned a name, the Emperor Yao recalled his memory and expressed his impression on the named. It indicates that the Emperor Yao had reminiscent memory available for introspection and recall, a feature of subjective consciousness. To send a man in charge of flood control, the Yao Emperor disagreed with the tribal chiefs about the candidate they had recommended. But those tribal chiefs insisted, and the Yao Emperor gave in. Once again, it shows that conflicting opinions are commonplace in primary society, since there is no forceful authority.

The first text of *Collection of Ancient Texts* has the following phrases to describe poetry and songs, "Poetry is the expression of earnest thought; singing is the prolonged utterance of that expression; the notes accompany that utterance, and they are harmonized themselves by the standard tubes. 詩言志， 歌永言， 聲依永， 律和聲。 " Those words clearly indicate the presence of subjective consciousness.

If we accept the divination around 4000 BC in China as an indication of subjective consciousness and accept the authority of the ancient Chinese texts from 2356 to 1400 BC, Chinese history is more consistent with the weak form of Julian Jaynes' theory that consciousness must have begun shortly after humans acquired language.

An alternative interpretation of the burial goods with the deceased and the Chinese ancestor worship is that a subjective conscious mind has impassable difficulty to understand death. Some philosophers even noticed that man cannot imagine one's death and cannot imagine a world without him while he can vividly imagine how he was born. In other words, one cannot understand and cannot imagine how his or her subjective consciousness stops to exist. The death of one's subjective consciousness is only a culturally constructed idea enforced on man.

A culturally constructed subjective consciousness does not have death but the body does. An analogy is the computer with which, the software is immortal but the hard hare is not.

The concept of immortal souls itself indicates the presence of subjective consciousness rather than a bicameral mind to hear the voice of the deceased. Therefore, I agree with those who put the time for the emergence of human subjective consciousness much earlier around forty thousand years ago along the tool explosion and the first ritual burials.

Primates groom each other to solidify their social bond, and anthropologists believe that naked humans chat with each other in stead of grooming. Such chat does not necessarily function as exchange of information, but it can be only for the enjoyment. Such chat is a piece of pure art. Through such chat and other collective activities, all members integrate into a whole psychologically and emotionally in primary society. Thus subjective consciousness might be an unintended side product while humans enjoy themselves by doing nothing, and secondary society uses subjective consciousness as the basic engine to promote its goal.

One goal of meditation is to seek a state of mind: thoughtless awareness. Thus it is not an easy job to stay wake and have nothing in the mind. No doubt ancient primitive people might have a drifting or wandering mind when they had nothing to do. Julian Jaynes thinks bicameral people do not have reminiscent memory, and their memories are supposed to be random and unorganized. The content of the drifting mind of primitive people includes such unorganized memories plus imagination. When they mastered enough words, nothing could stop them from communicating with each other about what was going on in their wandering minds. What they so expressed is called hallucination or imagination or spiritual experience or whatever you prefer but the result is the same that they relaxed and enjoyed themselves just as many animals do when they have nothing to do. This process eventually led to the stage that their collective imagination had created a world of their own which has a set of metaphors or mental representations to describe the created world with the mind-space. That is exactly what subjective consciousness is. Of course, this collectively imagined world by our ancient primitive people was a mixture of hallucination and reality, the real world in Jaynes' term.

In response to a danger situation, one or two primates call out and the rest primates only hear the voice of the call but they do not see the danger situation themselves. Most of those primates take the same right action in response to the call. According to Jaynes, primitive people would similarly respond to a certain situation with the right words in their minds as auditory hallucination. The result is the same: They all response to the situation with the right action.

John Hamilton reports auditory hallucinations in nonverbal quadriplegics [15]. He found nine out of 13 (69.2%) such quadriplegics showed auditory hallucination.

Hamilton even suggests, "…auditory hallucination, which for certain physically handicapped populations may be the rule, not the exception." Those people are completely dependent on others for their physical and mental well-being. As mentioned above, our civilization made uncivilized idle people all labouring themselves day and night like ants, especially in the early stage of civilization. Their conditions may be in a way similar to those quadriplegics. On the other hand, those quadriplegics hear voices when they have nothing to do lying in bed. To hear those voices certainly requires mental concentration to a certain degree. Those voices may be more a result of subjective consciousness than a result of the bicameral mind, since mental concentration is no doubt an action of free will that directs the thought to certain direction. Of course those voices affected the way those quadriplegics respond to their care-givers afterwards. If those quadriplegics had only randomly drifting minds when they were alone and did not have any mental activity concentrating on certain topics, they would not have heard the voices they had. Those voices are all persistent and meaningful to the hearers. If the voices they heard were only part of their randomly drifting minds, they would not have been able to report any voices. Again it favours the weak form of the theory that subjective consciousness coexists with the bicameral mind: Some heard voice because they had searched for the voice consciously, and some heard the voice only as a way to follow the authority.

Hamilton discusses intuitions at length. Primitive people had quite different intuitions from modern civilized people. Primitive people's intuition is the result of human nature. Our intuition is the working of our minds without our awareness. Such intuitions have integrated into them all the information we have learned by subjective conscious experience.

Since hypnosis, trance, religious experience, and even including poetry writing, are all considered as a temporary bicameral mind. Subjective consciousness and bicameral mentality can transform into each other in modern individuals. It is understandable that subjective consciousness and bicameral mentality could transform into each other in ancient society. Thus once acquired subjective consciousness could be lost afterwards in a small society. Sophisticated writing and sophisticated social structure based on subjective consciousness might have acted to prevent such loss. Of course, a large subjective conscious population itself is the ultimate blockage to such loss. One way for the loss of subjective consciousness is that some content of subjective consciousness becomes inheritance of the society such as mythology or divine voice heard by members, the bicameral mind. Thus the bicameral mind could be the relic of the previous conscious minds that had been lost.

If subjective consciousness could be lost during the early stage of human development, the weak form and the strong form of Julian Jaynes's theory do not contradict each other. The West happened to be the strong form while China happened to go through a pathway of the weak form of the theory. The weak form indicates the coexistence of subjective consciousness and the bicameral mind in early Chinese history while the strong form indicates the absence of subjective consciousness before the documented presence of the bicameral mind in the West. Both remain speculative and unfalsifiable. Furthermore, the author believes that subjective consciousness likely first appeared with the tool explosion around forty thousand years ago and switched to a full blown bicameral mind in the early Mediterranean civilizations but not in Chinese civilization.

Julian Jaynes made it clear that this weak form of his theory is almost unfalsifiable. He says, "I think we should have a hypothesis that can be disproved by evidence if we are going to call it a scientific hypothesis." Thus Julian Jaynes did not necessarily believe less in his weak form than in his strong form of the theory.

References

[1.] Julian Jaynes (1976): The Origin of Consciousness in the Breakdown of the Bicameral Mind. Boston: Houghton-Mifflin.

[2.] Julian Jaynes (1986): Consciousness and the Voices of the Mind, Canadian Psychology, April 1986, Vol. 27(2).

[3.] Wang Yuzhe 王玉哲 (2004)：Ancient Chinese History, Shanghai: People's Publishing House, 2004. (in Chinese)

[4.] Ted Remington (2007): *The Origin of Rhetoric in the Breakdown of the Bicameral Mind*, The Jaynesian Newsletter, Summer 2007. (http://www.julianjaynes.org)

[5.] Marvin Harris (1977): Cannibals and Kings. New York: Random House. p9.

[6.] Marvin Harris (1988): Culture, People, Nature. New York: Harper & Row Publishers. P377-78.

[7.] Xia Zhenhao (2001): A General Cultural History: Xia and Shang. Shanghai: Shanghai Art and Literature Publishing House, p608-747. (in Chinese)

[8.] David Keightley (1990): Early civilization in China. In Paul S. Ropp, eds: Heritage of China. Berkeley, University of California Press. p37.

[9.] L. Levy-Bruhl (1973): Primitive Mentality. New York: Macmillan. (p61-62).

[10.] Erika Bourguignon (1971): Psychological Anthropology: an Introduction to Human Nature and Cultural Differences. New York: Holt, Rinehart and Winston.

[11.] Michael Carr (2008): The Shi "Corpse/Personator" Ceremony in Early China. In Marcel Kuijsten, eds, *Reflections on the Dawn of Consciousness, Henderson*: Julian Jaynes Society.

[12.] Charles Q. Choi (2008): Do You Need Only Half Your Brain? Scientific American, March 2008, p104.

[13.] Julie Kane (2004): Poetry as Right-Hemisphere Language. Journal of Consciousness Studies. 11, No. 5-6, p21-59.

[14.] Wang, Baolin (2003): A Modern Edition of Collection of Ancient Texts. Shanghai: Shanghai Ancient Book Publishing House. P36-37. (Wang cites the 19th century sinologist Dr. M. H. Melhurst,

English translator James Legge, and recent studies by Dr.H. K. C. Yee in his book. YSLi) (in Chinese)

[15.]   J. Hamilton (2008): *Auditory Hallucinations in Nonverbal Quadriplegics*. In Marcel Kuijsten, eds, *Reflections on the Dawn of Consciousness, Henderson*: Julian Jaynes Society.

6

Serenity: The Lives my Mother and Grandmother Lived

(1) The Life My Mother Lived

At the supper table, my Mother suddenly collapsed in her seat and lost consciousness. She died three days later on her ninety third birthday, September 26, 2007. Autumn drought occasionally hits this rural area of China which hinders sowing winter wheat. Peasants had been worried that this year seemed to be one of those rare years. Miraculously heavy rain poured down almost the same time my Mother passed away, and it made farm work in the field impossible. The rain lasted several days but again miraculously stopped the day of my Mother's funeral. Sodden farm fields still prevented any entrance by peasants but the interment and its ceremony proved no problem at all as the graveyard was grassland. There was not a single drop of rain though it was gloomy all day. The local custom demands that no matter how urgent the farm work is, peasants have to stop for a funeral and no matter how horrible the weather is, a funeral has to be carried out on time. Chinese peasants are no longer superstitious, but they couldn't help uttering superstitious remarks on my Mother's funeral. They all said: What a nice lady! Even at the time going to heaven, she did not forget bringing the much wanted rain to her villagers and was reluctant to interrupt anybody's any farm work even for an hour.

Those remarks describe well the lives my Mother and grandmother had lived. The popular serenity prayer says: "God, grant me the serenity to accept the things I cannot change; the courage to change the things I can; and the wisdom to know the difference." I guess, it was the Chinese traditional culture that gave my mother and grandmother the wisdom to accept whatever came in their lives with serenity. Neither of them was born a broad minded person, but they never cried. I only occasionally saw them shedding tears silently. They never had any quarrel with anybody, and always yielded happily to other people's needs. But in the end, they lived a life better than the average materialistically and spiritually.

When I took English classes in China many years ago, our American teacher explained the word "sophisticated" to us, saying, "In comparison with the peasants who lived in the same villages one generation after another, you are all sophisticated." It makes more sense if we replace the word "sophisticated" with "complex". We all live a more and more complex life. The life has become so complex that our minds have to work continuously. To rest is either buried into a fifty page newspaper or emerged into the images and information of TV or Internet. Only after retirement, we realized that thoughtless awareness or serenity is almost impossible to achieve.

In the last twenty years or so, the life of Chinese peasants improved significantly. Every time I went home, my Mother expressed her satisfaction with life nonstop. But the words were more or less the same: How lucky I am to have such nice later years and not have to worry about how to fill up my stomach and how to clothe my body. In fact, my family never ran out of food or clothes. Even in the famine years, it was easy to get substitute such as tree leaves and grass roots in the countryside. We never threw away any cloth material even after many decades, and it thus was equally easy to keep us warm. What my Mother referred to as worries concerning food and clothes were probably related more to the rough social environment during her first seventy years. The family was quiet and safe with enough supplies, but it was surrounded by an unsafe society in turmoil. There were many wars before the late 1940s but there were many so-called political movements afterwards. The dramatic steps taken by the Chinese leaders shortly after Mao's death in 1976 were critical for the prosperity of the later years, but it was not peaceful for those who went through them. Chinese society was relatively peaceful only for the last twenty years or so.

The house I lived in as a child in the 1950s was all gone but remains in my memory. We had a twelve room bungalow, three rooms situated on each side of a rectangular courtyard. There were several secretive places built in for hiding and many features of the house were designed to prevent invaders from getting in. My grandfather joined a local network to co-ordinate efforts to protect the community against bandits and robbers, who were numerous and powerful in those warring years. Grandmother often complained: It was those years building this complex house that tired her into chronic bronchitis for life. Chinese peasants use the same word for tiredness and chronic lung disorder, since they both make one short of breath.

Both my Mother's and father's families were relatively better off than the average but their prosperity was really nothing in comparison to today's rich people. In 1993, I met one of my cousins on the way home. He said, "Wow, nowadays rich people are much larger and richer than the landlords and the capitalists we have confiscated and suppressed." That's only a few years after the new policy was in place. The rich people my cousin referred to had only twenty or thirty thousand Chinese dollars, equal to some three or four thousand in Canadian dollars. But they are richer than the landlords who might have been executed for their possessions.

My village has a fair every five days for peasants to sell and buy their farm produce. When I was in the elementary school, my

Mother once suggested to me that I should go to the fair and look for dropped watermelon and sunflower seeds. She said, the children of her parents' home often did so and brought home handfuls of seeds to share with the whole family. I never tried as my Mother suggested. Those poor peasants might be reluctant to pick up one or two seeds, but they will certainly bend over to pick them up if they drop a few. I might have had to fix my eyes on others' heels for days to get a handful of seeds.

Both my mother's and father's families had, however, their property confiscated during the political movement of the Land Reform when I was four years old. The slogan to guide this campaign was: "Sweep them out of their houses like rubbish." One day our courtyard was full of people carrying everything away. As Children had no toys in those years, I remember colourful objects that appealed to a child's eyes being taken away by young peasants. For days, we had nothing left except the clothes on our bodies. I followed my sister who was a few years older than me to beg for food door by door. We stood under the window, and begging, "Granny, Granny, be kind enough to share with the hungery people a mouthful of solid food." The solid food we got was nothing but steamed corn pastry, a mouthful a door if we were lucky. My father was in prison. My family, headed by the only two adult women, my Mother and Grandmother, gathered together to share a meal, each picking up a mouthful of solid food we had begged. We all stood in the dark room, since we had no light and no chairs. Grandmother and Mother suddenly had a great idea. They had dragged away everything except a huge jar of pickling turnips that they couldn't move. They sealed it. We stole some out to everybody. The next day Grandmother and Mother asked one of my grown-up cousins, who happened to be poor, to come and have a look at the jar and told him: I accidentally broke the seal while playing around there. So much salt was put in that it tasted exactly like salt itself. Such awful food was out the table of Chinese people some twenty years ago.

One characteristic of those political movements led by the Chinese Communist Party was that they always overdid it first and corrected the overdone parts later. The confiscation of my family's property was deemed to be a mistake. They released my father and returned most of the seized properties back to us. Years later, I read Mao's article about how to classify different classes. It was the guidelines for the Land Reform. According to Mao's criteria, which was based on how much land and how many helping hands one family had, the confiscation of my family's property was indeed a mistake.

A few days ago, former president Jimmy Carter said, "Obama should not take Hillary Clinton as his running partner to the presidency, and vice versa." Thus the social division into two parts fighting against each other for whatever reason it may be, generates hatred that cannot be conciliated easily. Those Chinese Communist political movements all left such long lasting effects. The many villagers who classified my family as a class enemy returned us the property they took away but kept saying that we were the class enemy. They kept writing such letters to the schools I went to. It caused me serious trouble when I was in the junior and senior high school. I had to keep my head low in front of other students. After I went to the University of Beijing, the teachers there had a much clearer mind. They treated such letters as pure nonsense. The mentor of our medical school class, a dashing young man, was so open-minded that he shared some of those letters with me. I am sure that those villagers, if still alive today, hold the same view: Our family was indeed part of the enemy class to the country and to the people because of our scanty possessions.

(2) The Life My Grandmother Lived

My Grandmother was born in 1882 and died in 1967. Grandmother and Mother lived together for more than 30 years since Mother married into the family in the 1930s. For some ten warring years, they were the only grownups in the family. Until the mid 1950s when modern commercialization spread to the Chinese countryside, Grandmother and Mother took charge of a broad array of so-called house chores: 1) keep and feed an ox, a pig, a dozen hens; 2) prepare the daily meals for the whole family, but they had to start with grinding the grains into flour; 3) prepare clothes for the whole family, but they had to start with spinning the cotton into thread. In addition, they had to keep the house tidy and clean. The above three categories of work were typical for all married women in the Chinese countryside.

This was the traditional Chinese division between men and women: Men's territory was outside the house, which, including the yard, was women's territory. Women had a lot of work to do but also had the power to make decisions. Men ate whatever women cooked for them and wore whatever women made for them. Only occasionally did women go into the farm field to feed the men when the urgent farm work did not allow them go back for lunch. Chinese traditions also asked women to obey their mother-in-law, though my Grandmother was not a bossy lady.

Neither Grandmother nor Mother was born broad-minded but their personalities were quite different. In the mid 1930s, the government waged a national campaign to stop women's foot-binding. Although both Grandmother and Mother had bound feet, they showed quite different attitudes towards this campaign. My Mother joined the majority of the population who were fiercely against this campaign. They said, "Sun Yat-sen, what a man. Why don't you take better care of your own wife, and stop bothering other men's wives and daughters?" Grandmother applauded it immediately when she first heard the news, "What a great idea it is! Women can then go anywhere as men do."

Grandmother was a gifted woman, though she never had any education. She was born with a clear mind, and as a result, shed many more tears than Mother. Since girls were not allowed to go to school, Grandmother stood outside the school watching through the window when she was a girl. In this way, she mastered a few hundred Chinese characters. She became a self-taught calligrapher and artist who was much better than the average of nowadays' Chinese university graduates, though her works were mainly folk arts and the regular Chinese calligraphy. She once recited her poem to me, but I was too young to understand it. I only remember that the poem sounded so great and so elegant as if it had been written by a highly educated professional poet. It did not sound at all like a folk song.

One might have expected that Grandmother would not get along with Mother. In fact, they worked together in a perfect harmony. They never quarrelled, and never complained against each other in front of children. In fact, they discussed very little before a decision was reached regarding what was the meal for today or who should do what. They went through extraordinary hardship together with the God-blessed serenity.

During the warring years that ended in the late 1940s, my grandfather and father were often absent from home. My grandfather was in a big city hereby on business, and my father joined the anti-Japanese guerrilla force. In my father's case, Grandmother and Mother worried about his safety. Only two young men from our clan's neighbourhood including my father joined the guerrilla. The other, my uncle, was shot countless times by a shower of bullets from an ambush when he came back near home one night. The Japanese invaders had got the message about his trip. During the warring years, Grandmother and Mother often took the children into hiding sometimes for days in the wilderness. They had to sleep in the open air and take care that the children would not reveal the hiding sites to the enemy, who were only half mile away.

The so called Great Leap Forward in 1958 created many unendurable hardships for the peasants that would last for years. Every family had to share meals in a canteen, and it was regarded as an outdated tradition that every household cooked their own meals. Guided by this progressive ideology, cooking utensils were used to make steel. My father had a good reputation as the village physician, and he was able to bury a cauldron which evaded the local official inspection. Traditionally the Chinese peasants cooked their family meals including steamed bread or corn pastry, steamed vegetables, and porridge altogether in this large cauldron. Well-to-do families could often prepare additional dishes by frying oil cooking. A headache in those years was that our cauldron had a hole. It was impossible to get a new one as too many had been melt to make steel. Grandmother and Mother had to seal it with pastry and the seal only lasted for one meal if they were lucky. It was often the case that the pastry seal was cracked by the fire, and porridge leaked out and put out the cooking fire. To make it worse, matches were hard to get, and the coal was difficult to set up burning. I often noticed the whole house and yard were shrouded by heavy smoke during lunch or supper hours.

In her late years, Grandmother suffered from senile dementia due to her chronic bronchitis. She also broke her hip and managed to make her way only by crawling. Even so, she was not regarded as suffering too much as she also lost her clear mind.

I often wonder what made Grandmother and Mother so submissive yet so serene but they played their roles so well. Nowadays, we have counselling everywhere but problems everywhere. Our suicide rates remain high. I cannot help thinking of their bound feet and what were the psychological effects on them after they went through so painful and so humiliating an experience in their pre-school or even in their toddler years. Maybe our civilized life on earth is like the foot-binding of Chinese women after all. According to Shakespeare, the whole human world is a stage, and we cry at birth because we drop onto this stage of fools. The foot-binding might have served as a rehearsal for this tragic drama of life. It was not surprising that the foot-binding custom was established during the Song dynasty (960-1279), which was the most intelligent dynasty in Chinese history and was by far the most advanced country in the world but it was defeated repeatedly and eventually conquered by Mongolia. Historians cannot identify who started this custom or when. It was the people themselves who started this foot- binding from the grass root level. Neither intelligence nor rationality fits well into civilization in human history.

*   *   *

Afterword: Traditional vs. Modern Lifestyle

Western culture had assimilated numerous traditional cultures before it assumed the dominant position in the world. When Western influence penetrated into China, it affected the cities first and affected the men first. Western culture entered into my family by transforming my grandfather from an ordinary young peasant into a city employee, and then a business man who lived entirely in a highly commercialized large port city, Tianjin. He returned home only after the Japanese invaded China as he thought it was safer to live in the countryside. My father moved into the city as a child to have his Western education. I consider the 1950s as the transition period when Chinese rural areas said goodbye to the traditional way of life that Chinese peasants had lived for thousands of years. Under communist rule, the education my generation had in the 1950s and 1960s was essentially Western except for the communist ideology which was only an hour or so per week. In conclusion, my mother and grandmother remained as the last two people in my family who lived their lives in the traditional way. My mother and grandmother were in their forties and seventies respectively when Chinese peasants started to live modern life. They had no need to adapt to the new life, since my family buffered a safe haven for them. My mother and grandmother lived in a typical Chinese traditional lifestyle almost entirely in the primary society setting of family and relatives, and were seldom in contact with friends from outside the family circle. Modern life is almost entirely based in the secondary society, and family life exists as part of the panorama of social life on a vast horizon.

In comparing their lives to ours, we wonder which is better, and which is more worth living? I would say modern life is more attractive to young people who are about to start their own life. For those who have lived the major part of their lives, the Chinese traditional life is more rewarding.

As to one's life achievement, both my mother and grandmother brought up several children, and supported their husbands and children as they moved smoothly into the new lifestyle. If we see this transition as the rocket that sent the first man to the moon, my mother and grandmother were the ground workers who made it possible. This transition took more than five hundred years in Europe but was crammed into Chinese history within a few decades. Historians like to talk about historical marks. If a Roman emperor expanded the empire's territory by invading its neighbours, historians would say this emperor left a historical mark. If a Roman emperor did nothing particular except for the routines, the emperor was said to have left no marks. With such criteria, both my mother and grandmother left historical marks. They contributed to some extraordinary historical marks as one of the millions of people who made those marks possible. Their names would not be mentioned in Chinese history or world history, but their contribution was a major part of our family history. To a historian, there is only one super tree exists in an entire mountain, and that is the one on the top even though thousands of trees cover the mountain forming the dense vegetation. In such a view, my mother's and grandmother's achievements are only meaningful to their family.

The dimensions of life experience may be quite different for those who live in primary society and those who live in secondary society. My mother and grandmother, who lived in the primary society, regarded the world outside the family circle as foreign lands to them. If anything happened in those foreign lands that affected them, they simply adapted to those changes the same way as they adapted to climate changes. They never bothered to fully understand what happened to China during their lifetime. My grandmother had an artistic mind, and she saw the musing and aesthetic side of her life experience. During the Boxer rebellion in 1900, my grandfather bought a sifter for half price when the possessions of the local Catholic churches were put on sale. My grandfather had to pay a small fine soon after when foreign troops invaded Beijing to protect their interests in China. My grandmother always chuckled a little when she told the story to me, as she sensed a musing quality of those dramatic events, but she knew nothing about the Boxer rebellion and foreign invasion. Those Boxers showed altered states of mind, trance. My grandmother told me several times about those Boxers in trance. It was apparently peculiar to her. To my observation, both my mother's and grandmother's spiritual pursuit remained in the realm of serenity, and they never relied on mysticism or the experience of an altered state of mind. I think they lived their lives almost entirely in serenity, and they did not have much experience of uncertainty.

The mystic pursuit or even altered state of mind is, in my opinion, related somewhat to life experience of uncertainty.

When my grandfather was dying, my mother and grandmother knelt down in front of the kitchen god, begging Heaven to allow them to donate some of their destined life years to my grandfather in order to help him to heal. Whether my grandfather would die or not was an uncertainty to them, but they called upon the emotional and psychological social bond with my grandfather itself to deal with this experience of uncertainty. When people stick together emotionally and psychologically, nothing including uncertainty will matter much to them. Considering the time they lived was one of the most tumultuous and uncertain periods in Chinese history with one war after another and one revolution after another, it was nothing short of a miracle that they lived their lives so serenely and so productively in their own world. With the knowledge and mind we have been brought up, we would have certainly fallen into deep depression or even committed suicide if we had been in their position. We live a life of our own choice while they lived the life they were born into. They made much fewer choices than we do today.

As to one's spiritual experience, they lived no doubt a much happier life than our modern men on average, though they might have laughed less and experienced fewer emotional ups and downs. My grandmother showed remarkable artistic talents that allowed her to spend some of her spare time more aesthetically. Although my grandmother often painted flowers and birds from life, she never painted anything to reflect her life, specifically like we would do if we were in her position. Both my mother and grandmother enjoyed watching Chinese traditional opera. Those operas, as were once criticized by the Communist government as being all about emperors, ministers, scholars, and ladies, did not relate to their life at all. Chinese women often sat together and chatted for hours while each was doing her needlework to make clothes or shoes. As a child, I listened to their chat a lot. Their chat was always about family life in their neighbourhood, and they laughed a lot but much less than we do in similar situations. To be precise, they only smiled and chuckled. They never talked nonsense or said anything obviously untrue or against the moral standards. Again, their chat was like the opera they watched and the paintings my grandmother created. They were related to their life only in a highly spiritual and abstract way. In other words, they were parts of their serenity. If they had talked nonsense or anything to denounce the moral requirement put on them as a woman by the Chinese patriarchal society, we think it would have served them as a much desired spiritual experience of liberty. But they never did, and it was beyond any doubt that they did not have such a spiritual need in their serene minds.

In the book, *A New Interpretation of Chinese Taoist Philosophy*, I divide our life experience, physical and spiritual, into six levels, namely the biological, social, cultural, intellectual, spiritual, and cosmic levels. We are almost identical at the biological and cosmic levels whether we live in a primary or a secondary society. The remaining four levels harbour the difference, and the middle two levels, the cultural and intellectual levels, the most. I guess my mother and grandmother lived their lives physically close to the biological level and spiritually close to the cosmic level. They were born that way, and only with great efforts, we may be able to achieve their serenity today.

To look back at my life, I moved away from serenity to a business mind. When I was a child, we had only occasionally a dim lamp light for the whole family in the long winter evening. When I just started to work as a physician in the 1970s, I used to sit along with other roommates on the balcony for hours in the early summer evening. We talked very little on those occasions. But today, I have to listen to radio or watch TV to go to sleep. It is no easy job to go back to serenity. Apparently, we have lost the ability to stay quietly within ourselves by doing and thinking nothing.

7

A Comparison of Confucius with Socrates

Summary: From primary to secondary society is a critical step in human cultural evolution, and it thus provides a new powerful perspective to understand Western and Chinese philosophies and their difference. Socrates is traditionally regarded as the father of Western ethics or moral philosophy, and Confucius holds that position in Chinese ethics. The two men lived nine or ten years apart. A comparison between Confucius and Socrates serves as an illustration to show how the two fatherly philosophers were hallmarked by their different social environments: primary and secondary societies. Data were presented and discussed under six subtitles: the top contribution, the life long quest, governing by doing nothing, the length of speech, religious philosophy, and the united One of heaven and man.

*   *   *

According to A. N. Whitehead, all philosophy is only a footnote to Plato. Such a statement always reminds me of Karl Jaspers'

Axial Age from 800 to 200 BC: a period of interregnum for liberty, a period of transition for critical thinkers to lay down the frame of thinking or the philosophical foundation for the coming years. Lao Tzu, Confucius, Socrates, and Plato are as relevant today as they were more than two thousand years ago. But the different social environments in China and in Greece during the Axial Age hatched different philosophies. The Chinese civilization developed on the basis of primary society while the Western started with secondary society. It provides a new powerful perspective to understand Western and Chinese philosophies and their difference, since it is based on a fundamentally critical step of human evolution, from primary to secondary society.

Confucius was the first Chinese critical thinker who tried to restore the social order and set up standards for human behaviour. Similarly, Socrates was the first critical thinker who shifted his attention to society and the human world. Their different thoughts and different outcomes are like hallmarks to label the different societies they were in. The Greek society had been a typical secondary society for at least a few hundred years before Socrates was born while the Chinese still lived in primary or quasi-primary society. But the Chinese society was in crisis during Confucius' time. Socrates is traditionally regarded as the father of Western ethics or moral philosophy, and so is Confucius of Chinese ethics. The two men lived nine or ten years apart, and both died in their early seventies. Neither of them wrote anything down, and far too much was ascribed to them by their followers. *Analects* and *Apology* are the most reliable sources for the two fatherly figures.

(1), **The Top Contribution**: Socrates' most important contribution is the so-called Socratic Method, which he largely applied to the examination of key moral concepts. The Socratic Method is a negative method of hypothesis elimination by asking a series of questions. With this method, better hypotheses are found by steadily identifying and eliminating those which lead to contradictions. The influence of this approach is most strongly felt today in scientific studies.

As a typical secondary society, the ancient Greek society was built to satisfy and also stimulate the materialistic needs of the population. Knowledge, techniques, and the social structure that supported such pursuits had to be tested to increase its odds of success. The Socratic Method reflects such a social need, and also reflects the need of a more stable life course by the ordinary people. Since secondary society faces all possibilities like a boat on uncharted high seas, people need the more grounded experience of primary society.

Confucius' most important contribution is the ethical code of benevolence and righteousness (renyi) which he set up for Chinese people. The core concept of this ethical code is benevolence (ren). Confucius once said, "Benevolence means loving people." In fact, ren (benevolence) and man are interchangeable words in *Analects*. Thus Confucian benevolence (ren) is very close to the meaning of humanity. When a primary society is facing the possibility of unwanted division, people rely on collective unconsciousness to make sure the society stay intact, since nobody has the power to force other members to stay. They call on people to search in their subconscious the feeling that they are humans and they are members of this society. In other words, they call on people to feel their subconscious bond with the society and with others. A primary society is a whole at the subconscious level because the members are linked together emotionally and psychologically.

Confucius came up with a similar way to call on people's subconscious, and remind them: "Please remember, you are human beings and behave like one!"

In secondary society, humanity is pretty much a creation by man and culture. Socrates would have responded to Confucius' call, "What kind of human beings? Please define it first."

It must be pointed out that people who lived in ancient primary society responded to those calls fundamentally different from us, since we are no longer as sensitive as they were to those calls. An analogy is that a toddler playing outside and ignoring his mother's call comes back immediately when his mother asks, "You do not want mommy any more?" A six month old infant knows to share his feeling with his mother by looking at her repeatedly when he is excited with a new toy. It is the subconscious bond between mother and child that the above toddler cannot part with.

(2), **The Meaning of Life**: Many people have a life long quest which serves as the meaning of their lives. Confucius' quest was to restore the social order while Socrates' quest was to find the truth. When a primary society was in trouble, every member felt the obligation to help especially the elite. In a secondary society, it was not Socrates' business to restore social order, and his duty was to fight bravely in the battlefield and work hard to make a living. In the remaining time, Socrates' quest was to examine everyone including himself and also examine many philosophical topics in order to find the truth. Such truth is ultimate in nature, not influenced by personal opinions. Such a concept of truth is characteristic of secondary society, of which the construction is based on rational thinking. Generally speaking, it is beyond the reach of a primary society to seek such truth. In the social affairs of a primary society, it is mingled with emotions and psychological feelings that rules out any rational thinking and calculation. The Chinese say, a law-binding magistrate keeps himself from meddling in family affairs. What Socrates sought was exactly the truth in life and in society. Unfortunately the truth Socrates finally found was unacceptable to the Athenian authority and the Athenian citizens, which led to his execution.

(3), **Governing by Doing Nothing as a Political Philosophy and as a Way of Life**: To govern by doing nothing (wuweierzhi) is often regarded as part of Taoist philosophy. In fact, Confucius himself held a strong belief in governing by doing nothing. *Analects* cites Shun, a legendary king, as the model of governing by doing nothing. Shun was said to have only five officials but the whole China was orderly during his reign. Once Confucius says, "The one who governed by doing nothing was Shun, and wasn't he? What did he do? He did nothing except for sitting in the throne solemnly and courteously."(*Analects* 15.4)

The Western social and political philosophy hardly had any thought in history close to such an idea of doing nothing to rule. Western civilizations were adventurous expeditions on a large scale from the very beginning.

Furthermore, Confucius gave a lovely picture of the life in the ancient Chinese primary society where there was no trace of any government. It is another way to express his belief in governing by doing nothing. He says, "When the Tao prevailed, the world was publicly owned, virtuous ones were selected and able ones were chosen, and people lived in harmony and honesty was valued. Everyone treated all the others as his own family, and treated all children as his own children. The elderly enjoyed their later years, the middle-aged made their contribution, and the young were nurtured to grow up. All those who had lost their families were taken care of. Males had their shares, and females had husbands. Goods were displayed on the ground, and nobody took them as their own. Everybody worked but not for themselves. There was neither plot nor scheme, and there was neither theft nor robbery. The outer doors remained open. It was called the World Commonwealth." (*The Rites: Liyun*)

If governing by doing nothing summarizes the social and political ideology of primary society, it can also be considered as a way of life. Thus it applies to every level and every aspect of life.

In a primary society, members spend their spare time enjoying themselves like most animals do after their basic biological needs are fulfilled. Enjoyment includes intellectual and philosophical pursuits, and also includes all aesthetic pursuits. If spare time is time left when one's basic biological desires are fulfilled, civilization can be built using spare time or its building process can be enjoyed by the people who build it. Thus the Chinese system did not hinder the development of their civilization though their early civilization may be less materialistic and ostentatious.

A secondary society often organizes its members to pursue its goal using their spare time. It is most successful if it makes its member regard the goal as their own. An easy way to achieve this is to link the goal to war, which makes any goal look like a survival issue. Such tricks worked in the Greek system but did not work with the Chinese super state of a two-level system.

The Chinese system was based on human nature and therefore unable to accommodate any big project like building the pyramids that was outside the survival needs of the population, since it was hard to get the consensus of the whole population. During the period from 2200 to 476 BC, there was no such project mentioned in Chinese records except for the flood control around 2200 BC. The vast flooded area itself was an urgent call to the population so that it could be regarded as a project for survival. On the other hand, in 841 BC, the angry citizens within the capital were enough to drive away the king. During the subsequent history after 476 BC, the two-level system was substantially changed but the traditions were still there. Two ambitious emperors, one built the Great Wall and the other, the Great Canal to link up the major rivers of China, both caused massive uprisings and immediate collapse of their dynasties. Their projects were far more useful than the ancient Egyptian pyramids and the Greek temples.

The Chinese system itself also means the separation of the two-levels: primary society and quasi-primary society. The former includes villages and the latter, the king and vassals. They both lived their lives inside their own societies, and the only connection between the two was tax and occasional military service. In the ancient Greece, all the slaves, free citizens, and government officials worked inside the same social and economic network. The close connection between slaves and their masters ensured the normal productive process. In the Chinese system, too many interactions between the two levels might lead to the emergence of a typical secondary society, which would have the potential to destabilize the whole system. Lao Tzu promotes the separation, and he says, "The best rulers are not known by their people... When the best rulers have achieved their goals, their people would say it is their own doing. (*Tao Te Ching*, Chapter 17)" Confucius held the same view. He said, "Let the people behave according to certain principles but never let them understand why." (*Analects*, 8:9) When a state inscribed its law in detail on a metal ritual vessel, Confucius voiced his disproval immediately.

As a result, Confucius and Socrates had radically different attitudes towards physical labour, though both of them were from poor families of the ruling class. Socrates was one of the free citizens who formed the ruling class over slaves. Confucius disliked physical labour and scorned those disciples who liked. He was said to have never laboured his limbs and was unable to tell millets from rice. Socrates was a mason. Some statues in the city of Athens were said to be his works. As the duty of a citizen, Socrates bravely fought several battles. Both as a teacher, Confucius apparently earned an income while Socrates refused to teach for money. Socrates regarded his teaching as part of the ideal philosopher's life he was pursuing. It is apparent that the ancient Greek life was more energetic and industrious while the Chinese, more peaceful.

(4), **The Length of Speech**: It is interesting to compare the lengths of Socrates' and Confucius' talks recorded by their followers. *Analects* that records Confucius' words during his whole life has only 27,000 words in English translation while *Apology* that records Socrates' speech at the court has 14,700 words in English translation. The way Plato recorded Socrates' words might be different from the way Confucius' disciples recorded Confucius' words, and the latter might be more concise. Both Plato and Meng Tzu (372-289 BC) expounded their thoughts in detail, since they both wrote for contemporary and future readers. Plato wrote more than two dozen books ranging from 20 to 300 modern printed pages while Meng Tzu wrote only one book with some 45,000 Chinese characters and less than 100 modern printed pages. The difference reflects the different functions of language in primary and secondary societies. China and Greece were at different stages of language evolution though they were both in the typical Axial Age.

Anthropologists believed that primates groom each other as a way to solidify the social bond while naked humans chat with each other to solidify their social bond. Even today when people spend most time working, watching television, they still chat at home. Such chat does not necessarily function as exchange of information or discussion of a current issue but can be only for the enjoyment. Theoretically people may break the boundary between hallucination and reality to talk nonsense in such chat but they usually do not. To my observation, some jobless outcasts do talk nonsense to denounce the social reality they are facing. I often see children of three or four years old chat this way: They giggle wholeheartedly at the nonsense they are talking. Such chat is a piece of pure art. Through such chat and other collective activities, all members integrate into a whole psychologically and emotionally in primary society. The cohesive force and the unity of secondary society rely on the uniform understanding of their collective goals. A highly developed system of communication that is based on exchange of information is a must.

Both Lao Tzu and Confucius lived in the late Spring and Autumn Period (770-476 BC) when the ancient Chinese super state of primary societies was in crisis, and a new system had not emerged yet to replace the old one. Both Lao Tzu and Confucius admired the past. Confucius' *Analects* is by no means a chat, and Confucius himself lived a life more like that in a secondary society since he traveled from state to state to promote his ideas. The friendly atmosphere among his disciples and himself is more like a typical primary society. Since people could live in primary or quasi-primary society with the ancient Chinese system, they lacked the experience of secondary society and lacked the sophisticated language. Plato and Socrates used to worry about the emotional effect of poetry and arts and ban them from their ideal republic except hymns to the gods and praise of famous men. Modern arts have lost such effects because we have all been exposed to too many arts already since our childhood. Similarly we have all lost our sensitivity to language, printed or spoken words. You can finish reading *Analects* within a few hours but it is not the way to read it. You have to read only a few lines a day and ruminating over those words the whole day. You may then appreciate the beauty and deep meanings of those words. You may even be induced into a particular mood that was precisely the effects of those words. You then may roughly have experienced what ancient people did when they heard those words because they were sensitive and we are not. Such effects do not apply to Socrates' speech in *Apology*, which is not much different from today's speech of a similar man in a similar situation. Ancient Greek secondary society had been well developed by Socrates' time.

A Chinese scholar says, *Analects* is one of the few good books that you can read any time under any circumstances and enjoy it. It will calm you down when you are in a bad mood. According to him, Meng Tzu's book does not have such effects on him. [1] Thus, *Analects* is not an ordinary piece of art like children's chats but one of the greatest masterpieces of art in thousands of years. Meng Tzu, though a loyal Confucian scholar he was, lived in the period of Warring States (475-221 BC) when secondary society was well established. The time required him to write differently from Confucius: There is more information and more insights but it is less like a piece of art.

(5), **Religious Philosophy**: In the early stage of secondary society, religion or belief in gods was often used to consecrate the form and course a society was taking, and thus provided a powerful cohesive force to stop its members from seeking other types of secondary society. It was certainly a contributing factor in the outcomes of ancient Greek wars. When Greeks defeated the Persian invasion in 480 BC, the Greek cities agreed to restore the Temple at Olympia and build a great temple to Zeus and a huge statue of him to thank the gods for their victory. When the Athenians were defeated in the Peloponnesian war (431-404 BC), Socrates was executed for blasphemy.

In primary society, the social cohesive force was human nature, and they did not face the possibility of different types of society. Their religion was quite different. Chuang Tzu says, "In the ancient time, yin and yang were in harmony. Gods and spirits were quiet and did not interfere with people. The four seasons followed their course. Animals and plants were not harmed. Humans lived to their full life span. People had knowledge but there was no use of it. This is called the big One."(*Chuang Tzu*, Chapter 16)

Under such circumstances, Confucius' principles regarding gods are: pay your respect to gods and spirits but keep a distance from them. A suitable interpretation of these principles is that gods and people do not interfere with each other. It is like in a primary society where nobody can force his will on others. Furthermore, Confucius had so-call Four No-Comments in his teaching and counselling practice, namely, Confucius never spoke about parapsychology, psychic power, mental disturbance, and ghosts (guaililuanshen). Confucius seemed to understand well today's psychology of religion. He was a practical man and did not want to go into these grey areas. His religious attitudes brought him no trouble, since gods do not interfere with people in a primary society setting.

A secondary society often stimulates its talents into free thinking but restricting it within its boundary, and often stimulates its talents into religious imagination but restricting it within its gods and beliefs. Socrates went too far both in religious imagination and in free thinking for his society to tolerate. Socrates talked about his inner voice that stopped him from entering politics. In a deep religious culture, such subconscious similar to Socrates' inner voice must be commonplace. The Athens government used Socrates to stop others, or even to use him as a scapegoat to silence complaints. Such political trickery is typical of secondary society that is not seen in primary society.

(6), **The United One of Heaven and Man (tianrenheyi)**: The Chinese philosophical phrase tirenheyi, (heaven and man are one, or the united one of heaven and man) is a concept that embraces a broad array of interpretations, including man's immersing himself in nature or losing himself in meditation. It is often regarded as the hallmark of Chinese philosophy that stresses the holistic thinking. As modern science shows, both man and the world are made by the same atoms and obeying the same law of nature. Furthermore, spiritual people pursue the high entity that guides both man and nature.

Confucius certainly had such a belief in the united one of heaven and man. He talked about the mandate of heaven and emphasized the heart and human nature. His follower Meng Tzu furthered Confucius' thought saying, "Once one knows human nature, he will know heaven." (*Meng Tzu: Jinxin*)

Mr. Fang, a notable Chinese scholar, has recently pointed out that both Western and Chinese philosophers believe in the united one of heaven and man, and there is no fundamental difference among their beliefs. He says, "Almost all Western traditional metaphysicians held and expounded the view of the united one of heaven and man, because one of the utmost ideals of Western traditional metaphysics is to seek the ultimate reality and the guiding principle for the whole world." [2] Socrates was indeed one of those metaphysicians. Thus both Confucius and Socrates believed in the united one of heaven and man.

I disagree with Mr. Fang, and I believe that their beliefs are fundamentally different though Western and Chinese philosophers may both hold the same view that heaven and man are one or the united one of heaven and man. Chinese philosophy was first hatched in a primary society while Western philosophy was founded in a secondary society. The words "heaven" (tian) and "man" (ren) may identify different entities in primary and secondary societies.

The Chinese word tian (heaven) can mean three things: God, nature, and ideology. All the three words, God, nature, and ideology, indicate different things in primary and secondary societies. In primary society, gods do not interfere with people, people are integral part of nature, and if they have an ideology, their ideology is based on human nature and instinct. Their ideology is shared by all primary societies. In secondary society, God often interferes with people and has the power to kill those who, like Socrates, offended God. Nature is something to work on and to conquer in secondary society while primary society has no intention or power to conquer nature as they see themselves as part of nature. The ideology of a secondary society is created by man, and different societies and different people have different ideologies. Primary society has no ideology in such a sense. Therefore, God, nature, and ideology indicate completely different entities though they use the same words.

With a fixed ideology and social structure as its guide, and with God as its inspiration, a particular secondary society can pursue whatever their goals may be in the environment of nature. Both Mesopotamian and Greek civilizations commercialized society to stimulate and satisfy the materialistic needs of the population. During the Axial Age, Greece had a huge class of slaves, but those slaves were part of this social structure built by man. Therefore, government officials, free citizens, and slaves were all well organized into the same system, the social machine, to pursue the same goals.

Finally, the word "man" (ren) also points to different entities in primary and secondary societies. In primary society, man is a natural man who is encoded by genetics and guided by human nature. As secondary society is created by man, and the man who lives in it is also of his own making. It is only in secondary society that a man can pursue a life of his own choice that is not dictated by human nature, though the majority of us are dictated by our culture. But our culture is largely a creation of man. Human nature remained the major topic in Chinese philosophy from the Axial Age till the last dynasty ended in 1911. The predominant opinion was that human nature is born good. In the West, the discussion of human nature involved many controversies though the latest thoughts tend to assert that human nature is the product of either culture or the result of our own free choice.[3, 4] In other words, man is of his own making.

As mentioned above (Essay 1), humans moved from primary to secondary society like fish moved to land. When fish moved onto land and became a land animal such as mammals or birds, they can no longer be called as fish, and it is only their ancestors that were fish.

Both Chinese Taoist philosophy and Confucian philosophy hold the view that heaven and man are one, but only Taoist philosophy holds primary society as its ideal model and holds itself back from secondary society. In Taoist opinion, a man can still become a natural man in the modern society. They call such man a real man.

(7) **Conclusion**: Many consider the ancient Greek city, Athens, as unique such as commercial activities, wealth, democracy, the pooling of different people from different places with different cultural backgrounds etc., to produce the most critical thinkers during the Axial Age. The Axial China had none of those. But there was one thing they shared with the Athenian, and that is freedom. The Chinese had no freedom to pursue wealth or any projects on the Athenian scale, but they did not have the bondage of commercial activities, wealth, democracy, etc. either. The first Chinese philosophers were able to think from the basis of the

born human nature and the genetically coded society, primary society. Although the whole world including China is now on the road built by Axial Greece or Western civilization, Chinese culture may still point to a different direction for the future.

References

[1.] Liu Mengxi(2004): Chuang Tzu and Modern/Post Modern (Zhuangzi yu Xiandai he Houxiandai). Hebei Education Publishing House, p24. (In Chinese)

[2.] Fang Zhaohui (2006): On the Traditional Concept of the United One of Heaven and Man in the Western History of Thought (Shitan Xifang Sixiangshi Shangde Tianrenheyi Chuantong). http://www.Confucius2000.com, 2006. (In Chinese)

[3.] Michael Ruse(1995): "Human Nature," in The Oxford Companion to Philosophy, ed. Ted Honderich (Oxford: Oxford University Press, 1995), 376-77.

[4.] Gordon Marshall(1994), The Concise Oxford Dictionary of Sociology (Oxford: Oxford University Press, 1994), 227.

8

The Cave Men

Prehistoric people used to live in caves, and they were called the cavemen.According to Plato, we are all cave men imprisoned to a cave of the tangible world. In his book *The Republic*, Plato gives us a vivid picture how the cave men live their lives: They are all chained to the ground and, furthermore, cannot turn back as their heads are chained as well. The only thing they can do is to look at the wall of the cave. Fortunately, light is coming from behind through some puppets of plants and animals moving on a raised walkway. Their lives are watching the moving shadows on the wall cast by those puppets. They are continuously naming the shapes as they come by. This, however, is the only reality that they know, even though they are seeing merely shadows of objects. They are thus conditioned to judge the quality of one another by their skill in quickly naming the shapes and dislike those who play poorly.

Scholars often compare Socrates (470-399 BC), Plato (428-347 BC), and Aristotle (384-322 BC) with Confucius (551-479 BC) and his two well known followers, Meng Tzu (372-289 BC) and Xun Tzu (325-238 BC). Those six men who lived roughly the same historical time may be the greatest thinkers of all time who laid down the philosophical frame of thinking for the next two and a half millennia. Their thoughts apparently developed along different tracks. God, the world, and I are three entities in the West so that Plato concentrated his thought on the objective observation of the world. God, the world, and I are all One in Chinese thinking, and the Chinese judged their world from how they feel, namely, from their own psychological and emotional experience.

The Chinese thinkers would say: If we are born to watch shadows on the cave walls, we should enjoy and treasure those shadows; if we are born chained, there are no chains at all because we cannot feel it. If there are any chains in our lives, they are inflicted by ourselves like social inequality, violent conflicts and wars. We should not accept them as natural, and we should fight against the social inequality forever until one day the ideal life comes down from heaven.

Such a striking difference was mainly the result of the different social environments that hatched different ideas. The Chinese society during that period was mainly primary or quasi-primary society at the edge of transformation into secondary society while the ancient Greek society had been secondary society for hundreds of years. Primary society was the society based on and stabilized by human nature while secondary society was a creation of human culture with a distinct ideology and corresponding social structure to support the ideology.

The allegory of cave men reflects Plato's understanding of secondary society. Secondary society broadened man's social horizon, and let humans, especially the well- educated, realize that man's ability to know the world is limited. The chains that the cave men wear is the symbol of the external force humans have to endure in secondary society but not in primary society. The external force comes from the outside of human nature, and humans often feel that they have to obey without knowing why. Secondary society is no longer the world you can judge according to how you feel.

When Socrates was sentenced to death by a jury of five hundreds for blasphemy in spite that he revealed to the jury: He was considered as the wisest man by the Delphic oracle ascribed to Apollo. There was no doubt that Socrates saw clearly the sentence was wrong. Reading Socrates'*Apology* by Plato, we feel strongly Socrates was innocent and wonder why jury thought otherwise. Socrates, however, accepted the sentence as part of his state for which he fought bravely in the battlefields.

Ancient Chinese thinkers judged their country and law according to how they felt. Confucianism has several ancient kings or ancient emperors as their models. One of them was Shun, a legendary figure who lived around 2255 BC. He was an ordinary peasant before he was promoted to the position of the Emperor of all China. He was not treated nicely by his family when he was young. His brother and father once tried to kill him. Thus someone came to ask Meng Tzu, the famous Confucian scholar at the time, what Shun would have done as the king of China if his father had committed murder. Meng Tzu said, Shun would have not stopped the arrest of his father, since the arrest was justified. But the arrest of one's dear father hurts his feeling so that Shun would have carried his father on his back to hide somewhere and leaving the country to others to worry. The answer reflects Meng Tzu's thorough understanding of Confucian principles: The family was far more important than the country. To the emperor or king, the country and his throne were worthless like a pair of worn-out shoes, but his father was worth much more.

In later years, the teachings of Confucius and his followers were compiled as the textbooks that all children had to study. They recited and chanted those words since the age they just began to say more than a few words. When they grew up, they either became government officials or a teacher who taught children how to prepare to be government officials. They lived a boring life, especially if their families were not with them. Confucius lived in the exciting Axial Age when human civilization advanced rapidly. But ever since, the Chinese social system was pretty much stagnant with an emperor of absolute power ruling this huge country. To be a government official, the job was only to serve as the representative of the emperor and carry out orders. They lacked the free space Confucius had to think and act out of their own judgment. On the other hand, they saw corruptions and social inequality everywhere inside the government structure, a reality contrary to what they had learnt from Confucius and his followers. They were even not allowed to utter their disagreement, let alone to change it.

Fortunately, Buddhism came to China during the Eastern Han dynasty (25-220 AD). As a matter of fact, both Taoism and Buddhism adeptly taught people how to extricate themselves from the mundane network of the tangible world. They taught people how to be lost into their own imagination, the meditation. This self-imagined world can be either colorful and fascinating in Taoist terms or supremely serene in Buddhist terms. To be precise, they moved themselves from Plato's cave of the tangible world into a cave of their own making, the self imagination.

Some even went further, and they were sitting alone in a cave in the wilderness facing the inside wall meditating for years. One of them was a famous one, Bodhidharma (?470-536), an Indian Buddhist who traveled to China, and found himself a cave of five meters in depth and three meters in width at almost the top of a mountain. He sat there for a total of nine years facing the wall of the cave. He was much less lucky than Plato's cave prisoners who can still watch the fascinating shadows cast on the wall. He had nothing to watch except for the bare rocks with his own shadow. Of course he had the feeling of the Buddhist super tranquility, the Nirvana, which was believed to be the most wonderful feeling in the universe. Since he sat there in one position, and his shadow was on the wall for nine years. There was said to be a permanent shadow left on the wall. This piece of rock with Bodhidharma's shadow was later removed from the cave and erected in a nearby temple as a sacred object worshiped by today's visitors.

*　　*　　*

Afterword: A Further Comparison Among India, Greece, and China

In the book *A New Interpretation of Chinese Taoist Philosophy*, I wrote:

"If we consider God, the world, and I as religion, science, and philosophy respectively, Chinese culture was inclined toward the philosophical or I side, while Indian culture was inclined toward the religious or God side. In the ideal realm or heaven after death, Taoists have both their individual souls and bodies, Christians have souls but Hindu-Buddhists have neither. Hindu-Buddhists lose their individual identities to join the cosmic pool of soul....Ancient Chinese philosophy developed in pursuit of an ideal way of secular life. Ancient Indian philosophy developed in pursuit of an ideal way of religious life. Ancient Greek philosophy developed as a way to deal with both God and the world." [1]

India, Greece, and China all had a voluminous collection of poetry as their earliest literary traditions. They were *Rig Veda*, Homer's epics, and the *Classic of Poetry* respectively for the three ancient civilizations. Those poems played a much more critical role in those people's lives. They were read, chanted, quoted, and listened to by the elite and by the common people as well. Thus those collections of poems provide us a perfect window to see what occupied the minds of those ancient people. Here I use those three literary traditions to illustrate the same point made in the book *A New Interpretation of Chinese Taoist Philosophy*.

Ancient philosophy was deeply rooted in the way of life ancient people lived. As Greek philosophy dealt both God and the world, their lives involved much more conquering and looting warfare. Thus Homer's epics are devoted to praising heroes, the half-god-half-human figures, who represented the kings or chiefs of the ancient Greek city states. The *Iliad* starts with the following lines:

Sing, O goddess, the anger of Achilles son of Peleus, that brought countless ills upon the Achaeans. Many a brave soul did it send hurrying down to Hades, and many a hero did it yield a prey to dogs and vultures, for so were the counsels of Jove fulfilled from the day on which the son of Atreus, king of men, and great Achilles, first fell out with one another.

Rig Veda is a collection of hymns devoted to the worship of gods. Their authors were supposed to be the priests. The book starts with the following lines:

I, Laud Agni, the chosen Priest, God, minister of sacrifice,
The hotar, lavishest wealth.
Worthy is Agni to be praised by living as by ancient seers.
He shall bring hitherward the Gods.

Except for a very few poems devoted to worship and religious rituals, the majority of the *Classic of Poetry* were authored by ordinary people. They describe the emotional experience of people at all levels. The book starts with a love song:

On the islet in the river '
Guan-guan go the ospreys,
The modest, retiring, virtuous young lady,
For our gentleman, a good mate she is.

The following table shows the different frequencies of various words to delineate the different lives for those three ancient traditions. The frequency of a certain word was greatly influenced by the topics of the poems. But the topics chosen for poetry also reflect the lifestyle of the people. Nevertheless, the frequencies of certain words do accurately reflect the different lives of those three early civilizations.

Table 9.1 The Different Frequencies of Various Words of the Early Literature [2]

	India: Rig Vida	Greece: Iliad/Odyssey	China: Classic of Poetry
Sea/ocean	0.05% (15/28017)	0.14% (74/53258)	0.015% (9/60856)
God/goddess	0.87% (244/28017)	0.36% (194/53258)	0.072% (44/60856)
I	1.1% (308/28017)	1.4% (737/53258)	1.1% (680/60856)
Ratio: I/gods	1.15 (280/244)	3.74 (737/197)	15.5 (680/44)
Battle/war	0.096% (27/28017)	0.13% (68/53258)	0.028% (17/60856)
Joy(ment,ful...)	0.14% (38/28017)	0.0094% (5/53258)	0.087% (53/60856)
Anger/angry	0.018% (5/28017)	0.092% (49/53258)	0.025% (15/60856)

As mentioned in Essay 2, the way of thinking of primitive people might have been deeply influenced by the sea and ocean. The frequencies of the words "sea" and "ocean" was well correlated with the distances of those three cultural traditions from the sea and ocean. A high frequency of the words "god" and "goddess" was noted with India. The frequency of the word "I" was, however, similar in all three traditions. When the concept of "I" is considered in relation to "god" and "goddess", Chinese poetry shows a remarkable high ratio I/gods.

As to the psychological and emotional experience, it clearly shows that the ancient Indian people had more joy and less frustration. Rig Veda uses the words "anger" and "angry" much less but uses much more the words "joy", "enjoyment", and "joyful. To be close with gods", namely the cave of self-imagination, might have been the most powerful way to make ancient people happy.

In their lives, the ancient Greek people had to deal with both God and the world while the Indians dealt with God and the Chinese, I. Both the words "world" and "science" were rarely used. Instead, the words "battle" and "war" may represent the dealings of both the human world and natural world. I use the words "angry" and "anger" to represent the motivation and frustration of the people in dealing with their world and with their God. As expected, a high frequency of those words was observed with the Greeks.

As a result, the ancient Greek people accomplished extraordinary achievements in science, philosophy, arts, architecture, politics, and wealth accumulation, which were unparalleled by either the Chinese or the Indian people. The Greeks also paid a dear price for those achievements, as they erected contradictions among the concepts of God, the world, and I. To conquer the world and to master science, man has to break himself free from the cave described by Plato. The cave in Plato's terms is mostly created by humans themselves. It is the culture one has been brought up with. The centre is God, who radiates light to illuminate the whole culture, or the cave. The execution of Socrates illustrates the pain those contradictions have brought to people.

If we calculate the value of all the creation by the Athenian people including science, philosophy, arts, literature, and wealth in modern terms of money and work out the GDP of the ancient Greece, it is certain that the Athenians had by far the highest GDP per capita in their contemporary world.

In today's world, the country and its people that correspond to the Athenians in the ancient world are the United States and the Americans. The American people seem to feel the same pain.

In a recent long essay published in *Free Inquiry*, Gregory S. Paul pointed out that among the industrial democratic countries, the United States stand out with the highest GDP per capita and the highest religious faith. Paul writes, "With its low taxes, relatively high rate of poverty, and huge disparity between incomes of the poor and the rich, the United States displays greater income disparity than any other industrial democracy and is, as we have seen, anomalously pious." In other words, to get the highest GDP and keep leadership in the world economy, they need a higher level of inequality and disparity to push themselves to work hard. They also have to try hard to break themselves free from the cave of self imagination. Consequently, they feel more pain and need more piously the religious cave. It astonished everyone in the world that in the last few years in the United States, there has been an ever accelerating nation-wide campaign trying to have both religious belief and scientific belief taught side by side in school. In other words, religious faith and science are the same. They may and may not have realized that they are approaching the Eastern view: God, the world, and I are One.

References

[1.] You-Sheng Li (2005): *A New Interpretation of Chinese Taoist Philosophy: An Anthropological/psychological view.* London, Canada: Taoist Recovery Centre. p4.

[2.] All the poems studied are in English translation. A full text was used for the Classic of Poetry but a random selection of 94 out of 1026 hymns was used for the Rig Veda and a random selection of five out of 24 books for the Homer's epics: Iliad and Odyssey. Their sources were as follows:

    1) Book of Poetry: http://etext.lib.virginia.edu/chinese.

    2) Vig Veda: http://www. sacred-texts.com.

    3) Iliad and Odyssey: http://www.sacred-texts.com.

[3.] Gregory S. Paul (2009): The big religion questions finally solved. Free Inquiry, December/January 2009 Issue, p24-36.

9

The Five Zone Territory and Early literature: Chinese vs West

Summary: According to the ancient records, the territory of China was divided into five zones, ranked according to each zone's distance from the capital during the first three dynasties, Hsia, Shang, and Chou. This organization was the result of the ancient Chinese super state of primary societies: The amount of political administration decreased progressively among the five zones as they moved outward as did Chinese cultural influence felt by the residents. To differing degrees in each of the zones, they all were influenced by the one universal mind of this super state, which reached out to embrace all humanity in the world known to them. In contrast, the bicameral mind prevailed in the West due to the psychological pressure generated by war and competition among city states. This essay compares the early Chinese and Western literature: the *Book of Mountains and Seas*, and the *Classic of Poetry* vs. Homer's epics: *The Iliad* and *The Odyssey*. This comparison shows vividly the different social environments that pertained in the Chinese and the Western worlds. The former culture was informal and relaxing and the latter was competitive and alienating. The former stressed the value of morality from the very beginning while the latter raised the concept of morality only during the fifth century BC. An extensive survey of the indigenous literature from both sides shows opposing trends of subjective expressivity measured by the frequency of the word "I". The Western subjective expressivity increased over time in history while in the Chinese world, it decreased. The West started with a secondary society that sought to improve its social environment afterwards while the Chinese started with a super state of primary societies that allowed the secondary society to emerge gradually over a period of two thousand years or so.

*   *   *

The two books of ancient Chinese records, *Collection of Ancient Texts: Yugong* and *State Remarks: Remarks of Chou,* both recorded the so-called five fu policy, with the Hsia and Chou dynasties dividing the territory into five zones according to the zone's distance from the capital. The most outward zone is called the Wasteland Zone. In the Hsia dynasty, all people were allowed to live in the Wasteland Zone without any restrictions. The Chou dynasty required the tribal chiefs from the Wasteland Zone to report to the king only once in their life time. At least one scholar thinks that the territory of the Shang dynasty was divided into similar zones. [1] This arrangement was the direct consequence of the super state of primary societies: Political territory equals the cultural influence that could be exerted on the people in their known world.

Thus the ancient Chinese considered the Wasteland Zone as the end of their known world. The Chinese regarded their government as the only government for all humanity, and they had to be responsible for all humans on earth. Subsequently their culture remained as a culture of primary society shared by all people of less developed ethics in their Wasteland Zone. Any particular culture of a secondary society failed to represent all of humanity.

In the book *United and Disintegrated: the Revelation of Chinese History*, a Chinese scholar Ge Jianxiong points out that what the

Chinese emperor and his court wanted from their peripheral ethnic states was only to win their regard. They did not want any ruling power to control them. As to the tribute and reward, the value of the reward given by the emperor to a remote state was usually more than that of the tribute paid by this state to the emperor. Those vassal states never received less than they contributed. The emperor and his court often opened their treasure houses to let the vassals take anything they liked. They wanted to show how rich they were in front of those remote ethnic states. [2]

The material exchange described by Ge is more like the social interaction in a primary society. Psychological and emotional value always overshadows any rational calculation. The ancient Chinese super state was not a social structure for commercial trade, and it was not a nation or country in a strict sense either. It was really a loose cultural construction for all humanity. Before the Opium War, Chinese government records show that they even mistook Great Britain as one of their remote vassal states. When a remote small country joins the United Nations, it does not lose anything materialistically nor its dignity.

The *Classic of Poetry: Xiaoya: Northern Mountains* has the following lines:

All land under the heavens belongs to the king,
All people over the world are subjects to the king.

The author of this poem was believed to be a petty official who expressed such a wish while making bitter complaints about his misfortunes. In face of the divided world, people expressed the wish of united humanity against land ownership and localized governments. It shows people have this intrinsic need.

Primary society allows people to enjoy themselves while the societies of ancient Mesopotamia and Greece were like those of 18th and 19th century Europe and America, with on-going wars here and there, all people labouring day and night like ants. Huge construction projects and the accumulation of wealth both skyrocketed, and the living conditions of the people were poor. The best witnesses of these contrasting living environments are neither historic records nor philosophical speculations but the early literature. Literature is the vehicle for people to express their psychological and emotional experiences. Homer's epics, *Classic of Poetry,* and *Book of Mountains and Seas* represent the earliest Western and Chinese literature. There are a few more literary works scattered among pre-Qin Chinese classics, but they are in the same style and along the same line of thought as the *Classic of Poetry and Book of Mountains and Seas.* For the same reason, the Mesopotamian epic *Gilgamesh* is more like an embryonic copy of Homer's epics. Homer's epics are the first volumes of literary works in European history while *Classic of Poetry* and *Book of Mountains and Seas* are the first compilations of literary works in Chinese history. The different effects of primary and secondary societies on those works are clearly visible.

(1) The Authors are Gods or Humans

For any cultural tradition, the earliest literature was fairy tales and folk songs. They are the *Book of Mountains and Sea* and the *Classic of Poetry* in China. They become one in the Greek traditions, the Homeric epics, *The Iliad* and *The Odyssey*. Homeric epics are legendary fairy tales in the form of poetry. The first lines of the two Homeric epics explain the difference between the Chinese and the Mediterranean traditions. *The Iliad* starts with the line: "Sing, goddess, the rage of Peleus's son, Achilles..." *The Odyssey* starts with, "Sing to me, Muse, of the man..."

As Essay 5 has discussed, American psychologist Julian Jaynes raised the theory of the bicameral mind in 1976. According to him, subjective consciousness only appeared some 3000 years ago. Ancient people had no subjective consciousness but a bicameral mind. Those people heard the divine voice through the right hemisphere of the brain, and the message coded in language was transferred to the left hemisphere where the orders were understood and carried out. Nowadays' psychotic patients represent the only remaining bicameral minds, and these were the normal people three thousand years ago.

With bicameral minds, ancient Greek poets created poetry through auditory hallucination transcribing what they heard from gods. In the imagination of ordinary men, gods would speak differently but their words should be understandable to men. Thus gods speak in a different voice; they speak in either aphoristic phrases or elegant verses. Gods never descend to the sort of language that a grandparent uses in telling a bedtime story. Thus as indicated by the above quoted starting lines from *The Iliad* and *The Odyssey,* the Greek epics are authored by gods while ordinary human beings created the Chinese poetry and legendary tales.

Most of the poems from the *Classic of Poetry* are folk songs, and therefore created by ordinary people. Although it is not known who authored the *Book of Mountains and Seas*, those fragmentary and simple legendary tales numbering in the hundreds were certainly created by ordinary people. Traditionally, Yu the Great and his minister, Yi, are credited with the *Book of Mountains and Seas,* though most scholars doubt this conclusion. We traditionally hold that the author of *The Iliad* and *The Odyssey* is Homer, but Homer was only one of many travelling bards who made a living by entertaining the aristocratic classes by singing those epics. The two epics were presented as the words of gods and not human beings.

(2) The Different Faith Systems Reflected in Chinese and Early Western Literature

Primary society has a headman and does not have the complex administrative system of secondary society. Early Chinese and Greek literature also reflects this difference. They both created many gods, but the gods of the former do not form the complex hierarchal theocracy of the latter.

It must be pointed out that primary society may also have a super god among other gods. This super god may be the spiritual reflection of the headman in a primary society and may also have been the result of speculation about the force behind the world that keeps the universe moving. This super god lacks a clear image and does not have much authority. It is like a headman who has an empty title with little power. That is exactly what God and heaven look like in the *Book of Mountains and Sea* and the *Classic of Poetry*.

The *Book of Mountains and Sea* calls this super god and the emperor of the Chinese super state the same name, di, emperor or God. It is even more amazing that when the word di, emperor or God appears, it is often unclear whether it denotes God in heaven or the emperor on earth. Such mixing up of the heavenly God with the secular emperor on earth was typical in primary society where God and man were perceived to operate at the same level. It was the spiritual reflection of the social phenomenon that the headman was at the same level as other members of a primary society. Only secondary society stresses the difference between gods and men. The Chinese God or di does not seem to be a powerful figure. The *Book of Mountains and Sea* carries a popular legend: "Form-Heaven (xingtian) competes with God for the throne. God cuts his head off and buries him under a mountain. Form-Heaven refuses to surrender, and he uses his nipples as eyes and navel as mouth, and he never stops brandishing his weapon." According to this description, God bloodies his hands killing Form-Heaven and buries the victim himself. Form-Heaven's rebellious spirits wear the air of charming naivety. This reflects the way in which the competing power was limited to physical strength in primary society and the social power of secondary society was missing. The authority of a powerful figure in a secondary society, either in heaven or on earth, is ensured by social organization, and he never needs to bloody his own hands.

The God or di in *Book of Mountains and Sea* becomes heaven in the *Classic of Poetry*, because the Chou dynasty believed in an even more impersonal deity, heaven. In the *Classic of Poetry*, the authors often let loose torrents of verbal abuse about heaven. Modern scholars interpret such verbal abuse of heaven as a way of criticizing the king of the Chou dynasty. It is a remarkable insight to compare the king with heaven. The king was the super authority on earth, equalling to the general secretary of the United Nations, and heaven was the super authority among all gods. They occupied similar positions in people's minds. An ordinary man hardly feels any influence from the general secretary of the United Nations on his life. Man is an animal of rich imagination who can link everything categorically. Thus people might connect any misfortunes in their lives to the king and to heaven. It sounded much more impressive when people blamed the king or heaven for their unhappiness. For example, the poem *Yongfeng: Cypress Boat*, repeats twice at the end of each of the two stanzas:

Oh, Mother! Oh, heaven!
Why don't you show understanding and sympathy for other people?

This is a young girl who dislikes her mother's lack of sympathy for her behaviour. She draws a parallel between her mother and heaven, seeing her mother as the super authority on earth. To match Mother with heaven, she stresses the intolerability of the situation she is in.

In *Chinese History: Pre-Qin*, the authors, Liu Baocai et al, regard cursing heaven in some poems in the *Classic of Poetry* as a sign of weakening religious faith in the late Western Chou dynasty. [3] I regard this as an invalid argument. In *Historical Records: Biographies of Quyuan and Jiasheng*, Sima Qian says, "Heaven is the origin of man. Man will come back to his origin when he is at the end of his luck. In bitterness and fatigue, man never fails to call on heaven." There are three poems (《Yuwuzheng 雨無正》《Zhaomin 召昊》 《Zhanyang 瞻仰》) that each starts with abusive words towards heaven, and devote the rest of the poems to condemning the secular world and complaining about the suffering of the people. Exactly as Sima Qian says, those authors came to their faith in heaven after bitter experiences. That's why they complained so bitterly. They think heaven is as close to them as their mother. The following is the first stanza of Yuwuzheng 雨無正:

Great and vast Heaven,
Your kindness has been rarely shown,
Sending down death and famine,
Killing people in all directions?
Why do you exercise no forethought, no care?
Arrayed in terrors is you, the Mighty Heaven,
Let alone the criminals,

You cover up their offences;
But those who have no crime,
Encounter sufferings with no end.

During the Hsia, Shang, and Chou dynasties, a few ministers lost their lives because they condemned the king's behaviour. Unlike in ancient Greece, nobody was executed for cursing heaven or gods in China. Therefore, the Chinese condemned heaven instead of the king.

The occasional execution of ministers by the king should not be taken as a sign of forceful authority. On contrary, it shows how hard the king had to push his ministers before his orders could be carried out. Since such executions usually occurred shortly before a dynasty collapsed, the king literally faced the choice between the execution of some ministers and the collapse of his dynasty.

Chinese religious faith remained much like that of a primary society long after the super state was established, because they never had experienced a typical secondary society as the result of this super state of primary societies.

Greek mythology from Homeric epics and other classic works has a strictly constructed hierarchy of gods at many levels. It is clearly the spiritual reflection of the ancient Greek stratified society. Ancient Greeks created a large number of gods under the command of the super god, Zeus. The union of gods and men gave birth to heroes. A hero equalled the king of a city state. Under the command of a hero were the armies formed by citizens. In *The Iliad*, the hero Achilles' soldiers were called Myrmidons, who were created from ants. So those men were brave, industrious, and blindly obedient. Thus even the main population of the city states lost their identities as human beings and became a screw or an ant in the social machine of secondary society. They became, in Julian Jaynes' term, the bicameral man. Under citizens were slaves.

As mentioned in Essay 1, man's move from primary to secondary society is like a fish moving onto land in the great process of biological evolution. This dramatic change of social environment was much felt in its early years. The society was neither controllable nor understandable. The cause of the Trojan war was the little bit unhappiness it caused to the goddess of discord, Eris, when she was not invited to a banquet. This Trojan war that lasted ten years and cost thousands of lives was entirely conducted by gods, and the two armies were like two massive groups of puppets whose movements were all operated by the finger tips of gods. Accidental offence to any god would cause tremendous disaster to the people. A Greek soldier killed a hare, and to avoid the subsequent disaster, the general commander had to sacrifice his daughter to console the unhappy god. When the Greek soldiers entered the city of Troy, a lesser chieftain pulled down a statue of the goddess Athena, and it led to the complete annihilation of the Greek army in a sea storm. This is the spiritual reflection of Greek social stratification on human minds, and it is not seen in the *Classic of Poetry* and the *Book of Mountains and Seas*.

There was an unshakable faith shown in Homer's epics and Greek mythology, a faith in fate. To ancient Greeks, fate was pre-determined and inexorable. Both the Chinese and the Greeks practiced divination, but only the Greeks kept such an unflinching faith in unbreakable fate. The death of the two heroes, Achilles and Hector, was preordained in the Trojan war. Everybody, including themselves, knew that they were destined to die in the war. They faced their destiny bravely to become heroes.

Here I will tell you about Sophocles' *Oedipus the King*. Oedipus was vexed for years about the oracle of his fate. The oracle said that he was fated to kill his father and marry his mother. To avoid the prophesied fate, he gave up his comfortable life as a prince and set out on a vagrant's life. While wandering around far from home, he accidentally killed a man during an argument. The dead man happened to be the local king, and Oedipus was chosen by the citizens as the next king after he solved the Sphinx riddle. Oedipus took the widow left by the former king as his wife. To his horror, he found out many years later that the king he had killed was his father and the wife he had married was his mother. The father and mother he had left were only his stepfather and stepmother. To avoid the fate, he travelled far from home but actually found the way himself to meet his fate face to face. His mother hanged herself in shame, and Oedipus blinded himself with needles and left the throne. This twisted oracle story is typical of many such stories that repeatedly reveal the irrefutable truth: Fate, how tragic it may be, cannot be avoided; fate, how twisted it may appear, will eventually be materialized. Despite the power of the social machine of an early secondary society to devastate people's lives, the only thing they could do was to worship and admire. It was exactly the right social environment that hatched the bicameral mind.

There was no typical secondary society in China, neither the *Classic of Poetry* nor the *Book of Mountains and Seas* shows any trace of such helplessness of the people in front of their society. The Chinese could at least let out a torrent of cursing words.

(3) Original Diversity vs. Directional Accumulation

Here is an important notion of this book that a primary society system is also able to develop civilization though it lacks the directional accumulation, typical of a secondary society. The development of civilization in a primary society system is a process of self-enjoyment, and does not need war to hasten its delivery and does not need an idle class to supervise the process from behind. In contrast to the West, Chinese civilization shows such characteristics.

An Egyptian pyramid is a piece of pure art without any practical value if we ignore the dead body of the pharaoh at its base. So are the millions of prehistoric drawings and paintings on mountain rock faces and in caves. The pyramids are the result of directional accumulation over a thousand years while those prehistoric arts are the original expression of human nature. We cannot determine which has a higher artistic value. Such a contrast also exists between Homer's epics and the two Chinese classics: *Classic of Poetry* and *Book of Mountains and Seas*.

Homeric epics, *The Iliad* and *The Odyssey*, have more than twenty seven thousand lines but describe only the Trojan war and how a hero, Odysseus, came home after the war. Traditionally both *The Iliad* and *The Odyssey* are credited to Homer, and they certainly appeared to be the product of one voice in comparison with the *Classic of Poetry*.

The *Classic of Poetry* has a little over thirty thousand Chinese characters and at most a few thousand lines. It has three hundred and five poems written by different authors with different voices. There are four sections, *Feng, Xiaya, Daya,* and *Song*, with the *Feng* more folk song like and the *Song* more like hymns and praises to the ancestors of the royal houses. The editor put the folk song like *Feng* first, indicating that the editor did not want to present those poems under the frame of a fixed ideology. The *Book of Mountains and Seas* has eighteen chapters, thirty one thousand Chinese characters. It describes more than a hundred states, five hundred and fifty mountains, more than three hundred rivers and animals, some hundred historic figures, and a few dozen gods. The book is arranged geographically, highlighting different locations, and does not have an unified ideology. It has no intention to compare those states and those historic figures, and it thus provides no commentary in addition to its plain descriptions.

A primary society consists of independent individuals, and the *Classic of Poetry* expresses the feeling and emotions of such individuals. The *Book of Mountains and Seas* records fragmentary legends from various geographic locations. Homeric epics use at least twice as many pages as the *Classic of Poetry* and the *Book of Mountains and Seas*, to praise gods and heroes, and to describe in detail their power and their great deeds. The ordinary soldiers and slaves are hardly mentioned, let alone their feelings and emotions. In comparison with the *Classic of Poetry* and the *Book of Mountains and Seas*, Homer's epics, *The Iliad* and *The Odyssey*, are apparently the result of directional accumulation over hundreds of years in a secondary society. Homer was one of the many travelling bards, who sang poetry to an audience of the idle class. Those bards and their idle audience were essential to stimulate the development of such a sophisticated literature form and its content under the guidance of their ideology. There were no such equivalent bards and idle audience in early Chinese history, and there are no equivalents of *The Iliad* and *The Odyssey* in China.

(4) The Measurement of Subjective Expressivity in Human History

In the ancient primary society that did not have a forceful authority, individual members were free to express whatever they wanted, and they were as casual and carefree as we are at home today. The order of a secondary society is not based on human nature but reflects the goals the society aims at. Such a social order is often a major factor in suppressing human nature and its expression. The historical transition from primary to secondary society was no doubt associated with a dramatic decrease of subjective expressivity.

The genetic term, expressivity, indicates the relative degree to which a trait caused by a gene is manifested in an individual. Subjective expressivity is the unsuppressed expression of one's feelings, emotions, imagination, creative desire and so forth that are dictated by our genetic nature. Subjective expressivity is part of human nature in primary society but may reflect a writer's ambition to achieve social goals in a secondary society. As there is no ideal secondary society yet, the subjective expressivity in a secondary society is always a mixture of ambition and human nature. The subjective expressivity is suppressed for the majority of people except a few in a secondary society. Confucius is an example, and he adapted to his social environment perfectly only when he was over seventy years old, when he followed whatever his heart dictated but it was always within the border of righteousness. So Confucius had to suppress part of his subjective expression for more than six decades, even though the social environment Confucius lived in was not a typical secondary society yet.

This book uses the frequency of the word "I" in poetry as a measurement of subjective expressivity. Poetry is the vehicle for people to express their feelings, emotions, and creative imagination. Although the frequency of the word "I" is influenced by many uncontrollable factors such as the literary content and themes, meaningful trends will emerge if a large number of poems from a large number of authors are surveyed. Here is a preliminary study, and more work will follow.

In the social model for the Chinese society before the Warring States Period (476- 221 BC), the village/tribal people still lived in primary society while the king, vassals, and their intellectual officials lived in quasi-primary society. This society falls between primary and secondary societies. The *Classic of Poetry* is the first collection of poetry in Chinese history, and it is divided into four sections: Feng, Xiaoya, Daya, and Song.

Modern editions often cite the possible author of a poem, and it is beyond any doubt that Feng is mainly folk songs from villages, Xiaya is authored chiefly by low ranking officials and Daya from high ranking officials including a famous prime minister, Duke Chou, who acted as king for many years. Song include poems for ritual purpose of the royal house, and its authors include the king himself. Thus from Feng, Xiaoya, Daya, to Song (風, 小雅, 大雅, 頌) is a gradual evolution from a typical primary society to a society that is close to a typical secondary society. In the following statistical results, the topic of each poem is also counted as words.

Table 9.1 The Frequency of Chinese Characters for I, me, my, mine in the *Classic of Poetry*

	Feng	Xiaoya	Daya	Song	Total
No. of Characters	11063	9900	6958	3219	31140
Wo 我	276	222	60	32	590
Wu 吾	0	0	0	2	2
Zhen 朕	0	0	3	1	4
Yu 余	0	0	0	0	0
Total	276/2.5%	222/2.2%	63/0.91%	35/1.1%	596/1.9%
Men 人	132	89	46	5	
Gods 神天帝	18	70	109	28	
Men/Gods	7.3	1.3	0.42	0.18	
Grief 哀	3	22	3	0	28

As Table 9.1 shows, subjective expressivity was decreased when the society was changing from primary to secondary society. Along with this changing trend, the Chinese character man (人) also appears less often but the Chinese characters for gods increase their frequency. The ratio men/gods changed from 7.3 to 0.18, which is statistically significant. It indicates that the ancient Chinese shifted their attention from man to gods while they were moving away from a typical primary society.

Psychological trauma often occurs during the transition from a primary to a secondary society. The authors of Xiaoya, low ranking officials, served as a bridge between the primary society of the village/tribal people and the quasi-primary society of the king and vassals. They lived in the bordering area, and their poems, Xiaoya, use many more expressions for negative emotions such as sadness, sorrow, bitterness, and so on. The Chinese character grief (ai, 哀) is only one of the many negative emotional expressions found in the *Classic of Poetry*. The Chinese character grief (ai, 哀) represents internalized emotions, which occur more often in secondary society than in primary society. The above quoted lines, *"Oh, Mother! Oh, heaven! / Why don't you show understanding and sympathy for other people?",* represent the typical expression of emotion in a primary society. Only after a negative emotion has stagnated in the mind for a period of time, does it become internalized emotion.

The Bible tells how Adam's son Cain killed his brother, and how God regretted having made men on earth, and then started the flood. God said, "Because the earth is full of violence as a result of them; and here I am bringing them to ruin together with the earth."(Genesis 6:13) This bible story reflects a social chaos that traumatized prehistoric people. The first order to emerge from this chaotic ruin was a forceful theocracy, an order dictated by gods in the Middle East. The dominating mentality was the bicameral mind according to Julian Jaynes. Subjective consciousness appeared afterwards, since Western civilization started with a typical secondary society. There are no parallel poems reflecting the transition from primary to secondary society, and instead, there was a shift from Gods to man in the Western history. According to Julian Jaynes, Homer's epics, *The Iliad* and *The Odyssey* represent different stages of the development of subjective consciousness. *The Iliad* reflects a typical bicameral mentality while *The Odyssey* shows the emergence of subjective consciousness to a certain degree. Dictated by gods, the bicameral people also spoke the word "I" but in the voice of gods. Nevertheless, *The Odyssey* shows more subjective expressivity than *The Iliad,* measured by the frequency of the word "I".

According to five randomly sampled pages from *The Iliad* and seven randomly sampled pages from *The Odyssey*, the frequency of the word "I" is 0.8% for *The Iliad* but 1.4% for *The Odyssey* in English Translation. I sampled the first, thirteenth, and twenty fourth chapters from both *The Iliad* and *The Odyssey* in Chinese translation. The frequency of Chinese character wo (I, me, my, mine) is 1.4% in the three chapters of *The Iliad* but is 1.8% in the three chapters from *The Odyssey*. I think, it is enough to say that *The Odyssey* does show more subjective expressivity than *The Iliad*.

Bernard Knox selected a total of 24 ancient Greek poets from *The Greek Anthology* arranged chronologically that are translated in English. I divided them into two halves at 100 BC. The first half has 11 authors and 942 words, and the second half has 13 authors and 962 words. The frequency of the English word "I" was higher in the later half than in the first half. The difference is statistically significant: 1.6% (15/942) vs. 3.1% (29/926), $X^2=4.81$, $P<0.05$. This is a further evidence to support the increasing trend of subjective expressivity in Western history.

I randomly sampled pages from another three chronological anthologies of poetry, two English translations from ancient Greece and Rome respectively, and the third is an anthology of English poetry. I divided each of them into two halves according to the number of pages but avoided to break the work of any author into two. All three anthologies show the same trend: Subjective expressivity is increased in the later half. The difference is statistically significant:

Greek   0.91% (67/7350) vs. 1.92% (121/6300) $X=25.4$ $P<0.005$
Rome   0.29% (8/2800) vs. 1.07% (30/2800) $X=12.8$ $P<0.005$
English 1.13%(203/18000) vs. 1.44%(286/19800) $X=7.4$ $P<0.005$

Without statistical analysis, one can see clearly that subjective expressivity was lower in Rome than either in Greece or in the English world. The Roman Empire was no doubt a more suppressive cultural construct. Nevertheless, subjective expressivity was an increasing trend in each of them, which is consistent with a gradual shift from gods to man in the order of a well established forceful theocracy.

As mentioned above, Chinese history was a gradual process of social transformation from primary to secondary society with a corresponding shift of power from the local governments to the central government. As shown in Table 9.2, a remarkable decreasing trend of subjective expressivity was associated with this gradual social transformation. The lowest frequencies were observed in the dynasties that were founded by foreign powers, the Yuan and the Qing dynasty. It is not surprising as Chinese intellectuals felt suppressed under foreign rules.

There is a theory among Chinese scholars that Chinese history was a gradual process of shifting from the battlefields along the northern border to the more peaceful southern part of China. The people along the northern border were usually tribal nomads, and moving to south. In this process, we see the shift from a primary to a secondary society. We can further divide the Six dynasties into Han, Wei, Jin, and the Northern and Southern dynasties, and their frequencies of the word "I" were 1.02% , 1.49% , 0.88% , 0.37% respectively. The Wei dynasty was mainly located in the north and the Jin dynasty mainly in the south. The former had a higher frequency (1.49%) than the latter (0.88%). The Northern and Southern dynasties were actually two separate contemporary states with one in the north and one in the south. The frequency of the word "I" was higher in the north (0.51%) than in the south (0.33%). The Song dynasty coexisted with other competitive powers and moved into the south later. This move of the Song dynasty from north to south was associated with a dramatic decrease in the frequency of the word "I" in poetry, from 0.45% to 0.00% (0/1222). I think that is enough to conclude that there was a decreased subjective expressivity in southern China compared to northern China.

Table 9.2 The Frequencies of Chinese Character "I" (我 , 吾, 余, 朕) in Chinese Poetry Along the History

Time	Total of characters	Subjective "I"	Possessive "I"	Objective "I"	Total/%
Shijing (1122-476BC)	31140	190	221	185	596/1.9%
Quyuan (352-278BC)	12107	90	46	50	186/1.5%
Six Dynasties (206BC-589)	24491	76	91	58	225/0.92%
Tang (618-907)	22690	34	24	12	70/0.31%
Song (960-1279)	5875	10	5	2	17/0.29%
Yuan (1271-1368)	3104	1	2	3	6/0.19%
Ming (1368-1644)	3911	3	6	1	10/0.26%
Qing (1644-1911)	9489	12	7	5	24/0.13%

(5) The Alienation of Human Morality

Social morality and the value system are a complex issue, and I will not go into this in detail. Both primary and secondary societies have their moral and value systems. But the former is based on human nature and the latter, on the goals of the society. To distinguish Homer's epics from the *Classic of Poetry* and the *Book of Mountains and Seas,* here I use the absence and presence of moral principles that betray basic human nature. The ancient Greek city states such as Athens mainly produced wine, olive oil, and silver, and well developed commercial trade was a must. Commercial trade hatched free minds and also a wealth-accumulating culture. Looting the less developed neighbours was inevitable.

The Trojan war as described in *The Iliad* and its sequels, such as *The Aeneid* by Virgil, was really a looting war. It gives details how children were killed and how women were transported back as trophies. Admiration and praise brim the pages for such wars, and the stories also give details about how those spoils of war were distributed. The rage of the heroic Achilles against the commander in general, Agamemnon, is the backbone of the story. That rage was caused by the distribution of seized women. Romantic love is part of our nature and is often portrayed as lofty and sacred, stirring our deep emotions. To reduce such a lofty love to the spoils of war, acquired by force, is not something that would ever be expressed in a primary society. In the primary society, hungry people might attack their neighbours for food but they would usually carry out an ambush in order to avoid violent conflicts and casualty. An ambush perpetrated by the hungry is fundamentally different from a formal war for looting. The former did not enter the *Classic of Poetry*. On contrary, the *Classic of Poetry* brims with condemnation of various immoral behaviours while the latter is the theme of a long epic poem. The culture of a looting war cannot be established in a short time, as it is against human nature. Aristotle expounded at length why it is natural to seize the defeated as slaves in war. Ancient Greeks had drifted far away from human nature.

It is not part of human nature to kill another human being. To admire the senseless killing of innocent people poetically is not a sign of the culture of a primary society. The protagonist of *The Odyssey* went off to the Trojan war for twenty years. In his hometown, almost everybody assumed that he was dead. A crowd of men came to pursue his wife. Acting as a stranger, Odysseus won a contest of archery with those men. Odysseus shot them dead one after another when they were all stripped of their capacity of protecting themselves. For twenty years, the wife remained chaste and faithful to Odysseus in front of so many pursuers. Such unrealistic chastity of women is again a characteristic of secondary society. Neither the *Classic of Poetry* nor the *Book of Mountains and Seas* has such over exaggerated details that go against basic human nature.

In summary, immoral violence does happen in primary society and due to the impelling power of human nature, people tend to suppress those memories. Thus people either fail to mention such violence or they condemn it in their poetry. A secondary society has to produce an effective strategy and put it into practice for a long time before it is able to create a culture that runs so contrary to human nature. Here is a more recent example:

According to G. Dyer (1995), humans do have a strong innate resistance to killing their own kind. The military has known about it for more than half a century, and has developed techniques to overcome it.

According to a trained psychologist, Lieutenant Colonel Dave Grossman (G. Dyer 1995), you can train and arm a man, put him on the battlefield, and expose him to the imminent danger of death, and in most cases, he still won't kill. However such non- killers were ashamed of their "cowardice' and did not talk about it. It was only in the final years of the Second World War that USA army historians conducting post-combat interviews with several hundred infantry companies under the promise of anonymity, discovered that only 15 to 20 percent of the soldiers ever fired their weapons on the battlefield. Some of them even fired their weapons deliberately aiming high so as not to hit anybody. It was the few who could endure the killing and were doing almost all of the killing. This had been the truth for thousands of years without being noticed or studied. For example 90 percent of the abandoned muskets picked up after the battle of Gettysburg (1863) were loaded but had not been fired.

The military overcomes this innate resistance by a combination of desensitization and conditioning techniques. The soldiers are asked to practise shooting at a target in the shape of a human being. They also make the shooting so easy and so automatic and reflexive that the soldiers have no time to think about it before pulling the trigger. Such techniques worked well during the Vietnam War, when up to 95 percent of American soldiers were firing their weapons at the enemy. As a result the Vietnam veterans suffered a very high rate of post-traumatic stress disorder since they were tricked into killing against their will.

From the *Classic of Poetry* and the *Book of Mountains and Seas*, we see clearly that ancient China did not know how to develop a culture that ran contrary to human nature, because they did not have the need. Their society was relatively stable and peaceful. From the descriptions of Homer's epics, such a culture against human nature was already in place in ancient Greece. How did they achieve this? According to Julian Jaynes, the bicameral mind prevailed in all Mediterranean civilizations. Those bicameral people did not have the slightest sense of morality. They did not have episodic memories as we do today, and they only had enough memories to enable them to carry out the divine orders they had heard.

References

[1.] Jack L. Dull(1990): The evolution of government in China. In Paul S. Ropp, eds: Heritage of China, Berkeley, USA: University of California Press. p56-57.

[2.] Ge Jianxiong (1994): Unity and Disintegration: The Revelation of Chinese History (tongyi yu fenlie: zongguo lishide qishi). Beijing: Three Union Book Store. (葛劍雄： 《統一與分裂：中國歷史的啟示》, 北京：三聯書店, 1994年。)

[3.] Liu Baocai (2001): Chinese History: Pre-Qin (zonguolishi: xianqinjuan). Beijing: High Education Publishing House. p125. (劉寶才：《中國歷史：先秦卷》, 北京：高等教育出版社, 2001年，第125頁。)

[4.] G. Dyer (1995): Learning how to kill humans. Globe and Mail, Dec. 23, 1995.

[5.] The analysis of the frequencies of the word "I" in poetry was based on poems from the following sources: 1) Chinese poems for the six dynasties, Tang, Song, and yuan dynasties are all from the website: http://www.xys.com., and they are from published books. The poems for the Ming and Qing dynasties were randomly sampled from the website: http://www.cnpoem.net. by the author. 2) The Greek and Roman poems are from: Bernard Knox(1993): Classical Literature. New York: W.W. Norton & Company, and the English poems are from: Harold Bloom (2004): The Best Poems of the English Language. New York: HarperCollins Publishers. The Chinese poems were counted word by word using the computer, and the English word "I" was counted by the author and the total English words were estimated according to the average number of words per page.

10

Writing Invented for Different Purposes

Writing is one of the signs anthropologists use to identify the emergence of civilization, also to demarcate pre-historic and historical times, since recorded history is fundamentally different from that interpreted from archaeological findings. Today writing serves many functions, and similarly, writing was invented by different people for different purposes in human history.

The invention of writing is, however, a simple idea that puts spoken words in representative marks to inform those who are absent. Theoretically, one man could invent a complete writing system within a few years. Complex invention such as religion or a political system may even need military action to spread to different cultures while a simple invention spreads itself rapidly like a virus. For example, all the alphabet spelling systems in the world are thought to have copied or derived from a single origin, the Phoenician alphabet. Of course the Phoenician alphabet may have derived from the Proto-Canaanite alphabet, but it was the Phoenician people who spread it to many cultures including the Greek. Now scholars believe that there are only three original writing systems, from the Middle East,

China, and Mesoamerica respectively. Why those cultures invented writing some thousand years ago still reflects the cultural difference today especially between the West and the Chinese.

Among the civilizations in Mesoamerica that possessed a system of hieroglyphic writing, the Zapotec was the earliest (600 BC) and, the Maya, the most complex one. Both civilizations recorded genealogical information about their hereditary nobles, emphasizing their links to former rulers and other nobles. Texts featured important events in the lives of the rulers and close family members. Judged by its contents, the Mesoamerican writing was literally the extension of the totem cultures, a more detailed representation of their clans. It is not surprising that their writings are similar to the totem poles by the Indigenous people of the Pacific Northwest Coast of North America. Those writings were likely invented by the tribal chiefs and their associates.

The Western writing developed under the influence of Mesopotamian civilization where writing first appeared in human history at the close of the fourth millennium BC. For thousand years, people in the Middle East used tokens to record numbers of sheep, goats, or other goods changed hands. A small clay token with certain marks on it may signify a sheep, and a large one with different marks, for ten sheep. Different tokens were used for goats and other properties. They sealed those tokens in a clay container, which was later hardened by baking. The outside of the container was etched with all marks representing what inside. The container was broken to show the content whenever a dispute occurred. Seals were also utilized to indicate the ownership of a property. A seal was typically a cylinder with specific marks on it, and the owner rolled the cylinder on the wet clay to leave its print as his seal.

Later on, those markings on the outside of the sealed containers were transferred onto clay tablets, which became the first writing in human history around 3100 BC. As the earliest writing in Europe, two writing systems, Linear A and Linear B, were discovered in the Greek island, Crete. Linear A, not deciphered yet, was related to Hittite and thus Asian in origin. Linear B was Greek, and it adapted the Linear A system. Linear B was deciphered in 1952, and the limited archaeological specimen were almost all records of goods and possessions. Thus the first European writing served the same function as those in the Middle East. Seals were also a feature of the Minoan civilization on the Cretan island. The Indian civilization developed between 2600 and 1900 BC along the Indus River valley. Their writing was not deciphered yet, but they also used seals to mark possessions, which was one of the many evidences for their contact with the Middle East.

From Mesopotamia, Egypt, Greece, to the Indus Valley, archaeologists had discovered huge remains of magnificent buildings, namely, the Ziggurats in Mesopotamia, the pyramids in Egypt, the Minoan palaces in Greece, the remains of the complex ancient cities in the Indus valley. They were all remarkable builders. It is conceivable that they all manufactured so many properties that they needed a good system to keep track of them. The inventors of their writing systems appeared to be the commercial traders.

China was different. Archaeologists had dug out the palace of the late Shang dynasty (1760-1122 BC). The palace was nothing more than a large mud thatched hut. There were some bronze vessels with sophisticated decoration indicating that their civilization was highly developed. They kept good records too. As mentioned in Essay 5, archaeologists had tried for years to confirm the presence of a writing system before 1766 BC but failed so far though two recent reports indicate otherwise. At a place (damaidi) in the Ningxia province, 8453 rock paintings and cliff carvings have been discovered, and more than 1500 of them were considered to be symbols bearing the basic elements of Chinese characters. More than a hundred inscribed bones from 4000 to 2000 BC were found in Shandong province and those inscriptions were considered as the precursors of the oracle bones from the late Shang dynasty. Those findings have to be examined and evaluated extensively before they are accepted as writing by the academic circle, which still take the oracle bones as the first Chinese writings.

In 1901, a traveling writer came to the capital of China, Beijing, as a visitor to a government official, who, as it happened, was taking some Chinese herbal medicine. Chinese herbal medicine contains herbs, minerals, and animal parts. A prescription usually fills up a pot in which they are boiled every day for the patient to drink the juice. This writer, while idle as a guest, observed each item of the medicine in detail to kill time. He suddenly realized that the strange marks on the so-called dragon bones are ancient writing. With a little money, the writer bought five thousand pieces and published them as a book. A different legend says, the government official himself found out that those marks are ancient writing but shared it with his friend, the writer.

In a place called Anyang, peasants often found those bones with etched marks while ploughing their fields. More than a hundred and fifty thousand pieces have now discovered. Most of them are oracle bones from the late Shang dynasty with a few as mere historic records. The king and his court officials carved their questions on the bones and then subjected them to fire. According to the cracks produced by the heating, interpretations were made as the final answer from God. It is a divination.

Those ascribed oracle bones are the earliest verified Chinese writing dated from 1400 to 1122 BC. The Book of Change says, ancient Chinese people, like the Inca Empire in the South America, used knotted strings for records but sages changed them to writing and etched marks. (Figure 5)

Chinese records ascribed the invention of writing to a legendary figure (Cangjie), who served the Yellow Emperor as his minister around 2600 BC. The records say, when he first invented writing, it rained with millets and ghosts were crying at night. The invention of Chinese writing achieved such a miracle that food became abundant, and ghosts could no longer bully people so that they were crying.

The archaeological findings are thus consistent with the above records. The Chinese writing was invented for divination, namely looking for answers to questions. As mentioned in Essay 5, those questions were often asked because of curiosity and the idle lifestyle of primary society. The inventors of Chinese writing system seem to be the intellectuals who served the king of the ancient Chinese super state. The king and his ministers neither needed to trade goods with anybody nor had to identify their clan among many clans of the same level.

Actually, the first intellectuals who served the ancient Chinese king were a combination of several professionals today, including witch, medical doctor, historian, and astronomer. Their writing was thus justified to be mysterious as well as miraculous.

Unlike any other writing systems in the world, Chinese writing, calligraphy, has been a major form of art. It is not rare nowadays that a piece of art can disturb its viewer's mental state. It is impossible for Chinese calligraphy to have such effects. On the contrary, Chinese calligraphy has great therapeutic effects, especially to the calligrapher himself. Many famous calligraphers make a decent living by their writing, and they usually lived a happy and rich life. Some patients of mental disorders such as anxiety and depression are cured by practicing Chinese calligraphy. Even today, some still use the unusual Chinese writing to heal or to exorcise. Superstitious people even swallow Chinese written words on paper to cure their illness.

The conclusion is an obvious one that civilization was not always paralleled with its material achievements or monumental constructions. Similarly, Chinese writing was not invented to track commercial transactions or anything material. For commercial transactions, a writing system had to be precise. The first Chinese writing had a mysterious and miraculous quality.

The first Hebrew writing was, however, the two carved tablets Moses brought to his people from Mount Si'nai, the Ten Commandments in the 1200s BC. It combines the mysterious and miraculous quality of Chinese writing and the powerful preciseness of the Western writing. It is the law written by God's fingers, and it is in alphabet.

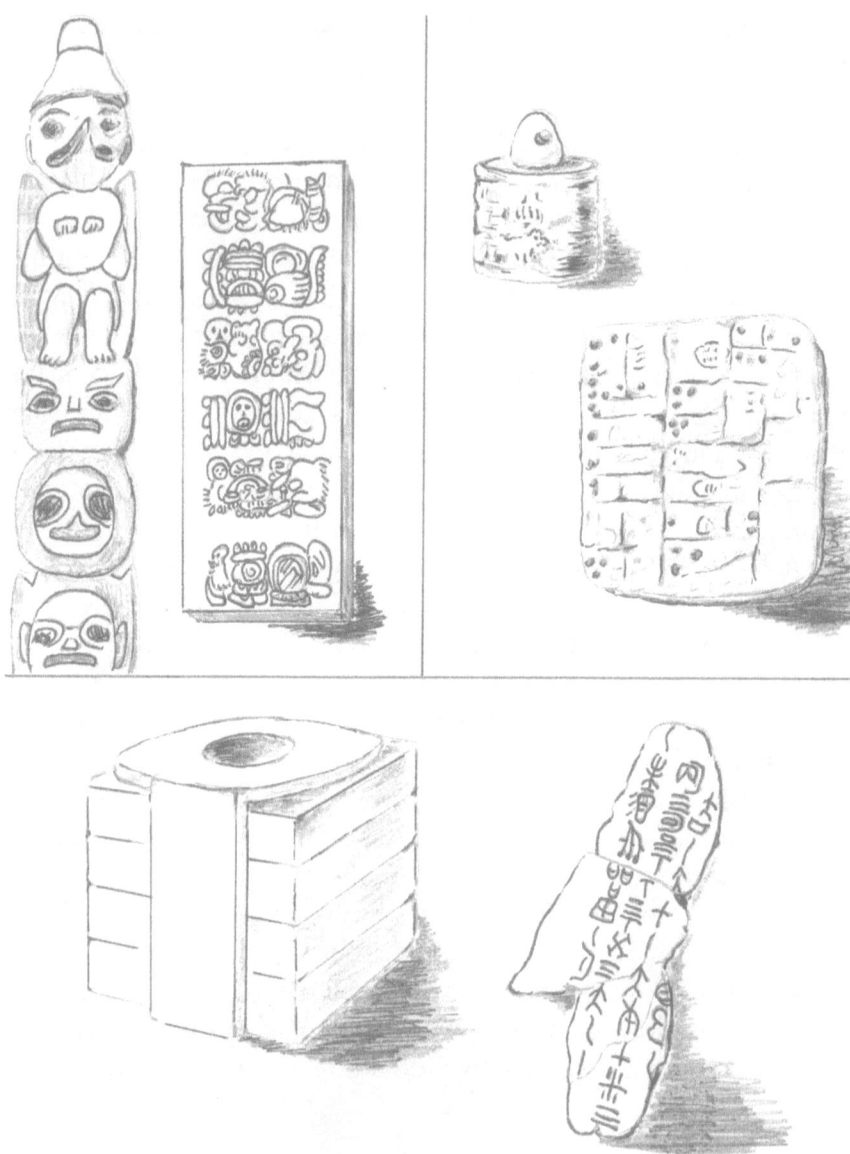

Figure 5. On the right side of each pair of figures are the early Mesoamerican, Mesopotamian, and Chinese writings and on the left side, their different artefacts which are supposed to have led to the invention of those quite different writing systems. Upper left, Mesoamerican; upper right, Mesopotamian; bottom, Chinese.

11

Where is God?

Christianity branched off from Judaism while Buddhism branched off from Hinduism. Neither Christianity nor Buddhism succeeded in their homelands but both flourished in foreign countries to become major religions in today's world.

Buddhism was created by Sakyamuni (Siddhartha Gautama), the Buddha, who was born about 563 and died 480 BC. The Buddha was a prince in a small state which is inside Nepal today. He gave up the luxury life of a prince and lived as a traveling monk preaching the religious truth in northern India where numerous independent states coexisted. In face of human sufferings everywhere, the Buddha asked, "Where is God?"

When there was a war, wounded soldiers and civilians were left dying in the battlefield. If there was a God, why didn't he stop the war and why didn't he heal the wounded? When there was a famine, hungry farmers travelled far from their homeland in search for food. If there was God, why didn't he feed those who were starving?

The Buddha then concluded that there is no God. The Buddha also denied the existence of the subjective I or the soul. Buddhism accepts the traditional theory of reincarnation but insists that both the world and I are illusory. Once the subjective I is lost, there is no more suffering. Thus the Buddhist religious truth resides outside God, the world, and I. Whoever realized and accepted this religious truth is called a Buddha, the enlightened one. So the pursuit of Buddhism is really a process of enlightenment. Contrast to the rigid unjust caste system suffocating the low caste talents, Buddhism emphasizes the equality of all humans in the sight of the Buddha. Everyone has a Buddha nature and everyone can become a Buddha, so they claim. The Buddha also taught whoever wanted to learn from him, regardless of sex, class, or caste.

The Western enlightenment movement started in the seventeenth century and ended with the French revolution in the late eighteenth century or early nineteenth century. Like the Buddha, the Western enlightenment employed rational thinking to examine the existence of God. They argued that if everything, physical and metaphysical, could be well explained in scientific terms by rational analysis, we do not need a supernatural being. There is no rational evidence for the existence of God.

Although there is no room left for God according to rational thinking, there is no proof for the non-existence of God either. Thomas H. Huxley (1825-1895) believed that the large secondary society of the modern human world is intended to be run by God not human beings, as he compared a colony or state with a farm or orchard. The intellectual gap between God and human beings equals the intellectual gap between man and plants or sheep or pigs. Lao Tzu said similar words, "The social world is not something humans can possess or grab in hand to meddle with. The one trying to possess it will lose it; the one trying to grab it and meddle with it will fail." The conservative political traditions in the West were based on a similar belief that the master of our world is God, and human beings had better not meddled with world affairs to create an ideal world. What we can do is only to solve the emerging problems, or the so-called pragmatism of piece-meal social reform.

The so-called fideism insists that religious truth is not, and ought not to be, based on rational knowledge but solely on faith. God exists only by faith. But why do we need such a faith to create a God who does not speak to rational minds but speaks to irrational minds with conflicting messages resulting in endless violence?

As discussed in Essay 1, the worldwide desertification around 4000-3000 BC resulted in a dramatic cultural transformation in the human world, namely from a peaceful motherly culture to a warlike patriarchal society. In his book, The Fall: The Evidence for a Golden Age, 6000 Years of Insanity and the Dawning of a New Era, Steve Taylor calls this social transformation the Fall. [1] Because of the ego explosion, social inequality, and war, the fallen people were suffering from psychic disharmony. It was those fallen people who created the concepts of God or gods. The hierarchy of gods or the world of God is really a psychological reflection of the secondary society on our minds. According to Taylor, even the idea of a prehistoric Goddess religion is a kind of error similar to the belief that some prehistoric societies were matriarchal.

We can today observe our children's behaviour to understand the religious faith in the ancient primary society, which was the golden age of childhood in human history. A toddler puts his or her little pillow on the top of a much larger pillow saying, "(The) pillow wants Mommy too!" So they see everything in the world have the same ideas and desires as they do. They thus have a psychological and emotional bond even with their physical world. In our children's imagined world, everything is golden bright and everything is motherly kind. Whether you call our children's world a godly or a godless world, it lacks the psychic disharmony and social inequality Taylor describes. It is also the Taoist ideal world. The following quotation from Leslie Marmon Silko's short fiction Lullaby that gives a more vivid picture of such a warm, friendly, peaceful, and interesting world humans once lived in:

The earth is your mother,
she holds you.
The sky is your father,
he protects you.
Sleep,
sleep.

Rainbow is your sister,
       she loves you.
The winds are your brothers,
       they sing to you.
Sleep,
sleep.
We are together always
We are together always
There never was time
When this
was not so.

When humans lost such a paradise of the ancient primary society, they consoled the pain of the secondary society by ego explosion, which often led to further pains. Taylor says, Buddhism provides a psychological method of transcending the fallen psychic disharmony. Can those Buddhist believers get rid of the idea of God or gods?

April 15, 2005 was the Buddha's 2567th birthday. I happened to attend the ceremony in a Buddhist temple in Ottawa. A baby Buddha was located in a tank of water, and every worshiper in turn came to bathe the baby Buddha by pouring water on his shoulders while being told the story of the Buddha's birth.

According to the custom of the day, the Buddha's mother traveled back to her mother's home to give birth. On the way she stopped to enjoy a beautiful garden, where the Buddha was born in a gesture with one hand pointing to heaven and the other to earth announcing, "In both heaven and earth, I am the only one superior to all." He then walked seven steps where seven lotus plants emerged and grew into full bloom immediately. Such a story indicates clearly that the Buddha is a supernatural being to those worshipers.

Then I observed, a middle-aged woman knelt down in front of the Buddha image in such a submissive way that five parts of her body attached to the floor, the head, the elbows, and the knees, and she stayed in that position for a long time.

With the advance of science today, in the well-educated minds of the worshipers, the Buddha was thus born a God, worshiped as a God while they were reciting the Buddha's teaching: There is no God.

During the Cultural Revolution (1966-1976), the American writer and journalist, Edgar Parks Snow (1905-1972) was once invited by the Chinese leader Mao to join the Chinese national day ceremony. Mao was worshiped as a living God inside China. Millions of Mao's worshipers were marching in front of Mao, shouting, "Ten thousand years to Chairman Mao!"

Snow asked Mao, "Isn't that a personality cult? Isn't that a superstition?"

Mao was silent for a long time, and then said, "If there is no God, people will create one. What can I do?"

In Mao, A Biography, Ross Terrill gives vivid descriptions of this Chinese living God, Mao's bitter life in his later years, lonely, being worshiped but deserted. Terrill concludes, the time of the hero is over, and people live their life without a hero. Unfortunately, Terrill isn't right yet. In a recent trip to China, I noticed a little Mao's statue dangling on a colourful pendant in front of the taxi driver seat. He said, Mao's statue has the magic power to protect people from any tragic events such as traffic accidents. The driver is apparently one of those Chinese who are unhappy, because their present national leaders are not godlike enough.

Reference

[1] Steve Taylor (2005): The Fall: The Evidence for a Golden Age, 6000 Years of Insanity and the Dawning of a New Era. Winchester UK: O Books, 2005.

12

Confucius and Jesus: Humanism Took Different Pathways in Chinese and Western History

The Chinese government first named Confucianism as its official ideology in the second century BC. Since then Confucianism remained as the mainstream culture to shape society and the way of life for more than two thousand years until the early 20th century when the first republic of China was founded. As the influence of Western culture entered China and it was followed by the subsequent revolutions, the fading out of Confucianism in Chinese life occurred in a relatively short time between 1840 and 1919. The Roman Emperor Theodoisius made Christianity, based on Jesus' teaching, the official religion in the late fourth century, and since then Christianity remained the dominant ideology to shape society and the way of life in Europe for more than a thousand years until recently. The fading out of Christianity as the main ideology in Western society was a gradual process. The underlying reason was the social movement of secularization started by the Renaissance.

If we see a culture and its people as a man, the two giant men firmly stood, one in China and the other in Europe, for more than a thousand years in human history, unmoved by the strong winds of various cultures and ideologies. Their brains were nothing but the teachings of two real men, Confucius and Jesus. Their successes were due to the humanist soul in their teachings, which represent the peak humanism ever reached during ancient time. It is most interesting and revealing to compare the two men, their ideas, and their influence on subsequent history.

(1) Definition of Humanism and its History in China and the West

Humanism is the tendency to emphasize man and his status, importance, his achievements, and interests. The definition of humanism thus varies within a broad category of ethical philosophies that support the dignity and worth of all people. Furthermore, humanism can be a component of a variety of more specific philosophical systems and is incorporated into several religious schools of thought. Humanism entails a commitment to the search for truth, morality, social justice, and an ideal society through human means.

It is worth noting that humanism as defined here is not in the narrow meaning that contrasts to the faith in supernatural being. Humanism in relative terms includes any ideology that is directed towards the improvement of human conditions, physically or spiritually. For example, human sacrifice was considered to be counter to humanism, but its complete disappearance in China was only witnessed about a hundred years ago. Confucius was so opposed to human sacrifice that he even cursed those who started to use artificial figures to replace real men, as Confucius thought that the dignity of man was buried with those figures that looked so real. This idea of Confucius' falls in the broad category of humanism as it contributed to the disappearance of human sacrifice in China. For similar considerations, Jesus' teachings and Christianity fall in too, though it is not a popular topic to write about Jesus' humanist contribution.

Early Greek people began to develop their thought by studying nature, and those early thinkers are called the natural philosophers. With Socrates and other sophists, attention was shifted to social, political, and moral issues. This shift is regarded as the beginning of Western humanism. The next important time in humanist history was when Stoicism appeared as a school of thought. Seneca's (2 BC- 65 AD) aphorism, "To man, a man is sacred", remains as a powerful slogan for humanists today.

In spite of the remarkable development of human thought along the line of humanism, the Roman Empire was still built on slavery. Millions of slaves lived inhumane lives. It was the emergence of Christianity and the collapse of the Roman Empire that brought an end to the Roman slavery system, though slavery was never stopped until recently. Many thought that Christianity contributed to the Roman collapse. There were many less slaves in the Medieval Europe, Christian teachings reac hed through to the bottom of the social stratification, and warmed the peasants' hearts with the conviction that God loves every man on earth. Christian bishops fulminated against the entertainments of the theater and amphitheater, and the baths. The baths were thought to be responsible for sexual depravity. Christian aristocrats gradually redirected their funding to churches, which were constructed in great numbers in the 400s and 500s. They also funded hospitals, orphanages, homes for the aged, and other institutions of caring which were established. It was for the first time in Roman history.

For a thousand years or so, Christianity remained as the mainstream culture to unite Europe and keep the social order. The Renaissance was a much broader social campaign to stress the value of mankind and the value of a man ahead of society and or ahead of nature. Therefore, the Renaissance denoted a move away from God to man as the center of interest. The Renaissance encouraged the ability of man to find about the universe through his own efforts, and more and more to control it. The official separation of governments and religion gradually led the way to where we are today when Christianity is no longer deemed relevant to our society and our life.

Chinese Humanism developed along a quite different historic pathway. Lao Tzu, Confucius, and other early Chinese thinkers all took the ancient society as the ideal model. Chinese records painted a clear picture of those peaceful yet humanist societies. Here I called it the natural humanism in contrast to the later development of humanism that is just one of many creations of man. The natural humanism was a product of the human heart and human nature. As a result, Chinese humanist thought appeared in a much earlier stage of civilization than in the West. Chinese scholars think there was a shift of attention from gods, ghosts, and other spiritual beings to man in the early years of the Chou dynasty (1122-256 BC), a few hundred years before any philosophical thinkers were born. Such a shift was due to careful thinking about why their new dynasty was able to replace the old one, and they concluded that human hearts were behind the change of dynasty. As discussed in Essay 1, the social structure during that time allowed all people to live in a primary or quasi-primary society, and human nature remained as the major force keeping that society stable. Such a shift was directed both by observation and by human nature. Rational thinking was present in a primary society but was not able to set up a leading ideology other than human nature.

This shift from gods to man covered such changes in ancient China: The impersonal sky or heaven replaced the original personal God (shangdi) as the new super god; divination used eight trigrams to replace oracle bones; a whole set of musical rituals was used to buttress the social ranking system and make it less inhumane. Humanism as a social movement affecting all levels of society appeared only during the Spring/Autumn and Warring States Periods (770-221 BC), and with Confucius as its leader. Both Confucius and Jesus were criticized in modern history, but such criticism cannot erase their tremendous contributions to the humanist history.

(2) The Fundamental Difference Between Confucius and Jesus: Jesus was More Like Mo Tzu

The following, though brief, is enough to show the fundamental difference between Confucianism and Christianity:

1. Confucianism relied on the government, but Christianity started as a movement against the governmental authority.

2. Confucius and his followers kept a distance from gods and spirits, but Jesus and his followers relied heavily on miracles and mysterious phenomena to preach.

3. Confucius held that gentlemen should not form parties and should not compete with each other, but Jesus painted his group as a unique one by criticizing others. To get a larger social space for their Christianity, his disciples struggled to spread his word to other sectors of society and other cultures.

4. Christianity had strict organization, going out to preach, but Confucianism remained at the level of academic thought and self-cultivation.

Confucius was from a family of the low level of the ruling class, equal to the intellectuals or scholars who worked in the government in later times. Jesus' father was a carpenter, and Jesus himself also used to work as a carpenter. Confucius said, "Inferior men are not afraid of heaven as they do not know the decree of heaven; they also take great men lightly, and laugh at the words of the sages." (Analects 16.8) Jesus was exactly such an inferior man who did not obey the local authority and laughed at their words. Jesus preached his religion, but he was not officially sanctioned to do so. This eventually led to Jesus' execution. Thus Jesus was a rebel under the name of God. Christianity was oppressed by the official religious organization, Judaism, and by the local authorities so that they left their native state, Israel, to preach abroad. Since Jesus' followers were all law-abiding, they were not noticed by the Roman Government for years. But they were still not tolerated by the government, and large numbers of Christians were executed.

Confucius preached his ideology of benevolence and righteousness that was based on loving people, but he did not go to the bottom level of the society to be friends with them. Those uneducated people lacked rational thinking and believed in miracles and mysterious phenomena. Educated people or people of the ruling class did not care much about those people except for exploiting them. They were particularly vulnerable to Jesus' preaching.

The Chinese ruling class had long gotten rid of irrational thinking about miracles and mysterious phenomena from the early years of the Chou dynasty and adapted rational thinking to manage national affairs. But this was only limited to the ruling class and educated people. The massive peasantry in the rural areas was still in the grip of irrational thinking.

Irrational thinking was partially due to lack of knowledge and was also based on intuition. Our inborn way of thinking is not rational, which becomes obvious when we observe the irrational nature of our daydreams and dreams at night. In the primitive primary society, rational thinking only occurred at times such as when they faced a task to be done. Systemic rational thinking on a large scale is part of our civilized culture, and it is a cultural construction.

Jesus' time came after the Axial Age, and without any doubt, the Roman authorities in Israel adapted rational thinking for their administration. According to the New Testament, Jesus' preaching was full of miracles and mysterious phenomena. Such stories spread rapidly among the people of the lower classes but raised the suspicions of authority. Contrary to Jesus, Confucius distanced himself from the lower classes and also from miracles and mysterious phenomena. He promoted a wary attitude towards gods and spirits: Be respectful to gods and spirits but keep a distance from them. Confucius had the principle of Four No-Comments in his teaching and counseling practice: He never talked about parapsychology, psychic power, mental disturbance, and ghosts. More than two thousand years later today, the attitudes towards religion, gods and ghosts are largely the same in the circle of Chinese intellectuals, who can be called the loyal followers of Confucius.

Confucius said, "Gentlemen have nothing to compete for. If they have to, they do it like in an archery match, where they ascend to their positions, bowing in deference toward other people who take part in the match. When done, they descend, and drink the ritual cup. This is the competition of gentlemen." Thus Confucians do not form any parties and do not usually compete. In modern Western politics, clerks and other staff in government offices are often discouraged to join the competitive parties in the parliament system. During Confucius' time, most of his followers took positions similar to today's clerks and other minor officials.

From the very beginning, Jesus competed vigorously with the local authorities for support of the people. It was well justified for the official religious staff to interpret the contemporary version of the Bible in certain ways in order to keep the society stable. Jesus ridiculed their interpretation of the Bible, and preached his own beliefs. Acting as the representative of God on earth, he sent his love to everybody he met. In doing so, I believe, Jesus challenged the authority of the local government, and on behalf of the poor people, he was in a rebellious position against the rich classes. But this rebellion was not one of violence but one of honesty, will, and commitment to social justice and love. Once Jesus suggested to a rich man that he should sell his belongings and give money to the poor, and doing so, he would have treasure kept in heaven. When the rich man was reluctant to do so, Jesus said to his disciples: "It is easier for a camel to pass through the eye of a needle, than for a rich man to enter into the kingdom of God." (Matthew 19:24) The early Christians were such well organized groups that they formed a more than egalitarian society, literally a communist society. Such teachings and organizations had a great appeal to the people of the lower classes, especially when the economy was poorly developed and people lived on meager supplies. It is no wonder why Christianity met such a rapid success in Europe.

Christianity followed Judaism as a monotheist religion. Judaism kept saying that their God was the only God, all other gods were only idols. Such statements kept Israel's people from being attracted by the gods from the neighboring cultures. When Christians preached within the Roman Empire, it had the effect of discriminating against other religions and their gods. Romans were typically polytheistic believers, and they worshiped any gods which happened to have worked for them, or who materialized their wishes, such as curing an illness. The Christian monotheistic explanation of God was not only philosophical but also unique in the Roman polytheistic culture. The lack of competition with Christian monotheist theory was another reason for its rapid success.

Among the various schools of thought in ancient China, only Mohism was close to Jesus and his teachings. Mo Tzu (476-390 BC) also came from a family of tradesman, and may also have been a carpenter himself. Mohism represented the voice of the people of the lower classes. Both Confucianism and Mohism were most popular during the Warring States Period (476-221 BC). Lu's Spring and Autumn Annals says, Mo Tzu had "masses of followers, abundant disciples, filling up all areas under the heavens." Like early Christianity, Mohism had strict organization. Their members were well disciplined, dedicated, frugal, hardworking, and were so brave that "they all could jump into fire and run on the edges of swords and would not look back for a moment until death" (Huainan Tzu: Chapter 20). Once one of their leaders committed suicide for his faith, and 183 disciples killed themselves to be buried with him. It is beyond doubt that if there had been good leadership, they would have been an ever-victorious and unbreakable force in all social conflicts, just as Christianity was in the West.

Mo Tzu said, "If all people in the world love each other, states do not attack each other, families do not interfere with each other, there will be neither robbers nor thieves. If kings and fathers are kind to their court officials and sons while court officials and sons are filial to their kings and fathers, the whole world will be orderly." Thus Mohists promoted universal love more than two thousand years ago in China. It carries the same message as Jesus's call for loving your enemies. If Mohism had been put into serious practice, Chinese history would have been different. Mohists would have been able to form a religious organization similar to Christianity, functioning as an internal restricting power to the centralized government, and this power, like the early Christianity, would have been unbreakable. Since the first centralized government appeared in the Qin dynasty (221-207 BC), only the emperor had the space for free thinking. What the people could have wished for was only a peaceful life without interruption. It was no longer possible to harbor the rapid pace of social changes that occurred during the Spring Autumn and Warring States Periods (770-221 BC).

(3) From Confucianism and Christianity to the Chinese and Western Pathways of Humanism

In contrast to Jesus' Christianity, Confucius fitted his Confucianism into the established frame of society where "a king is a king, a minister is a minister, a father is a father, and a son is a son"(Analects, 12.11), and then set up the standards for cultivating the spiritual characters and morals of Confucian scholars. Thus Confucian humanism could only be put into practice inside the established frame of the social order. Unfortunately, there was apparently not always an easily operable mechanism to push forward humanist policy in Chinese history. In the Book of Rites, Confucius says,

Use rituals to decide whether it is right or wrong. Use rituals to determine whether a man was sincere or not. Use rituals to point out the mistakes. Use rituals to set up good examples of benevolence and morals. Use rituals to show the benefits of being modest and conciliatory. Use rituals to show the regulations the people have to follow. If someone does not follow the rituals and regulations, he has to give up his position as a ruler, since people regard him as the cause of disaster. This is called the moderate means.

Here Confucius makes it clear that a ruler has to behave like a ruler, and follow the rituals and regulations. The ideology behind those rituals and regulations in Confucianism is humanism. There is no easily operable mechanism to remove a ruler who runs against Confucian humanist policy. The sentence "he has to give up his position as a ruler, since people regard him as the cause of disaster", clearly indicates that Confucius gave this important yet difficult task to heaven and to the people who did not have their representatives inside the government. If Confucius did not want massive peasant uprisings to serve as a checking system to make sure that the ruler carried on the Confucian humanist policy, then those would only be beautiful yet hollow words. Contrary to Confucianism, Jesus' Christianity combined Confucius' heaven (God) and people to form an unbreakable social force as an internal restricting mechanism to make sure that the government was on the right track of humanism.

Meng Tzu (372-289 BC), a famous Confucian scholar only second to Confucius, developed Confucius' idea further, and proposed some practical measures in a sequence. What could be done when a ruler repeatedly rejected humanist advice of a Confucian minister? Meng Tzu said: 1) The minister had the option to leave; 2) The ruler could be replaced by another one through the ruler's clan. In cooperation with the royal clan, ministers did sometimes change the emperor in subsequent history. Having this first measure in place certainly helped to keep the country and its administration on the right track of humanist policy. Changing rulers in this way often led to violence but usually on a small scale in Chinese history. The violence rarely went beyond the palaces.

Meng Tzu further confirmed the actions of vassal states that overthrew the national ruler when the latter departed from the right track of humanist policy in early Chinese history. Thus when a national ruler departed from humanist policy and his court and clan failed to replace him by another one, a local state could replace the unfitted ruler by revolution or usurpation. This was the second measure for keeping the country and its administration on the right track of humanist policy. Mindful of this theory of Meng Tzu's, Chinese emperors took preemptive action to demolish all vassal states during the Qin and Han dynasties (221 BC -220 AD) and dismissed all local military governors in the Song dynasty (960-1279). Thus no more local military powers could compete with the central government, even when the latter was weakened by its departure from humanist policy.

Meng Tzu did not mention the third measure to keep the country and its administration on the right track of humanist policy.

Confucius and Meng Tzu could not be blamed for the negative effects of the third measure directly, but they were partially responsible. Confucianism did not design an operable mechanism to restrict the emperor's power. As result, the emperor's power was expanded so that the second measure to keep the country and its administration on the right track of humanist policy by usurpation of local military powers was eliminated completely by the emperor himself. In Chinese history there were plenty of loyal ministers who gave up their lives to admonish the emperor. Those ministers were like Christians who gave up their lives for their faith. I think the above quotation from Confucius carries the connotation that massive peasant uprisings were the third measure to keep the country and its administration on the right track of humanist policy.

It was not an easy job for an ordinary peasant to run a county or a province. How could he all of sudden come to run a huge country? It was harder than climbing up the blue sky. This may have stopped some peasants from trying to rebel. Confucians did not wish to consort with the bottom of society like the Mohists and Christians did. In Chinese history, peasants were often stranded in situations where they were going to die whether they rebelled or not. In most such cases, the peasants accepted their fate and died painfully but uttered no sound. But quite a few chose to up-rise against their fate. Chinese peasant uprisings were frequent and massive on scale. They were like the waves in the Yangtze River that rolled one after another. These are the negative effects of less-well- designed Confucian humanism. Another negative effect was the impression Chinese history made on Western historians: The magnificent imperial culture stood in contrast to the primitive poverty of millions of Chinese peasants. One of the protagonists in the classic novel The Scholars raises a proposal to restrict the number of wives one could take in order to improve the situation that too many single men endured in the countryside. People say, there were three thousand beautiful women, including wives, concubines, and maids, in the palaces surrounding just one man, the emperor. If the Confucian ministers had had the rebellious spirit of Christians and Mohists, and had led those women to the countryside to marry those single men, it might have become the unique tale of humanism in Chinese history that was on everyone's lips.

Massive uprisings of peasants did climb up the blue sky by bare hands. There were two dynasties that were founded by the commoners in Chinese history, and their dynasties were stamped with the brand of Chinese peasants. These are the Han (206 BC- 220 AD) and Ming (1368-1644) dynasties. In many aspects, they were worse than the Tang (618-907) and Song (960-1279) dynasties that were founded by bureaucrats. After all, military power was in the hands of the emperor after the Song dynasty. The only source powerful enough to overthrow the emperor and its court when they were weakened by departure from humanist policy were either peasant uprisings or foreign invaders, which was exactly what happened in subsequent history. It is impossible to determine whether Confucius and Meng Tzu considered the foreign powers next door as part of their third measurement to keep the country and its administration on the right track of humanist policy. Foreign invaders did indeed enter in Chinese politics along with peasant uprisings as part of the third measurement. That is the Yuan(1272-1368) and Qing(1644-1911) dynasties, which saw the cruel blood shedding of a foreign invasion in addition to maintaining a much lower cultural level.

One of the reasons for the orderly prosperity during the reign of Emperors Literate and Scenery (Wen and Jing, 179-140 BC) was the presence of large vassal states inside their empire, which served as a restraining factor to keep the country and its administration on the track of humanist policy. Both Emperors Literate and Scenery were remarkably modest and self-refrained and stayed away from excess ambitions. During the rebellion of seven vassal states, Emperor Scenery executed his prime minister at the request of those rebel vassal states. The general who led the army to put down the rebellion refused repeatedly to obey the orders from the Emperor who asked the general to rescue his brother, whose capital city was under attacks by those rebel vassal states. Those two incidents indicate that the Chinese government was far from totalitarian because of the presence of vassal states at that time.

During the reign of King Li of Chou (?877-841 BC), the people of the capital rose up in rebellion. They swamped into the palace with sticks and farm tools in hand. King Li ran away and never dared to come back. The lord of a vassal state came to the capital as the temporary king for fourteen years, and then returned the throne to the royal family of Chou. Such a peaceful transition of the central power of the nation was praise-worthy but unfortunately exceptional in Chinese history. In contrast, when the totalitarian government was well established later in China, it usually took millions of lives to overthrow an unfit government or to put down a massive peasant rebellion. One example was the Taiping rebellion (1850-1864) that also lasted fourteen years, occupied almost half of China, and resulted in more than twenty million deaths but failed. From the records, we can see that the policies of the Taiping rebellion were much more humanist than the Qing dynasty (1644-1911). They even advocated equal rights of men and women, and public ownership of land.

(4) The Two Levels of Society and the Different Pathways of Chinese and Western Humanism

The genetically coded primary Society was the basic social organization of man immediately above families in ancient time. Bands and tribes are regarded as primary societies. Human nature or intuition was the major force to keep primary society stable and functioning.

Secondary society is a creation of human culture and has nothing to do with human genetics and human nature. Secondary society has limitless possible types, and each one may have its own evolutionary pathway. Modern secondary societies become similar, but ancient societies were much more diversified. According to Aristotle, ancient Greece had 158 political systems worth describing. The introduction of social stratification and other institutions that go against human nature is often necessary to keep a secondary society stable.

Our present secondary society is a strictly rational system that does not tolerate irrational thinking. We need rational thinking if we are aiming at social achievements such as well paid positions or if we are materializing a goal in the physical world such as building a house. Rational thinking enables us to reach our goals. But if we are relaxing on the sofa with our family and are aiming to enjoy ourselves, rational thought does not do us any good. Under such circumstances, it is quite okay if we talk nonsense or allow ourselves to entertain weird daydreams. Only primary society tolerates both irrational and rational thinking, living up to the dictum: *An' it harm none, do what thou wilt.*

Once Jesus' Christianity entered the center of secular social power, they too stressed the value of rational thinking. In history, some witches were in a state of irrational thinking, kept saying weird things, and expounding bizarre ideas. Many of them were tried and burned to death in so-called witch-hunts in many Christian countries. Nowadays, pastors and priests are graduates of theological schools, and the son of an ordinary carpenter will not be allowed to preach, unless he has the qualification. In many ways, ancient primary society was more humanist than modern secondary society.

In the West, the first secondary societies were city states, which arose both in the Middle East and in ancient Greece. Primary society quickly disintegrated to form a secondary society of free individuals. Secondary society, as a creation of man, has numerous pathways to take, and each one needs a set of ideology and corresponding social structure, often stratification, to support the ideology. As different individuals had different ideas as to what direction the society should go, political instability and violent conflicts were inevitable. In the Middle East, it was documented that the appearance of states was associated with shortened life spans. It was a chaotic nightmare to the people who had been accustomed to the much more humanist primary society. The only hope they had was God and other superpowers. On the other hand, no ruler could restore order overnight in a population that knew nothing about discipline and obedience. It was thus inevitable that the people would start to worship supernatural powers. Various magnificent constructions dedicated to gods appeared in the Middle East, Ancient Greece, and in Latin and South America. The master of such secondary societies was God, and people were only the servicemen to God. In the service of God, man more readily put up with inhumane living conditions.

After such an unusual start, human civilization was a process in which secondary society was being improved to better harbor human nature. Emphasis was shifting from God to man, and man was pursuing his self realization and self emancipation. In spite of the dramatic changes our secondary society has taken, human nature remains the same. Thus it was also a process in which man lost his way and then looked for his origins to set back in touch with himself.

As mentioned in Essay 1, the last five thousand years of human civilization of war were an upward spiral with a continuing increase in battles and imperial size and in social inequality. These increases in battles were all negative factors for humanism, and hindered its social movement. But human conditions were improved during the last few hundred years, and the shift from God to man did take place over a long time.

The process of Chinese humanism was quite different from that in the West. Both Lao Tzu and Confucius admired ancient society and regarded it as their ideal society. Lao Tzu says, "Heaven and earth coalesce and it rains sweet dew. The people, no one ordering them, self balance to equality." "The Tao of nature is to pare back abundance and add to the insufficient."(Tao Te Ching, Chapters 32, 77). According to Taoist philosophy, the ancient primary society was close to the ideal of humanism, and the following social structure in Chinese early civilization enabled people to remain in primary or quasi- primary society:

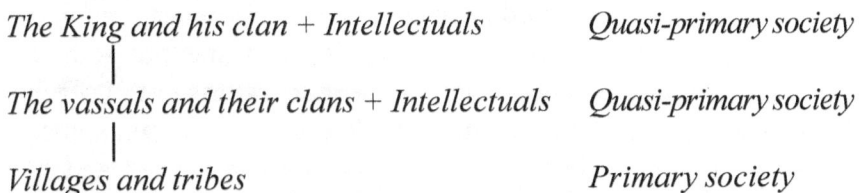

The King and his clan + Intellectuals *Quasi-primary society*

The vassals and their clans + Intellectuals *Quasi-primary society*

Villages and tribes *Primary society*

Under such a social structure in their early years of civilization, Chinese people were able to build their social network based on face to face interaction, which was not distorted by external forces other than human nature. (Essay 1) The above social structure covered nearly two thousand years and three dynasties. Ancient records regard the three dynasties, Hsia, Shang, and Chou, as a continuous cultural tradition but also outline the differences among the three dynasties. The following is my translated summary from The Rites comparing the three dynasties:

Hsia (2200-1766 BC): *The culture of Hia respects fate, pays respect to gods and ghosts but keeps a distance from them, is close to human nature and is loyal, delivers rewards and emoluments before punishment and power, is intimate but has no respect. The people are primitive, foolish, proud and wild, simple and uncultivated. The culture of Hsia does not take words lightly, does not require perfection, does not ask a lot from people, its people are not bored with their families and relatives, and its people have little to complain about.*

Shang (1765-1123 BC): *The culture of Shang respects gods, leads its people in service to gods, puts ghosts before rituals, delivers punishments before rewards, and its people are respectful but not close. Its people are restless and shameless. The culture of Shang does not take rituals lightly, expects a lot from the people.*

Chou (1122-256 BC): *The culture of Chou respects rituals and charity, pays respect to gods and ghosts but keeps a distance from them, is close to human nature and loyalty, rewards and punishes with a ranking system. Its people are close but have no respect for each other, are clever, cultivated, but cheating without shame. The culture of Chou forces people to meet its needs, does not take gods lightly, exhausts the system of rewards and punishments.*

From the above records, we can see the difference among the three dynasties: Both Hsia and Chou paid due respect to gods and ghosts but kept a distance from them. Shang stressed the service to gods and ghosts while relying heavily on force and punishment. More than a hundred thousand oracle bones were recovered, and they showed that Shang often waged military attacks on its neighbors, and human sacrifices numbering more than ten thousand. A notable Chinese historian (Wang 2004) held the view that class polarization first appeared during the Shang dynasty, and the Hsia dynasty was, therefore, a classless primitive society.

With the above social structure, especially during the Hsia and Chou dynasties, the society was mainly stabilized by human nature. There was no need to rely on forceful gods or ghosts such as those that cost Socrates' life. If the people harbored unnatural goals, they lacked the social mechanism to reach their goals. During the Shang dynasty, there might be such goals such as attacking peaceful neighbors and the drive to improve one's fortune, leading to the emergence of class stratification for the first time. The Chou dynasty abandoned the Shang's culture of gods and ghosts but used a more humanist way to stabilize any class polarization, the ritual system. Here I call the humanist policy of the Hsia dynasty, the natural humanism. The shift from gods to man in the early years of the Chou dynasty is comparable to the shift from nature to human society in the ancient Greek thinkers. These were the beginning of humanist social movement by man.

In the Middle East, parallel to the huge constructions dedicated to gods, the first center of social power was concentrated among religious staff, priests and witches. Even when secular kings were separated and had their own social networks to control the population, religious centers remained powerful entities that owned vast areas of land and employed massive numbers of people. In many ways, religious centers shared power with the government. Even the priests and priestesses of the Apollo Temple at Delphi of ancient Greece served as influential consultants to the local kings.

When the Israeli people developed their monotheist religion, they had a bible that lists the major laws and moral norms for the society as dictated by God. The priests (prophets) had the power to interpret and preach those laws and norms, and the government was only responsible to carry out those laws and norms. Thus those religious centers functioned very much like today's parliaments in the Western democratic governments. This contrasts well to the religious centers in ancient China.

For nearly two thousand years, the dominating religions in Chinese history were Confucianism, Taoism, and Buddhism. The function of those religions was comparable to that of a Minister of Culture in the imperial government, and had no power to interfere with any laws. The Minister of Culture could of course be dismissed at the emperor's will. Closing down temples and banning a certain religion occurred frequently in Chinese history.

Unlike Taoism and Buddhism, Confucianism was involved in politics. Such involvement was through the employment of Confucian scholars as government officials. Confucianism was never part of the imperial government. Nevertheless, the imperial government had the power to modify Confucianism at will. According to John King Fairbank (1902-1991), it was the emperor (Hanwudi, 140-87 BC) who created the first official version of Confucianism by hybridizing Confucianism with Legalism to suit his needs for a centralized government. Fairbank called it Imperial Confucianism, which was fundamentally different from the Confucianism founded by Confucius and Meng Tzu. The imperialist system with absolute power was a major setback for humanism in Chinese history, though it also kept local lords in check. This setback remained as the negative force to suppress the subjective expressivity in subsequent Chinese history. (Essay 9)

With the government being pressured by the continuous uprising of the peasants and influenced by Taoism and Confucianism, humanism did achieve some major progress in Chinese history against the increased social inequality and the further concentrated power of the emperor and his court. The following is what came to my mind while I was writing:

1). Taoist religion and Buddhism, first appeared during the late Han dynasty(25- 220), provided a place of retreat from the inhumane secondary society. Although no place was immune to the imperial power, religious temples were safer shelters to many who offended the government.

2). Taoist philosophy provided some practical techniques that helped the people to cope with the mental injuries inflicted by secondary society.

3). Confucianism developed into a so called Idealist Philosophy during the Song and Ming dynasties (960-1644), which further separated the spiritual cultivation of individual people from politics and the reality of secondary society. This provided an easily accessible and largely available spiritual retreat for those in need.

4). Human sacrifices were down significantly since the beginning of the social moment of humanism, though foot-binding and other customs against women appeared. Cruel punishments such as "ten thousand cuts" and "stripping the skin off" remained.

5). Shaped and influenced by the ideal egalitarian society of Taoist philosophy, class polarization in the countryside was much less evident than in the West. Before the Communist land reformation during the 1950s, the majority of land was roughly equally owned by the majority of the rural population. Both landlords and landless peasants were few.

6). Absolute poverty of lacking food, clothes, shelters and other basic requirements for living was never eliminated in Chinese history, and I would say, it was even worse than the early years of the Chou dynasty. The number of deaths in war increased significantly.

(5) Epilogue: The Spiritual Character of Confucian Scholars

Both Christianity and Confucianism emphasize the spiritual characters of their followers, though Confucianism does not rely on God to consecrate its followers' spirit. Confucius spoke in great details when explaining the ideal image of a Confucian gentleman (junzi), but he was reluctant to name anyone who met the criteria of benevolence. He apparently idealized and consecrated the spiritual characters of a Confucian gentleman. Thus Confucian scholars' spiritual cultivation became an artistic pursuit, and the spiritual character was seen like a piece of art that was detached from any social power or godly power. Like the early Christians found joy in poverty while willing to die for their faith, Confucian scholars displayed unmatched courage and spiritual character in spite of their poverty.

One of those scholars was Square (Fang Xiaoru or Square Filial-Confucianism, 1357-1402), who refused to cooperate with the new emperor in spite of a total of 873 people including himself, his family, relatives, and friends being executed. As he kept criticizing and even cursing the emperor to his majesty's face, his mouth was ripped across from ear to ear, and even that failed to silence him. He was made to watch his brother's execution, and tears welled out his eyes. The brother chanted a lofty and heroic poem to condole Square:

My dear brother, you need not wash your face with tears,
Die of benevolence and righteousness, and here's.
From the royal ornamental column and a thousand years,
We then travel home together, chanting to our ears.

After Square was cut in two at the waist as the execution required, he still managed to write ten and a half Chinese characters with his own blood to show his faith and condemn the emperor.

On the other hand, the new emperor was the uncle who dethroned his nephew. What difference was there as to which one of their families became the emperor? Was there any need to be so serious? It was at most a ritual issue but far from the issue of Confucian humanist policy. In the above quotation (Section 1), Confucius set up rituals as the criteria by which to judge a ruler's behavior. He clearly intended those rituals to promote his humanist policy. In fact, the nephew emperor violated the rituals first by trying to undermine his uncle's vassal state, and Confucian court officials, including Square, did not stop him. Paradoxically, the nephew's wish to substantially reduce the power of vassal states was only accomplished by his uncle. Wasn't the ascent to the throne the same whoever drafted the imperial edict? Why did the emperor have to force Square to draft it while the latter determined not to? This was an extremity of rational thinking in secondary society that never occurred in primary society. If Square was the lord of a vassal state, how did the emperor dare to ask for a rebuff to come to Square for the draft?

Therefore, those 873 deaths were not for such rubbishy issues as who was the right man for the throne from the same family. It was to defend the sacred nature of the spiritual character of Confucian scholars that Confucius and Meng Tzu outlined some two thousand years ago. It was like Pygmalion in Greek mythology who so loves the ivory figurine he has sculpted so that he gives up the happiness of sexual love and family. He thinks his figurine is the most beautiful in the whole world, and he is willing to sacrifice for the beauty he has created. Such sacrifice is radiating with beauty of the spiritual realm, far above secular pursuits such as the size and power of an empire that increased in the last five thousand years against human nature. Whenever I feel heartache about the dedication of Confucian scholars to their faith in Chinese history, I rely on my above interpretation to make me feel better.

Appendix 1. The Movie Hero and Chinese Taoist Philosophy

In Chinese history, intellectuals were Confucian in the government office but Taoist at home. Taoism became the guiding philosophy of Chinese spare time activities, including fine arts such as painting, music, calligraphy, and various ways to keep us in good health such as medicine and physical exercises. Typically, Taoists were nonofficial hermits who devoted their talents to admiring nature and the Chinese landscape. The moral spirit of Chinese swordsmanship was to cut the throat of social power and wealth to help the poor, therefore, nonofficial. Martial arts are also a form of physical exercise. As a result they have been deeply influenced by Taoist philosophy, which is the hidden message the movie Hero is trying to convey. It is impossible for a Westerner to fully understand and appreciate this movie without some basic knowledge of Chinese Taoist philosophy.

The first principle belief of Taoism is the so-called the united One of heaven and man. In other words, the human world and the natural world are one world, and humans should stay as part of Nature. In the modern scientific view, the whole universe including humans and animals are made of the same atoms, but Taoist philosophy emphasizes the spiritual side. The ideology of a good swordsman is that he is acting on behalf of both nature and man, or God in the Western terms, but not for himself. This is contrary to modern Western philosophy where a self actualization or individual freedom is the ultimate goal.

The movie Hero is the story of five swordsmen. There are four assassins headed by Nameless, played by Jet Li, and their target is the king, who is also the fifth swordsman. There are three minor characters: an elderly blind musician, an old calligraphy master, and Moon, the maid of one of the swordsmen named Broken Sword. These eight characters present different facets of the ideal image of a Taoist hero, or the Chinese traditional hero. The story is told and retold by Nameless to the king, and each of his retellings conflicts with the previous ones but brings the fighting sides closer to a spiritual unity of humankind and the universe, giving further dimensions to the movie's complexity and its high level of ideology.

When Nameless fights his duel with the assassin Sky, a trembling white-bearded musician gropes back to play his final tune for the two. Music and swordsmanship are said to be based on the same principles and share the same idea of spiritual perfection: The perfect tune makes no sound. This is a direct quotation from the first founder of Taoism, Lao Tzu, and it also alludes to the movie's final conclusion that a perfect swordsman uses no weapon. During their duel, the two stood still face to face for a whole hour with their eyes closed to fight each other fiercely in their minds. To an ordinary audience, this plot may sound mysterious and remote. This obscurity is a unique feature of Taoism. Some Taoist monks and nuns sat meditating on the mysterious nature of the universe as a religious practice. It is also worthwhile to notice that in the primitive primary society, dispute was often resolved by demonstration of power rather than a real fight.

When Nameless comes to fight Broken Sword and Snow, the third and fourth swordsman and swordswoman who happen to be lovers, calligraphy becomes the main concern of the movie. Broken Sword and Sky have developed new fighting techniques through the practice of calligraphy. Again, calligraphy and swordsmanship are said to base on the same principles. Nameless has to study Broken Sword's calligraphy to understand his new fighting techniques in order to beat them. Broken Sword writes the words SWORD and All UNDER THE HEAVENS for Nameless. "All under the heavens" indicates the whole humankind and the united One of man and nature. There is no room for fighting and killing in such a united world. To act in accordance with such a high ideology, the king gives his sword to his assassin Nameless, who then has the chance to kill the king but misses it deliberately. The king, the fifth swordsman, finally understands Broken Sword's calligraphy. The Chinese character SWORD written by Broken Sword, contains the connotation of perfect swordsmanship and refers to the notion that there is neither a sword in the hands nor a dagger in the heart but a broad mind to embrace the whole world.

When you embrace the whole world, you see only friends and no enemies. When you embrace the whole universe, you forget your own life and death. A Westerner will complain of the emotionless

216

faces of the characters, especially the protagonist or hero of the movie, Nameless. But it is the essence of the ideal hero who treats matters of life and death with a plain emotionless manner, neither hot-headed nor cold-hearted.

The Taoist aesthetic motto is: Heaven and earth have great beauty but do not say a word; perfect beauty has no shape. The Taoist aesthetic ideal is pristine simplicity. The movie Hero presents stunning two hours of flowing of artistic images. Many people are impressed by its beautiful scenes but understand little of the conflicting stories.

The producer has made every effort to make the movie fit in line with Taoist aesthetics. In a way, the movie tries to visualize Taoist aesthetics to its viewers. Although the images are impressive, they are simple in terms of colour. The landscapes are often mono-coloured, yellow, blue, or green. The swordsmen wear robes of a colour similar to the landscape. The whole movie has no images of flowers or any delicate ornaments, though one may expect to see those things in the setting of a royal palace.

Yin yang and the five elements, earth, wood, metal, fire, and water with the latter subduing the former one, i.e., water subduing fire subduing metal subduing wood subduing earth and earth subduing water, are now regarded as part of Taoist philosophy and religion. The king in Hero is based on the historical king of the Qin dynasty (221-207 BC), who believed in this theory. Each Chinese dynasty was said to represent one of the five elements, Chou (1122-256 BC) for fire, Qin for water, and so on. Each element has its own colour, yellow for earth, green for wood, white for metal, red for fire, and black for water. In the movie Hero, the king and all his court officials and soldiers are dressed either in black or in colours just as dark. The scene surrounding the five fighting swordsmen is shifting over the five colours: yellow, green including blue, white, red, and black. But the main colour is yellow that is both the colour of the first assassin Sky and the colour of the last scene when Broken Sword and Snow commit suicide together. The first one in the above list of the five elements is the yellow earth that represents the common ancestor of all Chinese people, the Yellow Emperor. The green colour including blue represents the Hsia dynasty. The

Chinese called their country Hua Hsia, which derived from the Hsia people. The only battlefield scene in this movie is when Qin fights with another state, the representative of Chou. A red-hued school of calligraphy becomes the centre beside the battlefield. It is consistent with the above theory. When Nameless is executed and buried as a hero, his body is covered with a large sheet of red cloth surrounded by black soldiers. The red fire of Chou is over, and the black water of Qin sets in.

The third and fourth lines of the Taoist bible, Tao Te Ching, read as follows:

Non-being names the beginning of heavens and earth.
Being names the mother of all things.

Ancient Chinese texts were not punctuated and the reader had to break at his own discretion. Depending on where the comma locates in those sentences, an alternative interpretation of the same Chinese words is as follows:

Nameless is the beginning of heavens and earth.
The named is the mother of all things.

In the place of God, Chinese Taoist philosophy designs the concept of Tao. Tao is said to be beyond human imagination. There is no name for Tao, since a name is part of our world, and Tao is beyond the universe. That's why Tao was able to create the universe. In the two versions of the above quotation, non-being and nameless are apparently referring to Tao. Swordsman Nameless in the movie Hero obviously hints at Tao, since the movies tries to create a Taoist hero Nameless. I consider such attempts a blasphemy.

As a movie, Hero is a pure fiction with a historical setting. If the audience knows the history, the movie will leave them in a deep fog, wondering what the producer really meant to say but could not get across.

The historical king of Qin was the most notorious figure in Chinese history. After his success in uniting China, he moved twelve hundred thousand rich families, more than a million people as estimated, from the conquered territory to his capital. To build new palaces that covered some fifty miles, he moved away eighty thousand households. He used 700,000 prisoners or three and a half per cent of the population to build his tomb, and all of those workers were doomed to be killed after they finished the job. Confucius and his followers promoted governments of knowledge and virtue more than two centuries before the king, and Alexander the Great led only 35,000 troops to conquer Persia a century earlier.

In history, there was a man who tried to force the king of Qin to withdraw his troops and return the conquered land by brandishing a poisoned dagger, since there had been a successful confrontation of this kind before. Two men had killed themselves to enable this man to have such a chance. The man tried to kill the king but missed, and the king escaped from his grip. Many details of this event were recorded. In more than two thousand years, this heroic story fascinated Chinese people and warmed their hearts. It was a beacon of hope in the darkness when people had to swallow their tears under a tyrant's rule. Their heroic deaths are remembered forever by the Chinese people. Although the history is similar to the movie of Hero in many ways, a failed assassination and a giving up make the difference even the latter is by the name of mankind.

The historical king of Qin was once attracted by and obsessed with the Taoist idea of immortal real people. He even called himself the real man instead of the king. His Taoist consultants decided that the king's behaviour was contrary to the ideology of Taoism, which emphasizes a non-assertive and natural way. In their view, the king would never become an immortal real man. They all escaped and left no trace. The king was so enraged that he buried 460 Confucian scholars alive who had nothing to do with those fugitives. The movie's attempt to beautify the king of Qin is groundless, farfetched, and runs against the Taoist ideology the movie is trying to convey. This contradiction leaves no clear message in the end, and the audience is left in a puzzle.

There has been a groundless belief in recent years that ancient Chinese people wanted a united nation to stop wars among the leftover states. There is no solid evidence to support such a belief. Except for a few with power, the majority of people certainly did not want to see millions losing their lives for this unity.

In this movie, the king is wise, and shares this same idea with his assassins: He conquers the world for the sake of humankind. The historical king of Qin did succeed in uniting China, but he succeeded only by militarizing his whole population and imposing marshal law, the total war policy. He sacrificed the people's basic needs for this unnatural goal that went against the more humane philosophical foundations laid down earlier by Lao Tzu, Confucius, and other thinkers. The historical king of Qin's policy was ridiculed by many in his time, and his kingdom was called the Beast State.

After the historical king of Qin died, there was a rebellion, and his dynasty was soon finished when the revolting force overwhelmed this oppressive regime. After six years of chaos and turmoil, a commoner rose to the throne as the new emperor of China. A scholar looked down upon this commoner emperor, and said: *There are no heroes in the world so that such a bloke has come to the fore.*

The founder of the Communist China, Chairman Mao, was often worried about his lack of education when meeting knowledgeable professors. During the Great Cultural Revolution from 1966 to 1976 when Mao waged his last battle against intellectuals who were better educated than he was, at least twice Mao lost his mind not knowing if he was a bloke or a hero. According to Mao's secretary Li Rui, millions of people died in a famine caused by Mao's errors in the late 1950s and the early 1960s. Mao admired the king of Qin and even compared himself to him.

There is a strong renaissance today in China of the long forgotten Taoism and other ancient ideologies. Since the young generations have not been taught about the recent communist history, they identify Mao as a national hero, believing he was as traditional as Taoism is. Mao might have been attracted by Taoism just as the historical king of Qin was, but neither of them was a sincere Taoist believer. Taoism teaches us to accept reality as it is without any emotion but with serenity, a wordless beauty of the mind. We need not to say that those such as the king and Mao, who did not genuinely believe in Taoism, are part of the beauty.

On the other hand, people who lived under a totalitarian regime had nothing to do except admired their leaders. Hero provides a way for those people to admire their own sacrifices which, they felt, had not been acknowledged. The two lover swordsmen, Broken Sword and Snow, are the most unforgettable characters. Their romance and their long endeavour to assassinate the king for the people's sake end as a futile sacrifice. What a pain it is! Fine arts sometimes have the same quality as religions: soothing the pain with beauty.

To be precise, there is no hero in the movie Hero, which speaks so clearly and beautifully: *There was not a hero either in the real world, but there is sacrifice by the people that has not been recognized.*

*   *   *

Afterword: The Tragedy of Chinese History

Ironically, the Movie Hero would become a masterpiece of tragedy if we replaced the king of the movie with the historical king of Qin. Its significance relies on the fact that it illustrates the tragic side of Chinese history. People with the loftiest ideology in the world gave up their lives heroically and nobly to enable a shameless bloke to become the emperor to muddle up with their national affairs and ruin their lives. Let us imagine:

Hitler did not commit suicide, and he met face-to-face with four generals of the Allied Force who first entered Berlin. They all had the desire to kill Hitler with their own hands. As Hitler had his gun, so their guns at one time were pointing to each other. All of a sudden, one of generals pushed his way into the front: "Please let me shoot Hitler! I have struggled for twelve years for this day. Please give all your guns to me!" He lost his whole family under the iron rule of Hitler, and both his father and mother died tragically in Nazi camps.

After he collected the three guns from the other three generals, he suddenly shouted, "For the sake of Europe and for the sake of the world, we cannot kill Hitler. Listen to me, Hitler is the only hope for a united Europe. Without Hitler, we will face a divided Europe and a divided world with endless wars and endless suffering! For the world's sake and for the people's sake, I forgive Hitler for his cruel killing of my family, because we need Hitler for a united Europe."

With tears streaming down his face, Hitler said, "Dear Friend, I am so happy to hear those words from the bottom of your heart. I have not been understood by the world, by the people, and even not by my ministers and generals. I applied violence for the world's sake, and I have killed for the people's sake. Finally, I have one man who understands my lofty purpose. With such a friend in the world, I feel content to die!"

After those words, Hitler threw his gun to the three other generals, and turned his back to them, and said, "Please make your decision for the world on this shot!"

The three generals decided not to shoot Hitler. Though it was a tough decision for him, Hitler ordered the execution of the four generals for assassination attempts as his government and people demanded.

Both Britain and Russia had a large territory outside Europe and the United States was an American country. If Europe were isolated as the ancient China, it would have been most likely that Hitler united Europe by force but his empire disintegrated immediately after his death to leave Europe in a political situation similar to what is now.

As mentioned in Essay 1, ancient China was like today's world with a powerless United Nations. The Chinese national king and his court had only the largest central state. This central state lost most of its territory in 841 BC because of the barbarian invasion and internal turmoil. During the subsequent Spring Autumn Period (770-476 BC), the national king was only symbolic, since his territory was no longer the largest among the hundreds of states. The ideal political situation sought out during this period was the puppet king plus a hegemonic state to function as the original super state. The first hegemonic state used to call on all states to form an alliance in order to keep out barbarian invasions and to enable cooperation among different states.

During the Warring States Period (476-221 BC) when seven major states competed with each other, a fundamental social transformation took place, which was comparable to the one that transformed the whole Europe after the French Revolution in 1789. The subsequent wars served no longer to select a hegemonic leader to form a loose confederation but represented the violent conflicts of different political ideologies and different ways of life. In both modern Europe and ancient China, the popular political intention was to keep a balance among different powers with different ideologies. That's why this dangerous situation lasted more than two hundred years, and many powerless small states were able to survive.

Like Nazi Germany, the State Qin with by far the largest military power represented a ruthless regimented lifestyle. Such a state though militarily powerful lacked the ability to unite Europe or China by pure force, since most people disliked such a way of life. Like Nazi Germany, State Qin applied the most dishonourable diplomatic policy: They bribed the high ranking officials of the other six states and assassinated those who refused the bribery. According to Chinese records, a Qin general once, at the end of a battle, buried four hundred thousand surrendered soldiers alive, which represented two percent of the Chinese population. No lofty political goal could be reached by such ruthless killing and such dishonourable diplomatic trickery. Such tricks only work once because nobody can be fooled twice. But once was often enough to change history.

After the Qin united China in 221 BC, there was a long debate and struggle between the original system of confederation with a super state and the later system with a centralized bureaucratic government of provinces and counties. It was only during the reign of Emperor Wu of the Han dynasty (140-86 BC) when the latter system took control of China and was set up as the norm for the subsequent history until 1911. Emperor Wu was indeed ambitious. The Chinese population was reduced by half during his reign. It means some fifteen millions of Chinese people lost their lives, either killed or died of starvation, for his historical achievement. Shortly before his death, Emperor Wu admitted that he had behaved exactly like the king of Qin. Nevertheless, during the reign of those two notorious kings or emperors, millions lost their lives. The author of the movie Hero took the liberty to assume that those people gave their lives willingly and nobly for a political system of centralized bureaucratic government. Thus those deaths were no longer tragic but honourable. I think we had better left those deaths remain tragic. A Chinese poet from the Tang dynasty wrote:

Mountains, rivers, lakes, and lands all become battlefields,
How can the people continue to enjoy their labour in the farm fields?
I beg you not to ask how to receive a title from the imperial order,
Ten thousand skeletons decay in the wilderness to achieve one general's honour.

Will our United Nations become a worldly imperial power when an accelerating warring phase occurs in the future like in ancient Chinese and modern European history? Let's hope Not.

Appendix 2. Taoism and Mao Zedong

I think the best words to describe Mao Zedong (1893-1976), the founder of Communist China, are those he said when he was young: Battling with heaven, the joy is limitless; battling with Earth, the joy is limitless; battling with people, the joy is limitless. As far as his life and his impact on the country he controlled from 1949 to 1976, Mao was as good as those words. The West and the former Soviet Union used to complain about the bellicose cock like China under the Communist rule. It was really the spirit of Mao himself, and it represented neither Chinese people nor all the party members. Mao turned his country, his government, and his family upside down many times over, and left no stone unturned. He certainly practiced those three phrases through his whole life. If we put what he said aside and study the way of his thinking, it is not surprising to find some strong elements of Chinese tradition, especially Taoism.

Mao was, of course, not a sincere and conscious Taoist thinker. But we can, nevertheless, understand Mao and his China much better if we adapt to a Taoist perspective. Karl Marx once said, I am not a Marxist myself. What Marx meant is that he did not practice Marxism but he certainly believed in the system he had developed and promoted. Mao used to say he believed in Confucianism in his early years but changed to Marxism later. However, I think Mao's thought is far away from either Marxism or Confucianism but close to Taoism. Marxism has often been criticized for its economy-determinist view. The influence of economic determinism on human thought and behavior became traceless in Mao's China. Mao stressed the importance of political ideology and carried out an ever-lasting battle against those who had a tendency to economy-determinism. In the Great Cultural Revolution, whoever had some connection with economy, or agricultural/industrial production was subjected to Mao's attacks. According to Marx, proletarian revolution only occurs after the whole world has entered into highly developed capitalist society. Mao labeled his revolution of peasants with Marxism. If we dismiss the part Lenin and Mao creatively added to Marxism, namely, separate Marxism from Leninism and Maoism, there is nothing of Marxism but old Chinese tradition in Mao's thought.

As to the Chinese traditional ideology, many authors have written on the influence of Confucianism on Mao. But I think Mao is closer to Taoism but farther away from Confucianism. In Chinese history, intellectuals were Confucians in the government office but Taoists at home. They relied on Taoist teachings to live an idle rural life, pursuing self-wellbeing. Both Lao Tzu and Chuang Tzu quoted the Chinese self-sufficient rural economy as their ideal society. As the result, the dominant ideology was not Confucianism but Taoism in the Chinese countryside.

If there was still some trace of Confucian influence in the Chinese rural areas, it was confined within the intellectual households. What peasants were fond of were Buddhism and Taoism, and they regarded Confucianism as something for educated people. Mao's family was not an intellectual one: His father was an ordinary peasant who had been a soldier and a merchant for a few years. He was fiercely opposed to Mao's further education to become an intellectual. Mao's mother was a Buddhist believer. Mao and his mother once discussed how to persuade Mao's father to believe in Buddhism. After running away from a tiger, his father did come to Buddhism and occasionally worshiped Buddha in the temples. In China most people could not tell Buddhism from Taoism but few failed to notice the difference between Confucianism and Taoism/Buddhism. Ordinary people like Mao's father never went to a Confucian temple, which was apparently not a proper place for them. Buddhism is far away from politics but Taoism is quite different. There is a strong political element in Taoism, which advocates egalitarianism. Mao's hometown was within the reach of the Society of Brothers, a peasant organization influenced by Taoist ideology. Therefore, Mao's family was at the level where the ideology was Taoism. Mao was soaked with the spirit of Taoism through what he saw and heard during his early childhood.

Chou En-lai's family was different, a traditional intellectual household. His lifestyle, graceful and poised, was close to the Confucius's golden mean, since he received a good Confucian education at home in his early years. Mao was also taught the five classics and the four books of Confucianism but during a period of cultural transition from the old to the new, it was not enough to let him surpass his family's influence.

Mao's many biographies mentioned how sympathetic to the poor Mao was as a child: He worked with his mother against his father's will; he gave rice to those who needed it; he even collaborated with the laborers against his father's interest. These are believable. It was however common in rural China where the father struggled to increase his fortune but children and women doled out alms. Lao Tzu says, "Heaven and earth coalesce and it rains sweet dew. The people, no one ordering them, self balance to equality." "The Tao of nature is to pare back abundance and add to the insufficient."(Tao Te Ching, Chapters 32, 77) Thus according to Taoist theory, it is our nature to self balance to equality by helping the poor, and wealth-building comes from our culture. Children and women are less contaminated by modern culture in comparison to men.

Taoism has the egalitarian primary society as its ideal society. In comparison with cities, the Chinese countryside is closer to primary society. In the mainland China, peasants are traditionally said to be believers in ultra-equalitarianism, which is in fact the Taoist ideal. Since such an ideal is not compatible with modern society, authority labeled it as ultra-equalitarianism. Among the Chinese Communist leaders, Mao's thought was much closer to Taoist egalitarianism than the others. That's why he put most leaders aside and was headstrong in pursuing some ultra-leftist policies such as the Great Cultural Revolution.

Some scholars say Chinese dynasties all adapted to Huang Lao (Yellow Emperor and Lao Tzu) at the core but dressed up as Confucianism. We can also say Mao was Huang Lao at the core but put on a face of Marxism. Mao led his country into an endless chaos, and people call it sarcastically running cycles of malarial fever. When one is suffering from malaria, he has a fever every two days but becomes normal between. Mao's political movements were all like that, and achieving nothing except for exhaustion. In the end, it was consisted with the Taoist principle: non-action though not intentionally. After Mao died, China has progressed rapidly in economy, arts, ideology and so on, and even the landscape changes with each passing day and passing month. Under such a contrast, Mao's China was really chaotic non-action.

Marx saw capitalism as the final stage in the evolution of human society, like a man of advanced age suffering from incurable cancer, and he prescribed communism as the remedy. Mao mixed it up with his childhood dream, which was also the Chinese poor peasants' dream, a simple, peaceful life free of inequality and exploitation. It is amazing that Mao as the leader of the most populous country in the world did not envision any necessary changes in the new horizons brought up by various revolutions in the West since the Renaissance. On the contrary, Mao battled fiercely against those who had some new vision. He literally suffocated all progressive ideas.

Half of Mao's bed was piled up with ancient Chinese books, from which one may speculate how his family life was. Mao envied other Chinese leaders' happy families and complaining his was an exception. He spent his last birthday with a group of young women, nurses and secretaries. His wife, Jiang Qing, cooked his favorite fish soup as a birthday present in order to ask for a chance to see him. He asked one of those girls to deliver his message: "Leave the soup and do not come in!" When I was a student at Peking University, Mao's daughter was there too. It was said that the daughter could see him only on special occasions. During the Great Cultural Revolution, Jiang Qing was once complaining with tears in front of an audience of more than ten thousand that class struggle had been carried out into her family. Her unusual remarks frightened Mao's daughter-in-law so much that she ran away hidden immediately.

According to his private physician, Mao lived a very simple life: He often wore pajamas all day and only dressed up for receiving guests. Even then he wore only shorts to show his scorn for world powers when he received Khrushchev at his swimming pool. He never brushed his teeth, and never took a bath or shower. Mao lived in the Imperial Park inside the Forbidden City where he grew vegetables instead of flowers in his garden. Once he said, "You may grow flowers in public places. It is no good having flowers in private areas, where we should grow more useful plants such as vegetables and fruits." After these remarks, thousands of potted plants were removed from private homes and left along the streets. Nearly three decades have passed since his death. His children have reached their later years but all of them lived as ordinary citizens, unlike later national leaders whose children either reached nationally prominent positions or became millionaires overnight. Mao's daughter's worn-out and patched clothes invited comments: *You are the only one in the capital who wears such shabby clothes.*

Land reform, or the equal distribution of land ownership, was not very successful in other countries except China. The equal distribution of land and the limiting of landholding had occurred in Chinese history as a persistent policy, though Mao was the original promoter of this policy in a new era. When Mao launched his land reform campaign, China was a country of peasants with a few landlords and a few landless peasants. The majority of peasants had a piece of land of their own. This was strikingly different from the Middle Age Europe where landowners and serfs were the rule. The major reason for this difference was the influence of Taoist philosophy which praised a simple rural life of equality. With landless peasants, Europe eventually commercialized its agriculture while under Mao's leadership, the Chinese peasant still abided by the piece of land, which became smaller and smaller with time passing, contemplating the same dream handed down through thousands of years.

In the first fifty years of the last century, there were numerous wars in China which eventually stirred up the peaceful peasants, by far the majority of the Chinese population. This let their demands enter the main political stage, and Mao emerged among rivals with their voice. Just think, everybody stood up with a weapon but did not have enough bread. Could it be anything else other than Communism? Mao read Lao Tzu and Chuang Tzu when he was young, but his mind was active with the gathering heroes of the popular Chinese novel *The Three Kingdoms.* Taoism, in Mao's view, advocates only non-action in politics. Some scholars have pointed out that Mao held a negative view over Lao Tzu until his late years. Those scholars drew their conclusions from Mao's words, speeches and articles. Psychological studies have clearly shown that we are still largely relying on our unconscious to make decisions in our daily life. One's unconscious is often linked to his childhood memories. Mao's childhood mind was no doubt dominated by Taoist ideology. Mao's self-sufficiency, rural communes and so on are all reflections of the Taoist utopia deep in his mind and have nothing to do with Marxism.

Mao often quoted from Lao Tzu and Chuang Tzu but it was often superficially coherent in context. For example, Mao wrote "Lao Tzu says no move is the first importance" in his article *On Physical Education* published in 1917 but Lao Tzu never said such words. Mao apparently quoted only from his vague memories and impression since Lao Tzu and Chuang Tzu were so deeply rooted in Chinese culture and vernacular, and no one can avoid them. When Mao was overexcited over his victory in 1949 after millions lost their lives, Mao wrote in his article *Goodbye, John Leighton Stuart* : " Lao Tzu says People are not afraid of death, how can you use death to make them fear?" Mao's mood and thought expressed in that article were only the opposite to Lao Tzu who advocates to celebrate military victory with funeral. The Comments Mao wrote on Chuang Lu's Biography, however, reveal the Taoist ideology in the depth of Mao's mind. From the following quotation, one can see clearly Mao had put Marxism aside and linked himself to those peasant leaders in Chinese history:

The mass health care movement described in Chuang Lu's Biography is like our People's Commune's free health care...free meals at the roadside shops are most interesting...it was the pioneer of our public canteens in the People's Communes. That's about 1600 years ago ...but it remains the same through those years that masses of poor peasants dream of equality, freedom, out of poverty, enough food and clothes...they showed the trend of primitive socialism without full awareness...our People's Communes are rooted far back in Chinese history...

Among the so-called a hundred schools of thought, Lao Tzu and Chuang Tzu are the only ones who ignored all authorities from both heaven and earth, and who acted independently on what they deemed proper. Chuang Tzu is noted by his bold and unconstrained remarks: "I, heaven, and earth were born together, and I share the same body with the universe." Modern scholars classify Chuang Tzu as one of those recluses and hermits, whose words, how heroic and boundless they may be, only affect their own lives. Mao once used the post-pause expression, popular in Northern Chinese rural areas, telling the American reporter Edgar P. Snow (1905-1972), "I am a monk holding an umbrella." The literal translation of those words caused serious misunderstanding: Mao was lonely, holding an umbrella in a gloomy rainy day. In fact, Mao meant through those words, "I respect neither God nor law." This Godless and lawless figure Mao was unfortunately a living God over his land and his people. The tragic results have been known to all.

Mao rebelled against his father when he was a child. He first rose to the top in the Communist party in the 1930s when he acted against orders from the Communist International. He later refused a peace proposal by Stalin and attacked the Soviet leaders publicly soon after Stalin's death. In spite of strong resistance inside the party, Mao pushed forward the agricultural collectivization, and eventually led to the disastrous Great Leap Forward campaign. Millions died of starvation, and Mao was left isolated in front of the popular opposition force inside the government. Mao had mastered the Huang Lao arts of political trickery hiding his intentions and biding the time. Several years later, he single-handedly launched the Great Cultural Revolution to condemn all government officials by the name of a new revolution. To Mao's dismay, the revolutionary cadres became bureaucrats once they were in the government office. Thus there was a need for another revolution to remove them. The revolution became continuous since one required another. No matter how many revolutions were there, Mao himself was the only exception, and no revolution could touch him.

In modern society, we all have several roles to play: We are husband and wife, parent and child at home, employees or workers in the company, and citizens in a country. Society uses those roles to organize all people into a social network. During the Cultural Revolution, Mao once said gangju muzhang, once you pull up the head rope of a network such as a fishing net, all its meshes open. In his view, among the complex social network of millions of

Chinese people there is a head rope which when pulled will move all Chinese people. This seemingly simple mechanism shows how our society works. In contrast to the money-based Western society, Chinese society was said to be official-rank- based. If this was the case, the official ranking system should be highly developed with noticeable differences between different ranks. But this contradicted Mao's egalitarianist ideology. As a result Mao launched the Four Clean-up Movement followed by the Cultural Revolution, which smashed the newly set up bureaucratic system. Thus the ranking system was no longer enough to motivate the officials, let alone the ordinary people. It was inevitable that it would fall back on violence and terror which Mao and his colleagues were fond of through their experience in the warring era.

Since the rebellion of the citizens in the capital during the rein of King Li of Chou (841 BC), Chinese peasant uprisings were particularly common. The Han and Ming dynasties were established by massive uprisings with upper classes changing their places with the lower ones, like tossing over a pancake, which was never seen in the West. In modern Chinese history, the Nationalists overthrew the Ching dynasty and had not stabilized their ruling yet when the Communist uprising succeeded in driving them out of the mainland of China. Only ten years after the People's Republic was founded, Mao directed his spearhead of attack at his party officials, culminating in the Cultural Revolution's seizure of the power and setting up the Shanghai Commune. This was apparently a copy of the Paris Communes in 1789 and in 1871. The society then split into two factions in a life-and-death struggle. Born in a family of old government officials, Chou En-Lai was familiar with such games. He called the two-faction-struggle, tossing over the pancake. When this faction was in power, the other faction was the downside being baked by the hot pan, either tortured in prison or locked inside a cowshed. Once the other faction was out of prison and in power, it started to bake this faction with the hot pan. The final goal of such tossing-over-the-pancake revolution is to achieve an egalitarian secondary society, which was apparently impossible in Chinese history. Mao's senseless tossing about was only a miniature of such maneuvers through Chinese history.

In the book *A New Interpretation of Chinese Taoist Philosophy*, I compared the Axial China with modern Europe and found amazing similarities between the two. But the French Revolution was the main driving force behind social reform in modern Europe while Chinese social reform was carried out by kings and their ministers. In fact Chinese peasant uprisings never aimed clearly at any social reform but only at tossing-over- pancake like dynastic changes. Such changes of dynasties were supposed to result in a final egalitarian society.

In the early 1950s, Chinese peasants called themselves the self existence king, which means they were leisurely and carefree but content with oneself like a king happy in their own world. Unless when there was war or disaster, Chinese rural life was peaceful and stable like Lao Tzu says: *Enjoy the tastiness of your food, admire the beauty of your clothing, delight yourself with your home and its environment, and be happy with your culture.* There was plenty of spare time and at least nothing to do in the whole winter. There were numerous festivals each year with a lot of entertaining activities in between, not to mention the grand ceremonies of weddings and funerals when more often than not, farming work was put aside and all villagers joined in. In comparison to modern urban life, Chinese rural life is much closer to the Taoist ideal lifestyle.

To organize the spare time of those peasants into new developments, either economic or artistic, at high levels, a social structure of secondary society is essential. Without such a social structure readily available, peasants have to spend their spare time in their traditional way. Under the influence of Taoism, Chinese history wiped out the middle class of vassals and lords and put peasants directly under the emperor and his court. According to some scholars, the class of vassals and lords finally collapsed in the Song dynasty (960-1279). As not much room left for intellectuals to actualize their ambitions, they turned into their inner world to develop the New Confucianism headed by Cheng and Chu. Mao's words, *battling with heaven, the joy is limitless; battling with Earth, the joy is limitless; battling with people, the joy is limitless,* sound as if he was very ambitious but still within the boundary of his childhood dream. His life struggle may become the last battle against the middle class in Chinese history.

In the Taoist traditions, there is no place for democracy. Taoism advocates equality, frugality, kindness, and modesty which may have similar social functions in creating a feeling of fairness. The water course way of thinking in Taoism, however, developed into the so-called art of political trickery, and the godless view developed into ruthlessness in power struggles in the hands of ancient Chinese politicians. Mao showed those characteristics once he was in the leadership position of the party after 1935.

When Mao joined the Chinese Communist Party, ideas of social reform, freedom, and democracy had spread to China. The Communist Party had its conventional rules for electing its leaders. Mao put all those conventions aside to build his personal web of power. Nobody could challenge him whether he was right or wrong. Before him, leaders had been changed every a few years but Mao held that position for forty one years until he died without appointing a successor. His Taoist style of political trickery and manipulation became apparent in his last fifteen years or so. In a way he played hide and seek with his high ranking officials. He relied on his secretaries, service people, guards, and even his dance partners for information. This also reflected his lacking of ability to deal with other people in equal terms but showing fully patriarchal behavior. As a result, Chinese diplomatic relations with other countries once fell into embarrassing isolation.

Chuang Tzu was one of Mao's favorite books and Li Po, a Taoist, was his favorite poet. Chuang Tzu's carefree boundless style was also seen in Mao's speeches and writings. Li Po's romantic unconstrained style was also seen in Mao's poetry.

Yin and Yang are important concepts of Taoism, seeing the opposite complementary forces inside all things and entities which lead everything to change toward its opposite: The weak becomes strong, and the strong becomes weak. That's what it means in Chapter 40, *Tao Te Ching*:

That which is converse is the action of Tao;
That which is weak is the use of Tao.

Tao Te Ching is short but elaborates this Yin/Yang principle repeatedly in different verses. By different names such as two point or two side methods or dialectics, this Taoist principle became Mao's favorite topic and appears everywhere in his works and speeches. This principle of course also applies to Mao himself: Such a glorious revolutionary life and such a super powerful figure ended his days in his isolated bedroom observing the keenly impatient desire of his colleagues to see his death. His voice was so a weak and tiny whisper when he begged, *Would you please lift your lordly hands and let them go (after my death)*! The Chinese official interpretation says the word "them" in those Mao's words refers to the rebels who reached high positions through the Cultural Revolution. From the context and circumstances, it is crystal clear that Mao worried about his wife and her friends, the Gang of Four. Did they let them go? No, and they didn't. Fifteen years after Mao's death, people celebrated again over the death of Mao's wife who committed suicide in prison.

Shortly before his death, Mao said that he did only two things in his whole life: He seized power over the mainland of China from the Japanese and the Nationalist, and he led the Cultural Revolution. His wife's death signaled that the latter had been completely overturned. If Mao were alive in heaven, he might have recited the following popular lines to express his pain:

Before seeing victory, in camp ground, the general dies,
With collars soaked with tears, his heroic soul weeps and cries.

Appendix 3. A Comparison of Confucius with Plato and Aristotle in Political Philosophy

Summary: Modern political philosophy lists Plato and Aristotle as its ancient founders but not Confucius. In fact, Confucius was a professional politician while neither Plato nor Aristotle was. Confucius practiced and taught politics for his whole life. Confucius' political philosophy is based on the genetically coded primary society while Western political philosophy including Plato's and Aristotle's are all based on the man-made secondary society.

Confucius political philosophy is nothing but human-heartedness plus examples, which are set up by the ruling class for the people to follow and set up by everybody for others to follow.

Both Confucius and Plato charted out the ideal universal state for whole humanity but neither thought they were the original creators of their ideas. During the last six thousand years, civilization and accumulation of knowledge and social complexity were only side products of upgrading wars until the two world wars. It is like the evolutionary process that fish moved onto land and became mammals and birds, which was created not by man but by God.

Both Confucius and Aristotle were practical philosophers with a wide interest covering both nature and human worlds. Thus Plato from his sophisticated thinking of various forms or ideas and Confucius from his traditional and practical human world both came to the universal state of humanity. The fundamental difference between Confucius and Plato, Aristotle was: The former was based the genetically coded natural primary society while the latter was based on the man-made secondary society. During Confucius' time, the Ancient Chinese Super State of Primary Societies was still intact and functioning like today's United Nations to keep peace among local powers while Plato's philosopher kings are also partially played by the United Nations in modern world. In a way, from Confucius, Plato, and to Aristotle was along a course from the original human world in pre-civilization to the modern world. In the post-modern era, we may have to go an opposite course from Aristotle, Plato, and to Confucius.

*   *   *

Confucius worked through his whole life as a local governor, minister, and a councilor and manager to various state leaders while only Aristotle worked as a teacher or councilor to Great Alexander for some years. Confucius was also a teacher who taught people how to prepare themselves for a position in the government at different levels. If politics is the art or science of government and a politician practices politics, Confucius was a professional politician while none of Socrates, Plato, and Aristotle was.

Why Confucius was not named as a political philosopher while the above mentioned three ancient Greeks were is only because Confucius' political philosophy was based on the genetically coded primary society. As Western civilization has led the world in the last five hundred years in modernization, post-modern era urges us to see Confucius' political philosophy in comparison with Plato and Aristotle.

When all human societies are divided into the genetically coded primary society and the man-made secondary society, it is found that the Western civilization started with the secondary society while the Chinese started with the primary society. The ancient Chinese super state was divided orderly into numerous primary societies including the ruling class, which enabled Chinese people to continue their social life humans have lived for several million years. This super state of primary societies remained intact until 476 BC when Warring States Period started. (Li, 2005, 2014)

1) The master of the primary society is man while the master of the secondary society is God.

The primary society is the society humans are born with, and so humans are the master just as monkeys are the master of their society. The primary society, based on face-to-face interaction, has about 150 members and the social order is esthetic/psychological. The social order is usually rational in a secondary society.

As a man-made society, the secondary society faces numerous possibilities and each has an uncharted course stretching into the future. As the result, the secondary society is uncontrollable by man.

Lao Tzu says: "The human world is a Godly thing, which cannot be operated, and cannot be owned either, the one who operates it will end in failure, the one who owns it will lose it." (Chapter 29) Confucius respected God but stayed away from God: He focused on the human society but did not astray away from the human nature: the human-heartedness. Both Lao Tzu and Confucius hold the view: Stay away from action- taking and the world will remain orderly.

Having seen various societies and states aiming at various directions and goals, Plato saw a pre-existing world of forms and ideas deep in our mind, which was created by God. Only philosophers could go deep in our mind and reveal those forms and ideas.

This is along the same line of thought as the Bible where God created Adam and Eve more than four thousand years ago when Mediterranean civilizations started. In fact, humans are created by themselves in the secondary society, and so modern scholars claim: "We are, in short, what we make ourselves"; "The most influential perspective in sociology...has been view human nature as a consequence of human histories and experiences, rather than any predetermined essence." (Wolfe, 2001; Marshall, 1994)

In fact, our civilized history has been a long process of upgrading wars with the humanity fighting against itself, which greatly sped up the process of cultural evolution and ended with this global village of sophisticated science and technology. Under the pressure of war, humanity traded its happiness for materialistic achievements and linguistic sophistication, so the suicide rates were doubled or nearly doubled even in Canada and United States in the twentieth century. (Macionis and Gerber, 1999). This sped-up six thousand years of human civilization was no way designed by man but by God.

2) Plato's World of Forms or Ideas and Confucius' Refusal of Original Thinking: The Plato's Problem

It is interesting to note that both Plato and Confucius insisted that they were not the original creators of their ideas. Confucius says his job is re-narration or re-telling but not creating; Plato insists that his ideas came from God, as mentioned above.

A linguistic philosopher so talked about how his young daughter learned to speak: As a toddler, she only managed to speak two or three words with visible difficulty in expressing herself. Then all of a sudden, she is chattering continuously with her mother or other girls around three and four years old. She speaks so freely without any visible effort and only has difficulty in stopping talking. There is nothing in the world that she cannot express and talk about. Furthermore, she is always correct in grammar though nobody has taught her any knowledge of grammar.

Noam Chomsky (1928-) first noticed this phenomenon in the 1960s. He thought we humans are born with a brain power of language, and so-called generative grammar, a grammar which grows itself among children. He called it the Plato's Problem. The question is, where does our knowledge come from and how does it become our possession when environmental conditions do not provide sufficient information? In a more general sense, Plato's Problem refers to the problem of explaining a "lack of input",or the so-called poverty of stimulus.

Plato was the first philosopher who systematically inquired into this issue. It is from the Meno that the modern instantiation of Plato's Problem is derived. Plato believed that we possess innate ideas that precede any knowledge that we gain through experience. Therefore, Plato himself must have been surprised in a similar way about the pouring out an endless stream of new ideas from his own mind.

I observed that when young girls of three or four years chat with each other, they apparently forget the difference between reality and imagination without any sense of logos. Chinese Taoist philosophy admires animals and children even infants, and take them as example to follow. Similarly, Confucius admires the color and beauty of the primary society. So he says: "I enjoy myself by eating coarse rice, drinking plain water, and sleeping on my own arms as a pillow. Riches and honors acquired by unrighteousness, are to me as a floating cloud." (Analect, 7:15)

Confucius' talks were often accompanied with musical instruments while none of Plato's and Aristotle's books were written for chanting with musical instruments.

Confucius says: "It is by poetry that one's mind is aroused; it is by the rites that one stands firmly in the society; it is by music that a man is completed." (Analects, 8:8)

Then we come to Confucius' refusal of original thinking. I have read the Analects thoroughly for several times, which led me to believe that Confucius was deliberately refusing to go into original thinking like Plato and Aristotle did. During Confucius' time, the man-made secondary society was emerging and had not established itself yet. In the background of the Chinese Super State of Primary Societies had been there for more than a thousand years, a new ideology or a new way of thinking had to pave the way for any secondary society. Confucius clearly saw it and to stop the emerging of any secondary society and to set up an example, Confucius determined to hold himself back from any original thinking along the way of a new secondary society.

Confucius praised people who were born with knowledge or Plato's innate ideas and saying: " I am not one of those, and I learned from others for my knowledge." Confucius further pointed out that some people created knowledge by themselves, and he was not one of them. (Analects: 7:19; 6:9; 7:27)

Confucius said: "A superior man, in regard to what he does not know, shows a cautious reserve." "thought without learning is perilous." "The study of strange doctrines is injurious indeed!" (Analects: 13:3; 2:16)

As in the Mediterranean world when Plato and Aristotle lived, the secondary society was built to pursue material gain and the society became, to certain extent, controllable by man like a hand tool. Confucius insisted that a gentleman does not pursue any material gain and does not become a tool controllable by man. In conclusion, Confucius clearly shows his opposition to the emerging man-made secondary society.

3) A Comparison of Socrates, Plato, Aristotle with Confucius, Mencius, and Hsun Tzu

By far the most comparable three Chinese philosophers to Socrates (469-399 BC), Plato (427-347 BC), and Aristotle (384-322 BC) are Confucius (551-479 BC), Mencius (372-289 BC), and Hsun Tzu (286-238 BC). Those six philosophers all lived during Karl Jaspers' Axial Age from 800 to 200 BC. Both Socrates and Confucius are the first ethic philosophers in their culture who for the first time focused on the human world, society and life. Socrates, Plato, Aristotle were teachers and students while Confucius, Mencius, and Hsun Tzu were all along the same line of thought as the founder and followers of Confucianism. Thus it is not surprising that the six philosophers showed the same trend of change in time: Plain (oral tradition), ideal, and practical. As the founders, both Confucius and Socrates did not write anything down; both Plato and Mencius were highly ideal pursuers; both Aristotle and Hsun Tzu were highly practical, namely empirical philosophers: they both accepted the cruel reality of the secondary society as normal.

Therefore, the six philosophers showed the same trend of change: from plain, ideal, to practical while both Greece and China entered into Imperial period during the late Axial age. A dramatic difference between the two reflects the fundamental different societies Greece and China started with: the secondary and the primary society.

If being practical means getting used to it, the Greek social environment improved while the Chinese worsened by the disintegration of the primary society shortly after Confucius' death. So Socrates was executed in Greece while Hsun Tzu's two students were executed in China; Confucius was the one most involved in politics in China while Aristotle was the one most involved in politics in Greece. Chinese poetry started with the folksong of The Poetry Classic but ended with Qu Yuan and his colleagues' poetry written both by and for the upper class of autocrats. The Greek poetry changed in an opposite way: from tragic autocratic to comic. If Socrates' death is tragic, facing a similar situation, Aristotle showed humorous attitudes: "I will not allow the Athenians to sin twice against philosophy!" It reflects the change of the life attitude of the population and society: from ideal though tragic to practical.

The three Chinese philosophers from Confucius to Hsun Tzu covered about three hundred years while the three Greek philsophers covered only about a hundred years. The Greek culture changed much faster, since they started with the secondary society.

4) What is the Question?

Plato opens book 1 of the Republic by asking: What is justice? Aristotle opens book 3 of the Politics by asking: What is a state? Confucius' book, the Analects, opens by asking: Is it not pleasant to learn with a constant perseverance and application?

Here we see clearly both Plato and Aristotle have a question to ask while Confucius only has some issue to emphasize by asking a question. This is the difference between the man-made secondary society and the natural primary society: the former face numerous possibilities and so they have serious question to consider about while what the latter needs is to remind themselves: Enjoy where you are and do not go astray and get lost.

To Plato and Socrates, ancient Greek people who lived in one of the numerous states like setting in cave with both their legs and heads chained and fixed in a position to look at the shadows on the cave wall casted by objects and animals from outside of the cave.

Such a cave is a man-made secondary society but not a primary society. Man is born with a broad view and sense of his social world, natural world, and his inner world, the human mind. The man-made secondary society only picks up a few of this broad and sense and overstretch them to form the base of a secondary society. In Plato's view, only philosophers can go out of the cave and have a broad view and obtains the philosopher mind with rational thinking of logos.

In fact, in a man-made secondaey society in their early years, residents face numerous questions and possibilities. Cave men and philosophers only represent those who have a practical mind and those who have a philosophical mind. In fact, Plato had a broader mind than Aristotle had, since Aristotle was more practical.

With Plato's cave as the metaphor, Confucius' ideal life in a primary society is a cave man with a philosophical mind, who live his life in the cave while his mind wondering outside the cave only as an enjoyable fantase. This man has to remind himself from time to time: do not apply his fantase ideas into his cave man life, otherwise it will become incontrollable by man.

Therefore, Confucius opens his book of Analects by asking: Is it not pleasant to learn with a constant perseverance and application? Another classic of Confucianism, Rites: Great Learning, summarizes this leaning and application as: Cultivate oneself, bring orderly equality to the family, govern the state, and bring orderly peace to the human world. In Confucius term, to learn is only to learn from their traditions and from senior members and from each other.

Therefore, both Confucius and Plato had a broader mind than Aristotle had while Confucius was just as practical as Aristotle was. Both Plato and Confucius are looking for an Ideal Universal Human World.

5) What is Politics

Politics derives from the Greek word polis, and so to Plato and Aristotle, politics essentially means city affairs, or governing a city state. In fact, Confucius faced the same political landscape as Plato, Aristotle did, state and its people. Confucius' motherland, State Lu, was about the size of Athens, less than half million in population.

When someone asks: What is politics? Confucius, as a professional politician, answers: Politics means you behave yourself correctly. (Analects, 12:17) The essence of Confucius' teachings is nothing but human-heartedness, and in other word, and the above Confucius' answer only means: You are dictated by human nature and do not go astray from human nature.

Confucius says: "If the people be led by laws, and uniformity sought to be given them by punishments, they will try to avoid the punishment, but have no sense of shame. " "If they be led by virtue, and uniformity sought to be given them by the rules of propriety, they will have the sense of shame, and moreover will become good."(Analects: 2:3, 2:4)

If Confucius had had been in Plato's and Aristotle's position, he might have said: If the people be led by material gaining, and uniformity sought to be given them by laws and punishment, they will have totally different senses of shame and eventually go on fighting each other until the whole human world divided into two campuses to fight the two world wars and exhaosting the resource on earth afterwards.

If Plato and Aristotle had had been in Confucius' position, they might have said: If the people be led by virtue, and uniformity sought to be given them by the rules of propriety, they will have the sense of shame and become good but they do not know how to deal with the conflicting situation accelerated by material gaining when they are in the secondary society, their society may periodically end with collapse.

The subsequent two thousand year history in Europe and in China after those six philosophers and their times was also characterized by the above difference between Confucius' and Plato's, Aristotle's political philosophies. European history was fulfilled by warfairs while Chinese history restricted non-human-heartedness among the imperial court and its officials at different levels. In the coming imperial age in China, human- heartedness was readily transformed into so-called shameless black-heartedness: violence and killing to promote the wishes of social power.

6) Conclusion

Confucius was as ideal as Plato and was as practical as Aristotle in his political philosophy.

As mentioned above, we are essentially what we make ourselves. Both Confucius and Plato refused to accept such a view: both man and his society are made by himself. Plato thought that all our ideas were created by God and sitting deep in our mind while Confucius thought that our human world was based on nothing but pure uncontaminated human nature. Mencius says that human-heartedness is nothing but human beings.

Since Plato and Confucius idealized different societies: secondary and primary society respectively. They showed quite different attitudes towards poetry and arts. In the super state of primary societies, the ruling class lived in their own primary societies but living an artistic life: chanting poetry and performing rites on social occasions as Chinese people did when Confucius was alive.

Clearly both Confucius and Plato faced the same dilema of early human civilization but idealized at primary and secondary society respectively: Confucius was headstrong in refusing to go into the field of original thinking while Plato forbid both the rulers and gardians to have families and properties. They both were far from reasonable.

The social structure of the period of early Chinese civilization from 2200 to 476 BC was idiographically modelled as follows:

The King and his clan + Intellectuals   *Quasi-primary society*
    |

The vassals and their clans + Intellectuals *Quasi-primary society*
    |

Villages and tribes   *Primary society*

Theoretically the kings and vassals in the above idiogram live in a secondary society since they are functioning as the ruling class, but in fact they still lived a nearly primary society or quasi-primary society. Vassals are the state level where Confucius lived. Both kings and vassals functioned like the United Nations in our world, namely, to keep peace and balance among local powers and societies. It must be pointed out that the social power was much less developed in the Chinese world where was a powerless king. With a United Nations, the modern world is like the ancient Chinese world but both modern world and the acient Greek world are in the secondary society.

In Plato's ideal world, there is no slave but is equality between men and women. Aritotle took slavery and inequality between men and women as normal. In today's world, economical classification has gone further than the ancient Greece though slavery is liminated while inequality between the two sexes is still there.

The function of the Plato's philosopher kings was partially played by the Roman Catholic Popes in the middle age Europe and by the United Nations in the modern world. Although the United Nations can be seen as the king and his court in the ancient Chinese world, they are fundamentally different societies. The six thousand years of upgrading warfairs up to the two world wars is essentially astray from Confucius' ideal human world of primary societies.

The six thousand year of civilization and upgrading warfare was only a proof that the secondary society is uncontrollable by man. The theory of two levelled society comes to the same belief as Plato: Our six thousand years of civilization was designed by God and not by man. Like fish moved onto land and became mammals, birds, and reptiles in the biological history, humans moved into the secondary society where they were fighting each other in order to accumulate enough knowledge and wealth for a new human world in the future, which will be more similar to the primary society we are born with.

(Submitted to and accepted by THE X×VTH INTERNATIONAL CONFERENCE OF PHILOSOPHY, 2016 in Ancient Olympia, Greece)

Afterword: Yu the Great and His Story of Controlling the Vast Flood

The Yellow Emperor and Yu the Great started and established the ancient Chinese super state of primary societies. The Yellow Emperor was worshiped as the ancestor of all Chinese people. But in the 1950s when I was a child in the Chinese countryside, people often talked about Yu the Great and how he spent 13 years controlling the flood and passing by his home three times and he was too busy to go into the passing home even once. I was also told: this river water was yellow because too much sand inside the water.

As shown in Figure 6, the Yellow River has a critical area where the river flows from mountainous high land to low plain land. When the river bank was broken here and it will result a vast flood in the low land area, and even led to a new river course. In the Chinese history, this river had more 1500 times of flood and 26 times of river course change. The top one in Figure 6 was between 2200 and 602 BC which might be created by Yu the Great. The bottom one between 1939 and 1947 when the government army bombed the river bank to flood the Japanese army during the Second World War.

Yu the Great's father was sent to control the flood but failed after 9 years hard work because he used traditional way to lead peasants to build new banks everywhere to stop the flood. His son, Yu the Great took over his father's job but changed to a new method. He stood on the high mountain and found a better course to lead the flood into the sea, and led the local peasants to create several new rivers and lakes, and eventually ended this flood successfully. Similar efforts and successes happened later on, since Chinese people knew to follow Yu the Great's example in similar situations.

Since Chinese peasants still lived in the primary society in the 1950s, there was no formal village or clan leaders. Usually one or two volunteers came out to do the necessary work such as collecting tax, and they did not receive any payment for their work. My clan had a large graveyard and there was stone tablet describing the story behind. There was a local flood in 1777, and many hunger people came to my clan graveyard and cut all the trees down to sell it for some money. One of the clan member, Jingsen picked up the left over tree branches and used them to make farm tools and then sold for some money and plus his own donation, a total of three thousand dollars. He used this money to organize the whole clan working to rebuild the graveyard and buy more land to enlarge this graveyard. He also used the money to have all clan members enjoy a dinner together once or twice per year. More than a hundred years later in 1905, his later generation sons asked a scholar in the neighbor county to write this story and engrave it on this stone tablet.

This Jingsen and Yu the Great were the same to voluntarily lead their people to solve the problems in their natural primary society. Jinsen had no need to become the local king since the government had provided a peaceful environment already.

According to the bible, God was not happy because of the human sin and then sent the flood to wipe out all humans except the righteous Noah and his family. This God flood lasted only 150 days while Yu the Great's flood lasted more than twenty years. It let me to conclude that the master of the primary society is man or people but not God while the master of the secondary society is God but not man or people.

The soul of the universe or God planned the five thousand years of upgrading war civilization to accumulate knowledge and wealth for a new world. I recently wrote a novel in Chinese: The Taoist Utopia in the 23rd Century where humans and AIs have the same appearance and live together; they can fly in the sky and swim in ocean, they can go back history to live hundreds years ago; there is no difference between imagination and reality. It will take much longer time for humans to evolve into different secondary society humans like lobefin fish became different land animals.

References

[1.] Li, You-Sheng, A New Interpretation of Chinese Taoist Philosophy: An Anthropological/Psychological View. London, Canada: Taoist Recovery Centre, 2005.

[2.] Li, You-Sheng, Confucius in Another Perspective. Suchou University Press, 2014. (in Chinese)

[3.] Eckhardt, William, 1995, A dialectical evolutionary theory of civilizations, empires, and wars. In: Civilizations world systems studying world-historical change, ed by S. K. Sanderson. Walnut Creek, USA: AltaMira Press. p75-108.

[4.] Macionis, JJ and L. M. Gerber. 1999. Sociology. Scarborough, Canada: Prentice Hall Allyn and Bacon Canada. p587.

[5.] Marshall, G, 1994. The Concise Oxford Dictionary of Sociology: Human Nature. Oxford University Press.

[6.] Miller, GF. 1998: "Sexual Selection for Cultural Display." In Evolution of Culture. Edited by R. Dunbar, C. Knight, and C. Power. Edinburgh: Edinburgh University Press.

[7.] Wolfe, A., 2001, "Human nature" in Encyclopedia of Sociology, p1233-36. New York: Blackwell.

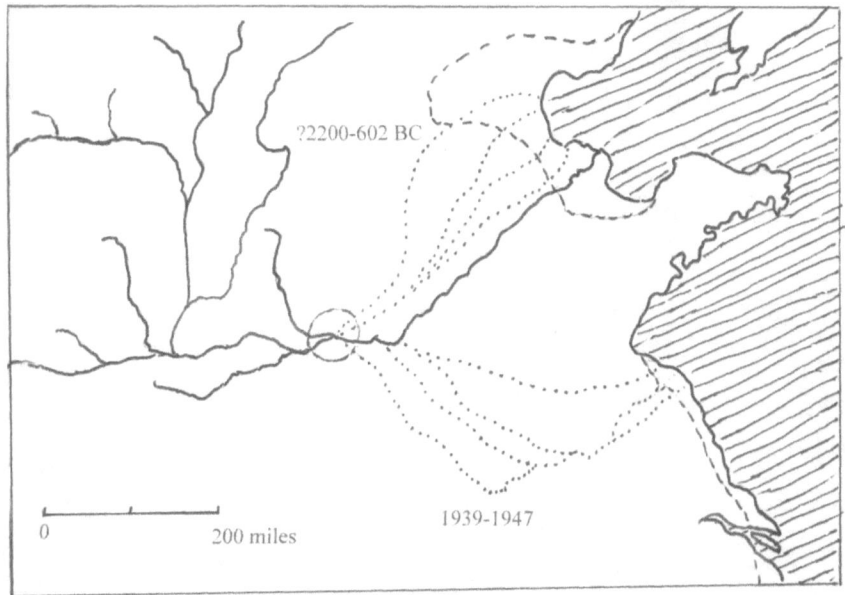

?2200-602 BC

1939-1947

0   200 miles

Figure 6, The Yellow River: The broken line represents the coast in Yu the Great's time , and the dotted line represents the main Yellow River courses in history. The top one might be the one created by Yu the Great and it was so stable because his hard work and it lasted more than a thousand years.